Generative Man:
Psychoanalytic Perspectives

Books by Don S. Browning
Published by The Westminster Press

GENERATIVE MAN: PSYCHOANALYTIC PERSPECTIVES
ATONEMENT AND PSYCHOTHERAPY

GENERATIVE MAN: PSYCHOANALYTIC PERSPECTIVES

by

Don S. Browning

THE WESTMINSTER PRESS
Philadelphia

Grateful acknowledgment is made to the following
for permission to use copyrighted material:

International Universities Press, Inc., for quotations
from: Heinz Hartmann, *Ego Psychology and the
Problem of Adaptation.* Copyright 1958 by Interna-
tional Universities Press, Inc. Robert White, *Ego and
Reality in Psychoanalytic Theory.* Copyright 1963 by
International Universities Press, Inc.

W. W. Norton & Company, Inc., for quotations from
Erik H. Erikson, *Insight and Responsibility.* Copyright
© 1964 by Erik H. Erikson.

Random House, Inc., for quotations from Norman O.
Brown, *Love's Body.* Copyright © 1966 by Norman O.
Brown.

PUBLISHED BY THE WESTMINSTER PRESS®
PHILADELPHIA, PENNSYLVANIA

PRINTED IN THE UNITED STATES OF AMERICA

Library of Congress Cataloging in Publication Data

Browning, Don S.
    Generative man.

    Bibliography: p.
    1. Psychoanalysis.   2. Man.   3. Technology and
civilization.   4. Civilization, Modern—1950–
I. Title.   [DNLM: 1. Psychoanalytic interpretation.
WM 460 B885g   1973]
BF173.B85   128'.3   73–1248
ISBN 0–664–20969–6

To my parents, Robert and Nelle Browning

CONTENTS

Introduction   7

Chapter 1   Psychoanalysis and Modernity   11

Chapter 2   Philip Rieff: Psychological Man and the Penultimate Ethic of the Abundant Life   32

    A Theory of Culture   35
    The Sources of Psychological Man   38
      The Cultural and Social Forces of Modernity   39
      Freud: The Exemplary Character   40
      Psychoanalysis as a Moral Science   42
      The Rieffian Uses of Freud   45
    Psychological Man   54

Chapter 3   Norman Brown: Dionysian Man and the Resurrection of the True Christian Body   60

    The Disease Called Man   64
    Character and Modernity: Apollo and *Homo
Economicus*   74
    The Dionysian Christian   78

Chapter 4   The Ego, Play, and Individuation   83

    The Ego and the Principle of Constancy in
Freud   86
    The Ego in the Writings of Heinz Hartmann:
The Fuller Vision   90
    Play and Individuation in the Thought of Robert
White   96

Chapter 5   Erich Fromm: The Productive Personality and the
            Coming of the Messianic Time   105

            The Human Situation   114
            Character and History: The Social Psychology of
               Modernity   118
            Psychology and the Science of Ethics   124
            The Anthropology of Productive Man   126
            Hope and the Messianic Time   131
            Productive Man: A Summary   135

Chapter 6   Erik Erikson: Generative Man and the Household
            of God   145

            Psychoanalysis and the Ethics of Human Ecology   151
            The Ego: Its Epigenesis, Virtues, and Necessary
               Rituals   155
            Care and the Anthropology of Generative Man   162
            Identity and Modernity   166

Chapter 7   The Empirics of Generative Man   179

            The Dialectics of Receiving and Acting   179
            Generative Man and the Meaning of Time   197
            Generative Man and the Social World: Life as
               Creative Ritualization   201
            Generative Man and the "Other"   207

Epilogue   Generativity and Advance: Postscript on Generative
            Man and Religion   218

Notes   229

Bibliography   253

Index   263

ACKNOWLEDGMENTS

I would like to express appreciation to the following people for their assistance with the preparation of the manuscript for this book. First, I want to thank my students—especially Stanley Brown, Jim Shackelford, and Lewis Rambo—for their help with editing and indexing. Deep thanks goes to Donna Guido, Minerva Bell, and Rehova Arthur for typing the manuscript at various stages. I profoundly appreciate the research grant from the American Association of Theological Schools which made possible several months in France, where I wrote the major portion of the book. Two deans of The Divinity School at The University of Chicago—Jerald Brauer and Joseph Kitagawa—have been supportive of the work that has gone into this volume. Perry Le Fevre of Chicago Theological Seminary read parts of the manuscript and made helpful criticisms. My wife, Carol, and my children, Elizabeth and Christopher, have shown remarkable tolerance and even occasional enthusiasm for the project which culminated in this book. And finally, an appreciation that words cannot express goes to my parents, Robert and Nelle Browning, to whom this volume is dedicated and who are generative people in their own right.

D. S. B.

INTRODUCTION

The major problem facing mankind in this last half of the twentieth century is now becoming clear. That problem is this: How can the runaway economic and technological expansion of Western society be slowed down without prematurely destroying the potential contributions to human good that our technocratic society might conceivably make? Events in recent years have made it abundantly clear that Western society cannot continue for many more years along its present path. The ecological crisis facing the world has put into question the mere physical survival of the human race. In addition, the quality of life in modern societies, especially in American society, has steadily come under more telling criticism in recent years. Not only are there doubts about the continuing survival of man, but it is not altogether certain that if extinction is averted, life will actually be worth living.

The shock of recognition for the general population has come only within recent months. The entire world—but especially the West—has maneuvered itself into an unfavorable ratio between its expanding populations, its economic and technological growth, and the ecological destruction being unleashed upon the environment. There appears to be no possible way for the Western industrial societies to maintain their present standard of living, rates of population growth, and speed of economic expansion without finally burying themselves under a mountain of poisonous debris. The great liberal goal of raising the world population to a standard of living equal to the West must now be recognized as an impossible one. The resources of the world cannot even bear the burden of the present level of affluence in the great industrial nations; certainly, they cannot survive the strain of worldwide industrialization, especially at present levels of population increase.

And yet, we have already tasted the forbidden fruit. There is little chance that mankind can turn back the clock to recapture a preindustrial and pretechnological way of life. In addition, industrial and technological society does indeed contain the potential for bestowing modest yet important improvements in health service and education, values that men everywhere seem to want. The complete dismantling of industrial and technological society is obviously not the answer, even if it were a possibility. *Retrenchment* and *control*, not absolute dismantlement—herein lies the appropriate province for the solution to the problems facing Western society.

I can agree with Charles Reich and Theodore Roszak: the solution first of all requires a new cultural consciousness on the part of Western man.[1] But the new consciousness toward which I will slowly work in the pages of this book has little affinity with the emerging counter culture, at least as it is described by these men. Moving through the vision of the good man found in the four men reviewed in this study— Philip Rieff, Norman Brown, Erich Fromm, and Erik Erikson—will gradually take us through a narrower gate, one, I hope, that will lead to a more viable solution than anything presently to be found in the so-called counter culture. Also, the new consciousness toward which this study points will have more relevance to the political steps that must finally be taken if relief from our present predicament is to be found.

The new consciousness that man will develop must lead to a series of specifiable political solutions. First, it should be a consciousness that leads men all over the world to see the wisdom of drastically lowering the present level of population growth. This must be the first item on everyone's political agenda. Second, reckless economic and technological expansion must be checked, without, however, completely destroying either the will or the knowledge necessary to maintain a modest level of industrial and technological capacity. And finally, all of this must be done without undermining man's basic commitment to life and the preservation and enrichment of the human species.

The organizing symbolic for the new culture will be built from several sources. In this book I investigate what psychoanalysis can contribute to this new cultural symbolic. Psychoanalysis may indeed make a privileged—although not exclusive—contribution to the emerging symbolic. My effort in this book to examine certain psychoanalytic visions of the good man in the context of modernity is one way to assess the moral significance of the potential contribution of psychoanalysis.

I will argue that the concept of "generative man" implicit in the work of Erik Erikson is a trustworthy summary of the emerging psychoanalytic vision of the good man. I have not dedicated the entire book to his thought, simply because strength and clarity are added to his ideas if they are placed in the context of other commanding interpretations of the psychoanalytic vision of the good man. "Generative man," as we will come to know him, is precisely the man who is dedicated to the maintenance and ecological strength of the human race. He finds his fulfillment in the confirming recognition bestowed by children, both his own and those of others. In the name of preserving the race, he hopes that each child born into the world is both wanted and cared for. Because of his interest in the maintenance of the human species, he knows that its growth must be severely limited. Generative man is committed not only to the physical preservation of the race but to its wider ecological integrity; for this reason he is also dedicated to the curtailment of that uncontrolled economic and technological expansion which not only pollutes the natural environment but weakens the very fabric of social existence. In short, the image of generative man will tell us much about what mankind has always wanted; in addition, it will suggest much about what man must once again become if he is to survive his present crisis.

1

PSYCHOANALYSIS AND MODERNITY

The question addressed in this book is limited in scope. It is simply this: What is the moral significance of the emerging psychoanalytic tradition? My inquiry into the moral significance of psychoanalysis will center on an age-old philosophical concern: What is the nature of the good man? I pose this question, however, to the emerging psychoanalytic tradition. I will attempt to discern the particular organization of human energy that psychoanalysis, in its later forms, seems to envision as normative or good.

But, since man never stands alone and can never be successfully abstracted, in either theory or practice, from his social context, this question must contain a societal or communal pole. The most pervasive social fact of contemporary life, at least for Western people, is the relentless march of the forces of modernity. The definition of modernity will be a central concern of our study. For the moment, however, we can say that modernity seems to be the social impact of that conglomeration of forces associated with industrialization, technology, structural differentiation of basic social institutions, occupational specialization, and urbanization. In addition, it seems to be associated with a certain cultural vision that emphasizes, through a variety of contradictory values, the idea that man—both collectively and individually—can improve his lot through his own efforts. Hence, my question has grown. I ask now: What is the emerging psychoanalytic vision of the good man in the context of modernity?

One further word needs to be said before my question can be properly stated and understood. Throughout the posing of this question I have implied that there is an emerging or evolving psychoanalytic tradition and that the more recent expressions of this tradition constitute the focus of my concern. Therefore, this is not another book on Freud. Nor is it a book about the ethics of Freud. Rather, it is a book about other men who have attempted to restate and amplify the moral meaning of what was truly significant and lasting about Freud's discoveries. I concern myself in this study less with what Freud actually said or intended and more with what is being done with his thought by others. My task is to discern the variety of ethical implications of a growing tradition.

The bulk of this essay is dedicated to an analysis of the characterologies of four contemporary psychoanalytically oriented ethicists—Philip Rieff, Norman Brown, Erich Fromm, and Erik Erikson. Each of these writers has a normative vision of man, a vision of what one might call the *good man*. Philip Rieff writes about *psychological man*, Norman Brown about *Dionysian man*, Erich Fromm about *productive man*, and Erik Erikson about *generative man*. Each of these writers offers, in various ways and under various terms, an interpretation and evaluation of modernity. And each of them positions his normative characterology with reference to this interpretation and evaluation of modernity. All four authors say something about what the good man should do either to cope with, transcend, transmute, or escape those forces of modernity which now envelop more than half the world and which in some way touch us all. And each of these men makes reference to psychoanalytic experience and concepts in articulating and verifying his vision. Hence, each justifiably can be characterized as a psychoanalytic ethicist.

But why should we concern ourselves with the moral significance of psychoanalysis? What is psychoanalysis in the life of contemporary Western culture that it merits this kind of inquiry? If psychoanalysis were a simple therapy, a limited medical device for the cure of irritating psychological symptoms and habits, then one could argue that concern over its moral implications is truly a waste of time. But psychoanalysis and its various therapies is not as neutral in its cultural significance as physiotherapy might be for the physically ill or occupational therapy might be for the retarded or the physically handicapped. The premise that justifies taking psychoanalysis and its moral implications so seriously is nothing less than the claim, put forth by many, that psychoanalysis has become the dominant symbolic in the Western world for the organization of the character of modern man.[1] Such a claim is forcefully argued by Philip Rieff, the psychoanalytic ethicist to be reviewed first in this study. Whether there is an emergent psychoanalytic ethic of such power and pervasiveness to be the major influence on the formation of modern character, replacing all other character types and reigning victorious over all other influences, I am not prepared to argue. But I will readily admit that its influence is of such magnitude that its ethical meaning must not be ignored. And, of course, it has not been ignored. Witness the great avalanche of both the very poor and the excellent studies on the cultural and moral significance of psychoanalysis of which the four theorists under review here constitute only a small but most provocative portion.[2] The continuing scholarly and public preoccupation with psychoanalysis is proof in itself of its enormous cultural meaning for our time.

Rieff's own argument, which demonstrates the cultural ascendancy of psychoanalysis, is worth mentioning at this time. Rieff believes that "controlling symbolics" tend to be the product of the creative elites of a particular culture. By controlling symbolics he means the system of ideas and symbols that organize human potential into predictable types of character or personality. Social forces, such as a civilization's dominant technology, its economy, its social changes, its wars and catastrophes, certainly all influence the formation of the moral character of a people. But the final crystallization of a controlling symbolic always seems to be an imaginative act by an outstanding individual or group. Rieff claims that Calvin and the theology of the Reformed Church produced the so-called Protestant ethic and the Protestant man which have been dominant in the West from the sixteenth to the beginning of the twentieth century. Rieff believes that the Protestant synthesis has now collapsed and that in its place has come psychoanalysis. Where Calvin stood, now stands Freud. The Freudian symbolic and the commanding presence of Freud's own mind, siphoned off into the general population through a worldwide corps of psychiatrists and psychoanalysts, have become the basic source feeding modern man's self-understanding.[3]

This thesis, put forth with particular power by Rieff, is not unique to him. It receives both direct and indirect support from a wide range of quarters. It is generally admitted in sociological literature—especially in the writings of Peter Berger, Thomas Luckmann, Talcott Parsons, and Robert Bellah—that modern self-understanding is becoming more personal, individualized, and privatized.[4] This means that when a person begins to think about who he is and what life is about he is most likely to do this in quasi-psychological rather than institutional, political, or specifically religious terms. Since Freudian psychology is the dominant psychological system in the Western world, both for the scholarly community and for the general population, it may indeed be true that the self-understanding for more and more people is being articulated in terms of the psychoanalytic ethos and ethic.

It can be accepted without question, I believe, that there is a notable psychologizing trend in the self-understanding of Western people. In addition, it can be accepted as at least a tenable hypothesis that the major psychologizing influence is psychoanalytic. But here we run into a serious difficulty. Most of the efforts to discern the moral significance of this tradition have concentrated either on the figure of Freud and his writings, as do Rieff and Brown, or on the psychoanalytic tradition in its more orthodox forms, such as John C. Flügel's important *Man, Morals and Society.*[5] Richard La Piere's highly polemical and quite lamentable *The Freudian Ethic* is a study of neither Freud nor the orthodox psychoanalytic tradition. It is primarily a caricature of a few Freudian ideas rendered absurd because of La Piere's inability to transcend, even for the purposes of scholarly discussion, his own intense commitment to what he calls the "ethic of enterprise."[6] Even Heinz Hartmann's important little essay entitled *Psychoanalysis and Moral Values,* while going beyond orthodox psychoanalytic formulations and reflecting the advances in ego psychology to be found in his own work, does not finally help us to assess the moral significance of these later developments in psychoanalytic theory. His claim that the psychoanalytic theory of man is still basically scientific and therefore neutral perpetuates the unfortunate myth that a theory of human behavior which has implications for therapy and socialization (as all forms of psychoanalysis most assuredly do) can be considered as neutral to questions of value and purpose. After the work of Rieff, it can no longer be seriously claimed that psychoanalysis is ethically neutral, even if it is asserted, as does Rieff, that it is only a penultimate ethic.

Hence, there are no studies, except for the work of Erik Erikson which we will review in Chapters 6 and 7, that attempt to clarify and evaluate the moral significance of the *growing* psychoanalytic tradition, especially as this tradition reflects itself in the theoretical and clinical advances of what is commonly called psychoanalytic ego psychology. It is Erikson's work which I will use to give heightened visibility to the emerging moral meaning of psychoanalytic theory and practice. His work builds solidly not only on the writings of Freud but also on the important advances of men such as Heinz Hartmann, Ernst Kris, David Rapaport, and Robert White. To some extent, Erikson summarizes their work, and yet, of course, he transcends it. His work bears a distinctive stamp all its own. It places the major trends of psychoanalytic ego psychology in the context of the central movements of the allied disciplines of ethology and ecology. It contributes a fresh theory of social relations which is almost completely absent from the writings of these other ego psychologists. It extends ego psychology into socio-logical and cultural analysis, and finally, with his important studies of Luther and Gandhi, into historical interpretation. And at every step Erikson attempts to enlarge upon the ethical meaning of both his work and the broader tradition out of which he draws.

But there are other reasons why I have embarked upon this study. These additional reasons are at once more personal and professional. To understand them will illuminate the meaning of the kinds of questions that will remain at the conclusion of this book. As a professor on a faculty of divinity connected to a major Midwestern university, I have grown accustomed to reflecting on what people feel very intense about and to what they consider to be most important—what theologians, after the days of Paul Tillich, generally call "ultimate concern." My own speciality has centered in what is often referred to as a "dialogical" field of study—the attempt to establish the appropriate interrelationship between the psychological sciences and religion. In practice, this work has often consisted of pursuing the answer to two questions. What is the psychological meaning of various religious or theological expres-sions? The second question is the reverse of the first. What are the implicit ultimate commitments (the really important values) behind a particular system of psychology, psychotherapy, or socialization?

The present study grows out of concern to establish what one might call the "horizon" of ultimate meaning and moral significance in the major post-Freud interpretations of psychoanalysis. The word "hori-zon" seems appropriate because it suggests a shading effect where clear beginnings and absolute endings are difficult to perceive. Such is the case with the question of ultimate commitment for most inter-pretations of psychoanalysis. Since psychoanalysis claims to be a science, it has the tendency to bracket judgments about ultimate things. Yet there is clearly a horizon of ultimate meaning in the thinking of Rieff, Fromm, and Erikson. Norman Brown, of course, moves psycho-analysis into an explicitly religious mode of reflection. But we, in this study, will content ourselves primarily with the borderline between the "serious" and the "ultimate." We will leave to another day that grander confrontation between what our study will teach us to take "seriously" in psychoanalysis and what various cultural and religious traditions have insisted that man should regard as "ultimate." Insofar as the concept of "generative man" will summarize much of what I believe to be serious in the emerging psychoanalytic tradition, we will delay to another time a detailed dialogue between the concept of generative man and the idea of Christian man which has generally been raised up before Western culture as its goal.

So my task here is to bracket, for the time being, the fact that I am a listener to the Christian message. I, like most people in the modern world, listen to a variety of messages. Yet I never know that I hear any of these messages quite correctly. Certainly this is true for the Christian message. But it is true of other messages as well, not the least of which is the one associated with the psychoanalytic tradition. In this book I attempt to listen very carefully to the important ethical interpreters of the psychoanalytic tradition in an effort to grasp its emerging cultural significance. At the end of the book we will be left with the further task, perhaps to be carried on in later investigations, of determining what the psychoanalytic symbolic finally means not only for the Christian symbolic but also for the other great religious symbolics throughout the world.

But why have I chosen to listen to these four men—Philip Rieff, Norman Brown, Erich Fromm, and Erik Erikson? We have at least three reasons for focusing our study on these figures. First, these four men all have rather well delineated positions on the ethical significance of psychoanalysis. They give us, so to speak, something substantial to chew on. As we have already indicated, Hartmann's work on this subject ends, in effect, by asserting the neutral, scientific nature of psychoanalysis and denying that it has any ethical meaning at all. These four writers have the common virtue of giving up the shibboleth that psychoanalysis is a neutral science. Most other works either have been highly polemic attacks (Richard La Piere, O. Hobart Mowrer),[7] have failed to address the question of ethics directly (Paul Ricoeur),[8] or have omitted investigating the normative characterology implied by psychoanalysis (Joseph Margolis, John C. Flügel).[9]

Our second reason for limiting our study to Rieff, Brown, Fromm, and Erikson is this: they have all enjoyed unusual publishing success on the American scene. This means that each of these writers, by virtue of his style, the content of his writings, and his sensitivity to the condition of his readers, has managed to say something that many people in the United States have found quite meaningful. All these men have been widely read, widely quoted, and have something of their own following among both the professional and lay reading public. This, then, is very much an American book. It is about a special kind of American success story—the success of psychoanalysis as a controlling symbolic, organizing the minds and hearts of many people.[10] It is also the success story of certain specific authors who, because they knew something about psychoanalysis and because they knew something about what Americans needed and wanted, were able to write books that were believed. Hence the writings of these men stand as something of a cultural text, almost in the sense of the *Geisteswissenschaften* school first set forth by Wilhelm Dilthey and now, with a somewhat different meaning, by Paul Ricoeur.[11] These texts not only convey the point of view of specific authors, they give expression to the felt-experience of thousands of readers who both applaud and defend what they have read.

I am fully aware that psychoanalysis is not the only cultural force informing the self-understanding of modern man. Evolutionary theory, Marxism, behaviorism, and the third and fourth forces in psychology have had important impacts on modern man's organization of his energies and his inner life. The last two forces—behaviorism and the third and fourth forces in psychology—under the leadership of B. F. Skinner and Abraham Maslow are gaining a significant number of followers. But the varieties of psychoanalytic thought and practice have been of particular significance, still are, and appear to be growing in literary, artistic, and scholarly communities. It is a major source informing modern man's understanding of the nature of man and the kind of society he needs to be truly human. There is no other way to explain the popularity of the four men we have chosen to study.

This, then, leads to our third reason for the choice of these four psychoanalytic ethicists: they constitute diagnostic indicators to real cultural options that presently seem to be facing the American people and possibly people throughout the entire Western world. In other words, through the medium of psychoanalytic terms and concepts, many people are attempting to work out solutions to the problems of modern life.

A short review of the major ideas of these four men will illustrate this last point. Philip Rieff, for instance, strikes me as providing what can be called an *accommodational* answer to the facts of modernity. Rieff tends to look at the sociological indices of modernity through the prism of certain cultural changes that have both accompanied and helped rationalize the modernizing process. Hence, he tends to view such sociological phenomena as industrialization, technology, and structural differentiation from the perspective of historical relativism and Freudian skepticism. To him they all add up to the collapse of systems of public authority and commitment. In the place of symbolics of public commitment, Rieff sees emerging, with the assistance of psychoanalysis, a not-very-rugged type of privatism and individualism. The normative personality type will be what Rieff calls the *psychological man*. This is the new modern man, primarily concerned about his own internal psychic economy and balance. He is man who lives dedicated to the modalities of prudent release. Clearly, psychological man is one who knows how to live in an affluent, basically capitalistic society. He lives for enjoyment, but his primary virtue is that he knows how to control himself. He does not believe in—that is to say, he does not expect too much out of—his pleasures, just as he jealously preserves the right to be skeptical about most everything. He is undoubtedly a consumer (*homo consumens*), but a prudent one. What distinguishes him from David Riesman's "other-directed man" or Erich Fromm's "marketing man" is his restraint and his heightened self-consciousness.[12] All three live basically in a modality of release (that is, consumption); the difference between them is that psychological man knows it and he does not expect too much from it. In addition to restraint, the other saving virtue of psychological man is his resistance to fanaticism and blind loyalty. To be a disciple of Freud is finally, according to Rieff, to be released from all discipleship. Psychological man's one great political virtue is his knowing apathy. Being free from fanaticism, he is also free from cruelty and other warlike tendencies. He is somewhat unheroic; war will not be his métier; yet it is not entirely clear, from what Rieff has to say, what will be the disposition of psychological man toward knowingly, consciously, and quite unfanatically sending others to fight for him.

Norman Brown, on the other hand, offers what can be called a *regressive* answer to the problems of modernity. His interpretation of modernity is thoroughly negative and completely rejecting. To him the modern world denies to man everything that man truly wishes. To Brown, the earmarks of modernity—industrialization, technology, and economic individualism (capitalism)—are all the results of repression. They are the consequence of man's unconscious fear of dying and his tendency to repress his body in an effort to avoid his death. Under the conditions of repression, the life and death instincts (which are in union in the unrepressed body) are split apart. Modernity is the culmination—the last gasp, so to speak—of the history of man's estranged and externalized death instinct. Brown's solution to the situation of modern man is a regressive one. But to call it regressive is not necessarily to reject it. In fact, it is one of the theses of this study that every good response to modernity must contain a regressive element. The problem is that the regressive element in Brown is thoroughgoing and complete. Brown's answer to the death-producing forces of modernity is the *Dionysian man*. Dionysian man is the man who accepts his death by first of all living his life. He tries to escape neither life nor death. In him, in fact, the life instinct and the death instinct are in union. He lives the life of playful release and "no line goes unlived." But playful release, for Dionysian man, means giving free expression to his oldest and most persistent wish. This is the wish for union, and union especially with the mother. Dionysian man seeks not the higher union, the progressive union, about which we will hear Fromm speak and to some extent Erikson. Instead, he seeks union with the first and oldest object of his love. Dionysian man's play is permeated with a nostalgia for return, a return to that early state of primordial existence where life and death are one. Many may question whether Brown's regressive solution to the tensions of modernity is really a solution at all. Most probably it is to be taken more as a cleansing than as a solution. The question is, however, Does Brown's attempt to radicalize our consciousness do more to confuse than it does to liberate and restore? Isn't there an element of literal-mindedness about Brown's vision of Dionysian man that requires either acceptance (and hence actual resignation and regression) or a firm rejection?

In contrast to Brown, Erich Fromm presents a *progressive* solution to the ambiguities of modernity. Erich Fromm stands as one of the outstanding publishing successes of our time among psychological and social scientists. His writings are a testimony to both the worries and the fading hopes of the 1940's and the 1950's in the United States. Although there is something dated about the style and the tone of his writings, his analysis of modern Western society emerges now in the 1970's as one of the most perceptive and powerful to be found. Fromm was forging a synthesis between psychoanalysis and Marxist humanism as early as 1941, the year he published *Escape from Freedom*. Fromm's *The Sane Society* (1955), published the same year as Herbert Marcuse's *Eros and Civilization*, was only the culmination of efforts toward such a synthesis he had been working on for at least two decades before Marcuse turned to psychoanalysis to enrich his own Marxist-humanist perspective. Although Wilhelm Reich was the first of the Freudian Marxists, Fromm is far more believable. On the other hand, the differences between Fromm and Marcuse are not as profound as is often thought. They differ primarily with regard to their theories of sexuality and their respective understandings of the role of revolution in political action. Their interpretations of the ills of Western society are quite similar, and here Marcuse is more indebted to Fromm than he has ever acknowledged. In addition, whereas Marcuse is often thought to be currently far more influential than Fromm on New Left thinking around the world, evidence suggests that there are important exceptions to this. Certainly Fromm's influence is extensive in South America, as can be seen in the writings and thought of Ivan Illich and Paulo Freire.[13] Students all over the United States are making pilgrimages to Illich's Center for Intercultural Documentation in Cuernavaca, Mexico. Here they learn of the close association of Illich and Fromm. Fromm also lives in Cuernavaca, and has close contact with the Center for Intercultural Documentation. He wrote the introduction to Illich's book *Celebration of Awareness.* Many of these students return to the United States, dust off their parents' copies of Fromm's *Escape from Freedom* or *Man for Himself,* and discover that in the 1940's Fromm was setting forth a critique of Western society very consistent with the current mood of many of our youth.

The main thrust of Fromm's message is actually quite simple. In a variety of ways he has been saying for over twenty-five years that what happened in Nazi Germany during the 1930's and 1940's can happen in the United States. Today, both his warning and his explanation of how it can happen appear more convincing than ever before.

Fromm's analysis of modern society is informed by nineteenth-century European sociology. Societies tend to go through evolutionary processes of structural differentiation which leave, in the end, the various aspects of the social system relatively autonomous from each other. This differentiation process means that individuals gain more and more freedom from the direct control of centralized institutions. Modernity, for Fromm, brings with it a certain kind of *freedom,* but a freedom that is deceptive and potentially destructive. It is a truncated and incomplete freedom, a negative freedom that tells man much about what he need no longer do but very little about what he should do— about what it might be good to do now that he has the liberty to choose. This kind of freedom, Fromm feels, is terrifying to man, and, in the end, he prefers not to have it. In fact, man actively flees it. This escape from freedom will invariably take the form of a regressive quest for the security of the undifferentiated and womblike matrix from which man comes. But for modern, differentiated man, regression to the security of primitive innocence is an impossibility. It is likely to take the form of masochistic loyalty to a totalitarian leader or sadistic tribalism in the name of a diffuse commitment to an already passing way of life.

Fromm's answer to the anxiety of modernity's vague freedom is his vision of the *productive man*. The very choice of the word "productive" to characterize his normative personality type suggests the reason why we are justified in including Fromm in this study of the emerging moral meaning of psychoanalysis. Fromm, in spite of his revisionism, gains his major inspiration for his vision of productive man from Freud's conception of the genital level of character development. Productive man is man with free access to his potencies, both in the area of genital sexuality and in the wider life processes. Productive man does not shrink from the vague freedoms of modern existence. Instead, he converts this negative freedom of modernity into a positive freedom through the active exercise of his own potentialities. Productive man is like Dionysian man in at least one respect—he seeks union. But the union he seeks is not a regressive return to a womblike existence; it is a higher union based on an affirmation of his own individuality and the exercise of his own powers. Productive man actively *achieves* union; he does not passively *receive* it. Therefore productive man does not falter before modernity. He seeks to actively control and shape it. Yet there is a constant tendency throughout Fromm's writings to place in opposition the passive and the active, the infantile and the mature, the primitive and the civilized, and to associate his view of productive man with the latter term in each polarity. This habit of mind in Fromm leads us to call his position an *undialectical progressivist* point of view. By this we mean only to say that Fromm does not balance the *high* in man with a deep enough appreciation for the *low*. In the end, productive man seems somewhat more alienated from the infantile, the primitive, and the passive in man than need be the case, even for the good of his own higher powers and the higher union that he seeks.

Erik Erikson presents us with a more dialectical view of the good man in the context of modernity.[14] By the word "dialectical," we mean to convey nothing unique to any particular school of philosophical thought. We only intend to suggest the rather simple idea that for Erikson the high in man must not exclude the low, just as the civilized must not exclude the primitive, the mature become dissociated from the infantile, or man's progressive advance become estranged from his more regressive renewals. The high and the low remain together for Erikson in a way which is not the case with our other psychoanalytic ethicists. This is the fruit of his *epigenetic principle*. According to this principle, all advances to the higher and later stages of development —toward independence, responsibility, maturity—must include and carry forward, while restating, a lower level of development. Without the early and the low, in both ontogenetic and phylogenetic development, the late and the high in human development is not truly better. Nor is it truly stronger. Unless the high in man somehow includes and restates the low, the high is weak, anemic, and unstable.

Hence, *generative man* (Erikson's normative vision of man) is at once more mature and more childlike, more civilized and more primitive, more human and more animal than any of the other character types considered in these pages. Generative man contains more dimensions and represents a more complex synthesis than either psychological, Dionysian, or productive man. For Erikson, the so-called lower in man—the animal, the primitive, the child (never, of course, to be considered as simply equivalent to each other)—contains important regulatory and organizing powers essential for the maintenance and restoration of man's ecological integrity. Yet the lower in man never functions with the precision and specificity that instinct does in the animal world. Hence, the lower in man must always be restated in the context of man's more progressive capacities for autonomy, conscious reflection, responsibility, and purposeful activity. It can be said that in Erikson's concept of generative man we have restored to us much of what is both truly animal and truly human, much that is both childlike and adult, and perhaps a great deal that is both primitive and civilized.

Generative man has much to offer for the wise use of the opportunities of modernity as well as for the prudent control of its excesses and dangers. Erikson's analysis of modernity takes account of many of the same sociological facts and theories present in the work of Rieff and Fromm. But he highlights a different set of consequences. Erikson is most struck by the breakdown in the fabric of modern life of those meaningful shared rituals which give integrity and coherence to every civilization. By ritual, Erikson means those patterns of mutual regulation and activation which simultaneously order behavior and meet human needs. The structural differentiation, the rapid social change, and the multiplication of options that characterize modern societies—all these trends and others besides add up to the failure of this single ingredient so necessary for the health of any community.

Without the existence of these stable yet flexible patterns of mutuality, neither society nor individual identity has the one resource indispensable for modern life—the capacity to submit to meaningful change in the context of commonly acknowledged continuities.

Generative man emerges in Erikson's writings as a *creative ritualizer*. This is his essence. Neither innovation nor tradition is his god. Yet he has an appreciation for the necessities of both. Hence, generative man does not withdraw from the challenges of modernity. He maintains the hope that inspires evolution among the animals and that led man to risk the wager that we now call modernity. This is the belief that life, at least in a few of its elementary features, can be slightly improved. Generative man's very animal and very human aversion to the spectacle of suffering in himself and in his children still leads him to believe that the techniques and technologies of modernity may indeed be able to remove a bit of the toil and disease from human life. However, he doubtless will take a strong hand in scaling down much of modernity's irresponsible expansiveness—its unbridled technologies, its unchecked inventiveness, and its ecologically unsound giantism. For generative man, all human activities are judged from the perspective of what they contribute to the generative task itself, i.e., the establishment and maintenance of succeeding generations. All human activities gain only a relative autonomy from this one mildly dictatorial central principle of sensibility. From the point of view of generative man, there are no completely autonomous human enterprises; there is no such thing, from his perspective, as art, or knowledge, or pleasure, as ends in themselves. And finally, generative man will have a capacity that now seems strangely absent in our reputably child-centered culture—the capacity to enter into serious, firm, yet understanding dialogue not only with his own children but with the children of others, as well as the child in himself. In fact, it is for the very reason that generative man has such free access to his own childhood depths that he also can so creatively enter into dialogue with his own and other children.

It is too early to endow generative man with the dignity of a complete anthropology; it cannot be found in Erikson's vision, nor in the meager extension of his thought to be found in this book. But commanding visions of the nature of man seldom enjoy the elegance of systematic articulation. In fact, Erikson's view of generative man is nowhere consciously and specifically set forth in his writings. Erikson never speaks of "generative man" as such; rather, he speaks of "generativity" as a stage of growth—as, in fact, the adult stage of maturity. But it is clear that the stage of generativity is the normative center of his thought and that the concept of generativity has great general significance for all of his writing. It can be safely asserted, then, that Erikson does possess a positive vision of what man should be like in the context of modernity. It is also clear that this vision has direct influence on his clinical judgments, his understanding of human development, and his interpretation of such phenomena as delinquency and adolescent identity confusion.

Erikson is, at this time, probably the most widely read psychologist in the United States. Training programs in all the human relations specialties—psychology, psychiatry, social work, nursing, industrial relations, secular and religious education, and religious or pastoral counseling—make wide use of his thought for instructional purposes. His work may well sum up, more than does that of any other psychologist or psychiatrist, the emerging consensus of values and commitments to be found in the helping professions today.

The question is, Who speaks for psychiatry today? It is my conviction that Erikson speaks more for main-line psychiatric thinking than does Rieff, Brown, or Fromm. It is also my conviction that Erikson's vision of man, although not a finished anthropology, is, among all the visions of the psychoanalytic ethicists, the one to be reckoned with in the grand dialogue over what symbolic will finally organize the energies of modern man.

The conceptual status of Erikson's thought is far from clear. His conceptual scheme is grounded on a combination of hard scientific principles, clinical observations, theoretical intuitions, and creative imagination (he was an artist before becoming a lay analyst). Erikson, like Freud, is constantly bringing together data from diverse realms. Freud correlated the data of dreams and free association with the physics, ethnology, and biology of his day. Erikson has correlated the data from his therapeutic interviews with adolescents and his play therapy with children with his own ethnological fieldwork (his famous studies of the Yurok and the Sioux), current trends in biology, ethology, and ecology, as well as his own remarkable psychohistorical biographies of Luther and Gandhi. His conception of generative man is not based on pure science. Yet scientific facts and theories play a suggestive role in grounding and engendering his vision. Generative man is born out of Erikson's experience as a human being, most especially his experience as a working therapist. Scientific facts and theories from clinical and experimental psychology, from ethnology, ethology, ecology, and biology, serve as "diagnostic indicators" (as Paul Ricoeur uses this concept)[15] which help to clarify the depths of his own experiential encounters with people. Hence, Erikson gives us a new scientific myth. Like Freud's doctrine of the Oedipal struggle, it is a combination of scientific fact and speculation. If Erikson's scientific myth is better than Freud's (or better than that of Rieff, Brown, or Fromm), it is because his science is more up-to-date and his speculations more sympathetic to the totality of the human situation.

In general, the response of these four psychoanalytic ethicists to the prospects of modernity tends to range from cautious to overtly reactionary. None of these men shares the unqualified enthusiasm for modernity that marked the liberal mentality that led us with such glowing predictions down the current path we have taken. Certainly Norman Brown recommends a radical and not-too-slow reversal of the modernizing trend. On the other hand, strangely enough, Philip Rieff comes the closest to affirming certain important features of the liberal vision, in spite of his avowedly pessimistic Freudian view of man and his bracing criticism of liberalism's naïve trust in the application of reason to human affairs. If liberalism means living in a world of penultimates without unifying philosophies of either man or society (which Charles Frankel suggests is part of the liberal vision),[16] then Rieff is at least a liberal in this sense. Fromm, on the other hand, who seems to share the liberal belief in the perfectibility of man, on the whole holds a vision of man and society that calls for a far more unified social ideology and a far more controlled economic and scientific environment than liberalism ever believed necessary.

Erikson says little about the perfectibility of man; but he does appear liberal enough himself to desire a little less suffering for mankind and progressivist enough to hope that humans can become considerably more responsible about their individual and corporate lives than they have been in the past. He shares with Fromm, however, a variety of reservations about the liberal mentality and its great hopes for modernity. Both of them seem to be searching for a more unified and universal ideological framework to guide the modernizing process and to give modern man a sense of identity. Neither is interested in eliminating the pluralism and individuality of modern societies, but both believe it necessary to find a vision of life sufficiently commanding to give these pluralisms a sense of special territory in the context of a larger, more meaningful scheme.

Both Fromm and Erikson believe that man needs, more than pleasure, a sense of "power" (Fromm) or "mastery" (Erikson). By this, neither means to suggest the kind of neurotic domination and exploitation so often associated with the clinical use of the words "power" and "mastery." But they do intend to convey the idea that man needs to feel that he has some influence over what happens to him and that he is a part of things, not simply in the sense of *conforming* but in the sense of *forming* that to which he belongs. Both of them realize that man seeks union and love, but both understand these phenomena under the rubric of mutuality. This means that love and union are always a matter of mutual responsiveness, mutual regulation, and mutual satisfaction between distinct individuals.

Yet one cannot avoid the impression that the ideas of power and mastery (whichever word we use) have a more organic, less Apollonian or Promethean character for Erikson than they do for Fromm. Both men want to overcome modern man's sense of powerlessness and estrangement and both want to restore his sense of responsible and active participation. In part, both want to do this by arresting the runaway expansiveness of modern civilization. It seems that Erikson and Fromm share the desire to reduce the gigantic dimensions of modern life. Or to say it differently, they want to stabilize and anchor some of the centrifugal forces that seem to be pulling modern man apart. Fromm's vision of society is explicitly aimed to accomplish this and contains far more programmatic particulars than can be found in Erikson. He has set forth, especially in his *The Sane Society* and *The Revolution of Hope,* a detailed blueprint complete with worker-controlled industries, community forums, citizen debate and action groups, etc. He calls his social philosophy communitarian socialism. On the other hand, Erikson offers no concrete vision of society; he has no clearly visible social philosophy. Yet one quickly gains the impression that his skepticism of modernity is even more profound than Fromm's and that there is an important qualitative difference between productive and generative man in their respective responses to its prospects.

I believe that we can safely say the following: Fromm wants to restore to modern man his sense of potency by greatly increasing man's capacity for active, conscious, and responsible activity. Hence, Fromm will restore to each man his sense of efficacy by making each man into a god. This is what he means by the perfectibility of man. This is the meaning of the title of one of his books, *You Shall Be as Gods.* Erikson, on the other hand, would restore to man his sense of efficacy by reducing the world of modernity to man-sized proportions. If it requires a god to live with modernity, Erikson is skeptical of the possibility. Erikson is committed to the principle that man can be made strong enough as man (but only as man) to harness and control modernity to fit his own quite remarkable yet quite finite capacities. Both in content and in style, Erikson is less inclined to commit the sin of pride than is Fromm.

The central moral witness of all four of these psychoanalytic ethicists has to do with the essentially conservative character of human life. In different ways, each of these men bear witness to the idea that human nature is not as malleable and open to change as the liberal mentality has supposed. Man has certain capacities for change and, up to a point, even somewhat enjoys change and variation. Psychoanalysis, however, has always resisted—and rightly so—neo-Freudian and certain social-psychological and behaviorist views of man that overemphasize the indeterminate character of human nature. In a variety of ways, psychoanalysis has made appeals to the animal foundations of human nature as a method for asserting that some things in man simply cannot be changed. Freud, Rieff, and Brown do this on the basis of Freud's conservative understanding of libido energy and his belief that the quest for pleasure is a conservative desire to restore and retain the equilibrium of sexual energy. Erikson and the ego psychologists assert the conservative element in human nature by making appeal to certain phylogenetic ego givens that evolved for and tend to demand an *average expectable environment.* Implicit in Erikson and the ego psychologists is a new ground for the "great refusal" which contemporary man may now be giving to the horrible spectrum of endless and ever-accelerating technological change.[17]

In contrast to the spirit of Erikson, Marcuse speaks of the id or eros as the ground for the great refusal which man must give to the inhuman justification of work and domination to be found in capitalism and its chief cultural sanction, the Protestant ethic. Eros may be the source of the grand refusal to the toil and the domination of modern capitalism, but the ego itself, I believe, will provide the grounds for the great refusal to the fragmenting rush of an unpredictable future which modernity and technological change seem to promise. Even Fromm, although devoid of the resources of both the orthodox view of the id or the later developments in ego psychology, shares in this conservative (or should we say conserving) ethos and speaks of a human nature that likes to grow but that does not submit, indeed cannot submit, to every change its environment might seek to impose.

During the last two hundred years in the Western world, most serious intellectual enterprises have addressed themselves, in one fashion or another, to the question of modernity. The grand debate over modernity is likely to intensify in the coming years. The recent social upheavals in the United States have led even the most optimistic American to question the soundness of the direction in which we are going. And liberal Europeans who have only recently overcome native European resistance to American ways of doing things ("because they are too modern") may enjoy only a short period of ascendancy.

Yet the grand debate over the meaning of modernity often proceeds under a variety of labels. Theologians are likely to discuss the issue under the rubric of *secularization*. However, the meaning of secularization is variously defined and its relationship to the question of modernization is not always clear. For some, secularization refers to the decline of the influence of the church in the affairs of Western men. For others, it means the apparent inability of modern man to believe in God. For others, it means that God is "dead" and that man is now free to build his own future. Still others believe that God is not dead but that he is now immanent in the secular process itself. Yet others insist that God is very alive but very transcendent, thereby leaving man with vast areas of secular experience over which to exercise his own prerogatives. And then there are those who hold that secularization is equivalent to man's rebellious sinfulness, a sign of man's prideful forgetfulness of God in the affairs of men.

The category of secularization, in addition to the great confusions surrounding its meaning, seems more confining, for our purposes, than does the category of modernization. With the rubric of modernization one can include the religious factors involved in the question of secularization as well as address a variety of other psychological, sociological, and cultural factors.

The same is true with the issue of language, which is another increasingly important umbrella under which the debate about modernity has progressed. The grand debate over the meaning of language is really a disguised debate over the meaning or evaluation of modernity. The central question is this: Is there more to life, truth, and reality than can be captured adequately by the scientific and mathematical models of language in which modernity has put so much faith? If modernity narrows its language to fit only the certainties of the mathematical and physical sciences, will it not impoverish and perhaps destroy civilization by establishing a language that can neither account for, guide, control, nor give appropriate expression to, the full range of life and reality? In contrast to the Bertrand Russells and the Alfred J. Ayers of this world, there are leading scholars in a variety of disciplines who have been tirelessly working to correct the narrowing pressure of technical reason upon the function of language in the modern world.

Mircea Eliade in the history of religions, Martin Heidegger and Paul Ricoeur in existential phenomenology, Claude Lévi-Strauss in cultural anthropology, and Paul Tillich in theology are only a few examples.

Our inquiry could be rewritten from the perspective of the current debate on the nature of language. But to impose the question of language on the men reviewed here would be to impose an alien category on their thought. Both Rieff and Erikson have little directly to say about language, and it is actually a secondary concern for both Fromm and Brown. Yet even in this study, the question of the nature and function of language is not completely overlooked, and we hazard the conjecture that the results of our study will not be completely without implications for this particular perspective on the even more fundamental debate about modernity.

Therefore, we address the question directly. What is the meaning and what are the prospects of modernity? And what kind of man should come along to do what should be done about modernity? These are the questions we bring to these thinkers. Posing the questions that interest us in terms of the problem of modernity is probably more congenial to the tradition of the social sciences in the United States. Persons such as Talcott Parsons, David Riesman, Winston White, C. Wright Mills, William Whyte, Edward Shils, Shmuel N. Eisenstadt, Daniel Lerner, and Cyril E. Black have been some of the leading figures in this discussion.[18] Even here, the discussion often proceeds under the category of "mass society." Yet the idea of modernity is also explicitly used by these men and is probably the category most congenial to the four thinkers we are studying as well as the broad discussion as it is progressing on the American scene.

To focus the question of the good man in the context of modernity will leave us with a few other concerns to pursue as well. Since we are bringing this question to four psychoanalytic ethicists, we will always want to know what each of these men believes to be the role of psychoanalysis as a moral science. Because ethics generally receives some kind of religious articulation and justification, we certainly will be concerned to know how each of these men understands the nature and function of religion. Since their respective interpretations of modernity are at the heart of our study, we will want to know something about the general approach to "interpretation" taken by each of these thinkers.

To give form to our discussion of the vision of man of each of these thinkers, I will summarize each position in terms of four specific categories: (1) man's relationship to himself, (2) his relationship to the

FOUR THEORIES OF THE GOOD MAN

	Accommodational Response	*Regressive Response*	*Progressive Response*	*Dialectically Progressive Response*
Categories	RIEFF: Psychological Man Modernity as the collapse of communal obligation	BROWN: Dionysian Man Modernity as repression	FROMM: Productive Man Modernity as alienating freedom	ERIKSON: Generative Man Modernity as identity-diffusing change
1 Man in relation to himself	Modality of release moderated by the insight and technical reason of the ego	Recapitulation into consciousness of the regressive wish for union and acceptance of death	Progressive restatement of need for union	Incorporation of child, animal, and primitive into generative ethic of care
2 Man in relation to his social world	a. Uses human relationships for comfort and balance b. Is detached from political process c. Experiments with religious symbols for balance	a. Sees all human relationships as shadows of repressed desire for union with the lost mother b. Sees politics as substitute quest for the lost body c. Sees all religions as disguises for true religion of resurrected body	a. Enriches others and self through active giving b. Is politically active in all spheres of life c. Has secular religion of positive ethic	a. Sees human relationships as mutuality of activation and reciprocity of giving and receiving b. Has generative politics of establishing, maintaining, and ritualizing institutional fabric of society c. Integrates religion, synthesizing ideological and universal elements
3 Man in relation to time	Lives in the prudent present, detached from the past, with cautious hopes for avoidance of pain in the future	Recaptures the past in order to live in the eternal present	Lives for the future and actively brings it about	Lives in the present, toward the future, incorporating and transforming the past
4 Man in relation to the "other" (the stranger)	Learns very little from the other, be it stranger, child, ancestor, or primitive	Under particularity of diverse traditions sees brotherhood of those who quest for union with lost body	Believes in universal brotherhood built on common ethical capacities	In dialogic relationship with the other, respects and learns from the particularity of the other while aspiring for a universal identity

FIG. 1

social world, (3) his orientation to time, and (4) his attitude toward the "other" (the stranger). Research in the relationship between culture and personality has suffered from the lack of stable categories to guide and organize comparative research.[19] The use of these four categories in the following pages is designed to overcome this shortcoming.

Figure 1 presents a summary of our comparative analysis of the vision of the good man in Rieff, Brown, Fromm, and Erikson.

We cannot hide our conviction that Philip Rieff, Norman Brown, and even Erich Fromm do not speak for the emerging consensus to be found in the later developments of the psychoanalytic tradition. We believe, instead, that Erik Erikson gives ethical form to many of these later developments. Yet it is profitable to set Erikson and the tradition of ego psychology side by side with these other psychoanalytic ethicists. Particularly is this true since their positions are doubtless representative of important cultural options with which Western people are experimenting, often in the name of psychoanalysis. Yet because of our bias toward Erikson and the broad tradition of ego psychology which he represents, we will often refer to this tradition in both testing and sometimes correcting some of the shortcomings of the other three writers. Most especially will we focus on the limitations of Rieff's concept of reason, Brown's ontology of individuation, and Fromm's undialectical progressivism. But always our major concern is the particular theory of the good man in the good society which each of these men, using the psychoanalytic tradition, has made an effort to illuminate.

2

PHILIP RIEFF

*Psychological Man and the Penultimate Ethic
of the Abundant Life*

No one has been more successful in demonstrating the cultural significance of psychoanalysis than Philip Rieff. While other writers have busied themselves exposing Freud's biological reductionism, his bondage to late nineteenth-century mechanistic models of scientific inquiry, and his general disregard of cultural and social factors, Rieff has taken a different road. He has demonstrated with the kind of intellectual force which discourages further debate that the main thrust of Freud's work was cultural and, in fact, even moral. After Rieff's work, there is very little more to be said on this subject. Freud knew that man did not live by instinct alone. His own criticisms of the culture of his day were designed to exorcise and reshape it but certainly not to destroy it.

This is why we begin with Rieff. He establishes the best argument available for one of the primary assumptions that justifies this study—the cultural meaning and influence of psychoanalysis and its view of man. More specifically, by giving it a name, Rieff crystallized Freud's vision of the way man should organize his energies to live with modernity. The concept of the "psychological man" is Rieff's name for the Freudian vision. Rieff takes the unformed vision of the master and, as disciples are prone to do, endows it with increased clarity, amplifies it, and finally advances it as a specific program with no small credit falling, in the end, to himself. Disciples of great masters tend to become famous and respected themselves.

But Rieff is a disciple of Freud in a special sense. He is not a practicing psychoanalyst aspiring to refine his therapeutic skills. By profession he is a sociologist although he is more of a student of the humanities than the academic discipline over which he specifically presides. He is primarily interested in how man's cultural vision shapes the way man lives and organizes his energies. Rieff is interested in the relation of culture and character, and it is with this question that he comes to his study of Freud and psychoanalysis. Rieff is convinced that there hovers around psychoanalysis as a therapeutic science a cluster of ideas, attitudes, and practices that contain a commanding vision of both the nature of the modern world and the way man must organize his character in order to live successfully within it. This configuration of ideas and attitudes is centered in the character of Freud himself. Freudian theory and the psychoanalytic movement are secondary to and finally mere conveyors of the matchless mind and character of Freud himself. If psychoanalysis has engendered a new symbolic, a new myth, which is in the process of reorganizing the character and self-understanding of modern man, it is further the case, Rieff believes, that this symbolic is animated by the very person of Freud himself. Although he would shy away from the comparison, it is clear that, for Rieff, Freud and the psychoanalytic movement constitute something of a new hierophany, complete with saving doctrine, disciplines, and human exemplar. Freud and his teachings may have given birth to a new controlling symbolic that will fulfill many of the same functions as the old religions. But this new controlling symbolic is distinctively modern in its antihierophonic, antireligious stance. It is the ultimate strategy for teaching modern man the art of living without ultimates—the last word in therapies for the unbelieving.

It is psychoanalysis, and more specifically the exemplary character of Freud, that has given the modern world a symbolic and a technology uniquely suited to the new kind of man who is emerging. Psychological man is different from all other personality types that have been dominant at various times throughout history. He is different from the religious man of our Hebrew and Christian heritage, the political man grounded in our Greek origins, and the economic man formed by the Enlightenment and then reshaped by Protestant ideology and piety. Near the end of his book *Freud: The Mind of the Moralist*, Rieff gives us the following preliminary introduction to this new man and briefly distinguishes him from his predecessors:

> He [psychological man] is not the pagan ideal, political man, for he is not committed to the public life. He is most unlike the religious man.

We will recognize in the case history of psychological man the nervous habits of his father, economic man: he is anti-heroic, shrewd, carefully counting his satisfactions and dissatisfactions, studying unprofitable commitments as the sins most to be avoided. From this immediate ancestor, psychological man has constituted his own careful economy of the inner life.[1]

According to Rieff, psychological man is learning how to live neither by "the ideal of might nor by the ideal of right"—two concepts that so profoundly confused "his ancestors, political man and religious man." [2] Rather, psychological man lives by the ideal of "insight—practical, experimental insight leading to the mastery of his own personality." [3] Psychological man has turned away from his Occidental preoccupation with transforming the environment and converting others. Rather, he now more nearly imitates the Oriental "ideal of salvation through self-contemplative manipulation." [4]

Even this brief characterization of psychological man should be enough to convince any honest mind that Rieff has identified some characterological movements within contemporary life which are only a little less than obvious. Whether his interpretation of these trends is correct and whether he can defend his belief about the importance of Freud and psychoanalysis in forming these trends—these are questions we will submit to more careful analysis in the process of this chapter. Rieff knows that Freud did not create *de nouveau* this emerging psychological man. Certainly psychological man is a synthesis of several different cultural fragments and sociological trends. The Protestant ethic, democracy, urbanism, structural differentiation under the impact of advanced industrialization, science, historical relativity—these are only a few of the cultural and social forces simply assumed by Rieff as sources setting the stage for the appearance of psychological man. Rieff makes no effort to systematize or verify some of the conventional conclusions of the social sciences which he freely employs but which are now tattered from the thoughtless usage that time and familiarity bestow upon all privileged theories.

Although Rieff acknowledges the manner in which social systematic changes and conflicts influence the formation of new character types (a favorite thesis of David Riesman and his followers), Rieff finally believes that cultural factors are far more important. In a footnote near the beginning of *The Triumph of the Therapeutic,* Rieff clearly states his rejection of the assumption, widely held among professional sociologists, that conflicts within the social system *or* conflicts between the social system and the cultural system constitute the fundamental theoretical framework for all sociological explanation. Rieff suggests, however, that it may be "necessary to develop a theory of tensions *within* a culture." He writes:

> Suppose it is from the superior level of the cultural system that organizing (and disorganizing) higher principles thrust into the social structure. That thrust of higher (cultural) principles into the myriad particular activities of man, enacted by cultural elites even in the most highly differentiated social structure, would then establish the modalities of societal integration and disintegration. Moreover, the study of smaller units of the social self would also take its direction from these modalities.[5]

The major cultural conflict out of which we have just emerged was the battle between Freud and Calvin. The symbolics that surrounded these men, their thought, and the social movements that followed them have constituted, during the first half of the twentieth century, the major cultural options contending for supremacy in organizing those "smaller units of the social self," i.e., the character and self-definition of modern Western man. Rieff believes that the battle is largely over and that Freud has clearly emerged as the victor.[6] But new battles are emerging. Now the question has become: Will Freud be heard and understood correctly or will modern man be seduced into moral chaos and cultural confession by Freud's remissive detractors?

A Theory of Culture

It is fitting that Rieff, who puts so much stock in the role of individual great minds and cultural elites in the formation of culture, should have his own favorite text upon which he bases his assessment of the cultural significance of Freud and his work. In view of the number of times that Rieff refers to it, one wonders if it does not serve as something of a sacred text. Rieff believes that this famous passage on the therapeutic "goals" of psychoanalysis reveals both the cultural and the normative implications of Freud's work. The purpose of therapy, Freud once wrote,

> is to strengthen the ego, to make it more independent of the superego, to widen its field of perception and enlarge its organization, so that it can appropriate fresh portions of the id. Where id was, there ego shall be. *It is a work of culture.*[7]

Certainly Rieff is correct in his assessment of Freud: in the mind of Freud, psychoanalysis was a method for civilizing the chaotic desires of the id, not with blind authority as had always been the case before, but with the cool light of psychoanalytic insight and interpretation.

But Rieff's theory of culture goes beyond anything that Freud ever contemplated. For Rieff, culture is *sui generis;* it is never to be reduced to a simple projection of psychological forces, sociological patterns, or, for that matter, even to the specific intentions of the creative minds of history. It is true that the great minds and the cultural elites of history tend to create culture, but their creations are always somewhat different from their intentions. With regard to his theory of culture, Rieff learns more from Max Weber than from Freud, and he learns very little at all from Durkheim or Marx.

What Rieff learned from Weber is simple enough. Culture is most generally the result of the *unintended* and misunderstood creations of history's cultural elites.[8] Weber demonstrated how this theory works out in several different historical contexts, not the least important of which, for Rieff, being the cultural consequences of the religious intentions of the Old Testament prophets. But the best-known example, and the most relevant for this study, is Calvin. The cultural consequences of Calvin's teachings cannot be inferred from his individual psychology, the social processes occurring during his day, or the specific intentions behind his theological doctrines. It was the unintended consequences of Calvin's two grand theological ideas—salvation through divine election and worldly blessings as a sign of this election —that they provided an ideological justification for a capitalist ethic and an organizing symbolic for "economic man." Culture is made from the top down, but seldom in the way that those at the top expected or hoped would be the case.

This does not mean that Rieff believes that psychological forces have been completely absent in the course of history from the formation of culture. Freud's Oedipal drama may well have constituted a subterranean current flowing beneath all cultural and historical processes in the past. But, for Rieff, the Oedipal analogy never exhausts the meaning of any specific historical or cultural expression; the psychological forces that animate the Oedipal struggle always take unique and highly specific meanings once they have been filtered through the creative imaginations of the cultural elites and suffered the unintended consequences of the ironies of historical misunderstanding. Rieff believes, along with Freud and Nietzsche, that psychology is the basic science, but this never means for Rieff that either history or culture can be understood as a simple eternal repetition of the primordial yearnings of the psyche à la Freud, Jung, Norman Brown, or, from another perspective, the work of Mircea Eliade. Rieff often, with good reason, likes to have his cake and eat it too. Cultural elites can make ripples flow in a variety of patterns, but Rieff grants that they throw their pebbles in the same old pond. Rieff believes that Freud overestimated the immobility and self-identity of the murky puddle out of which man for centuries has aspired to crawl. However, because of Freud's unswerving conviction of its silent presence, Rieff is convinced that the Viennese doctor may still prove to be man's best guide for escaping the vague and shadowy repetitions of history. Man escapes the repetitions of his psychological tendencies only through culture. Some cultures are better for this than are others, but for Rieff the best culture would be one based on the clear light of psychoanalytic insight.

What, then, is the function of culture? In order to answer this question, Rieff makes a distinction between all past cultures and the newly emerging culture. Rieff sees a certain formal similarity between the old and the new culture. The structure of the cultural equation will be the same, but in the new culture the calculations will be done in reverse.

All civilizations are based on cultures. Culture is the symbolic system of "restraints" and "permissions" operative in every civilization and every community. No community or civilization can exist without it. When this dialectical system of "Yes" and "No" is internalized and appropriated into the structure of a people's common character, Rieff likes to call it "faith." [9] This structure of culture, this faith of the people, serves as a cognitive and affective map of the social terrain, guiding people in their contacts with one another, censoring their exposure to novel and potentially disruptive or frightening stimuli, teaching them what to trust, and, most important of all, whom to trust.

Rieff's theory works like this: At the highest level of control stands the cultural system and the cultural elites who both invent and advocate its moral demands. Beneath this stands a cadre of therapeutic functionaries who administer its restraints and grant it permissions and consolations. Lower still is the social system itself, its institutional patterns, the daily life of the people, and the whole system of more proximate beliefs, justifications, prohibitions, and satisfactions which endow it with the appearance of meaning and solidity. [10]

Even the culture of psychological man, Rieff believes, will follow the same pattern, but with some important inversions. In all former cultures the system of restraints clearly outweighed and dominated the system of instinctual permissions and remissions. In the emerging civilization, the cultural algebra is shifting. Ours is a remissive culture. It is a culture in which the releases outweigh the controls. Whereas in former cultures remissions were in the service of restraints, in our culture prudent restraints and calculated controls are clearly in the service of richer and more varied releases. The cultural revolution Rieff is describing can be characterized in the following way: "From a predicate of renunciatory control, enjoining releases from impulse need, our culture has shifted toward a predicate of impulse release, projecting controls unsteadily based upon an infinite variety of wants raised to the status of needs." [11]

In all earlier cultures, the therapeutic functionaries administered consolations and educed conformity within the larger framework of a culture of restraint. In the new culture, the therapist instructs men in the disciplines of release, of self-expression, and of experimentation with the novel. In the new culture, the therapist is "anti-cultural" in the sense that he is subversive of the constraining functions of culture.[12] In fact, in this new civilization, the therapist and his patrons (the rich) are the new elites, and together they are busy developing a new culture, a new symbolic, and a new character type, all of which will be predicated upon motifs of release prudently ordered by the cognitive and interpretative controls of psychoanalytic insight. This will be control through self-knowledge and mutual self-revelation.[13]

At least this is what Rieff hopes will happen. The new culture may misfire simply because the therapist, the intellectual, and the rich may join hands with "instinctual everyman and his girl friend" and try to devise a completely remissive culture, a utopia of blind permissiveness, a community of faith where libido is god. This is the direction in which D. H. Lawrence, Wilhelm Reich, and Carl Jung are going. Along with them, Rieff believes, are going most liberal intellectuals, the liberal clergy, and far too many psychoanalytically trained therapists; all of them seem to be hell-bent on cultural suicide. Every culture must have its shared, deeply internalized, and institutionally regularized controlling symbolic. It is clear that although Rieff believes that control by insight would be superior to control by blind authority, he also believes that control by blind authority would be better than no control at all. And the tragedy of his analysis and his solution is that he can think of no other than these alternatives.

The Sources of Psychological Man

Freudian psychology did not create psychological man, but it may have been successful in bestowing a viable form to certain cultural and sociological fragments resident within man's unsteady march toward modernity. Psychological man will be a composite of (1) certain random cultural and social forces of modernity, (2) the commanding personality of Freud himself, (3) the procedures and moral implications of his therapy, and finally, (4) selected doctrines from Freud's scientific myth about the origins and nature of man.

The Cultural and Social Forces of Modernity

Rieff makes no effort to systematize the non-Freudian forces of modernity that have conspired to produce psychological man and his culture. That which other men, such as Shmuel N. Eisenstadt and Cyril E. Black, spend professional careers agonizing about, Rieff easily assumes or swiftly summarizes with striking epigrams, which have a persuasive force superior to their explanatory power.[14]

As is always the case with Rieff, the cultural forces are the most important. First, there is economic man (product of the Protestant ethic) who has bequeathed his individualism, his materialism, and his capacity to invest prudently and manipulate his inner emotional capital. But, of course, economic man has failed to pass on his asceticism and his moral rectitude. Then there is democracy itself: democracy, as De Tocqueville predicted long ago, tends to isolate people from one another and break down a sense of communal fidelity. In addition, we must list the historicist mentality which uproots our settled convictions about the past and the authority of the past. And finally, there is science (which always promulgates a neutralist attitude) which works to erode all our familiar canons about the true and all our accustomed beliefs about the good.

But there are social forces as well. Industrialization and urbanism differentiate our communities, destroying the integrating authority of village, tribe, and nuclear family, leaving modern man at once more free and more lonely. And finally technology itself has given modern man more leisure and released him from the clutches of necessity and the tyranny of community loyalty which is always demanded when scarcity is everyone's common enemy. Psychological man has been touched by all these forces of modernity. He is at once economic with his emotional investments, individualistic and lonely, enlightened and skeptical, liberated, self-centered, self-indulgent, and leisured. So far such a man sounds no different from the privatized urbanite who emerges when the sociological principle of "structural differentiation" is wrung until dry by such authors as Talcott Parsons, Peter Berger, and Thomas Luckmann.[15]

Although there are some points of similarity between the understanding of the character of modern man held by many sociologists and

Rieff's concept of psychological man, there are important methodological differences that separate them. For instance, Peter Berger and Thomas Luckmann believe that the processes of structural differentiation automatically work to loosen man's commitment to an objective social order, thereby freeing him to turn inward upon himself. Berger insists that even before the advent of Freud modern man was ready to buy what Freud would later want to sell.[16] Rieff sees it differently. He admits that modern man was well along with his disillusionment with old symbolics of communal and public obligation, but Freud came selling more than most moderns either expected or were at first prepared to buy. Try as they may, most sociologists, even the more enlightened such as Berger, have difficulty taking the cultural dimensions of social life with sufficient seriousness. The cultural symbolic generally ends up reflecting the structure of the social system; it adds little that is new.[17] Rieff errs in the other direction. For Rieff, the cultural system is so important that he hardly knows how to assess the significance of the social system itself. He promises to work out a fuller statement of their relation in a future book.

Freud: The Exemplary Character

For Philip Rieff, the dominant force in the modern world giving coherence and integrity to Western man's self-understanding is the psychoanalytic movement and, more specifically, the mind and character of Freud which this movement reflects.

Rieff conveys his personal reverence for the character of Freud when he writes that "the exemplary cast of Freud's mind and character is more enduring than the particulars of his doctrine." [18] In the preface to the Anchor edition of Freud: The Mind of the Moralist, Rieff writes with reference to the letters of Freud: "How rarely do great men retain their presence when we get close to them in the one way possible across the distance of history—in their correspondence. Freud survives, and grows in stature." [19] Later he adds, "The greatness of the man is beyond question, complementing the greatness of his mind." [20] Such unabandoned admiration will not be shared by all the authors reviewed in this study, and most certainly not by Fromm. However, this vaunted estimation of Freud is only preparatory to a major theoretical point— the importance of individual personalities for the formation of culture. In psychoanalysis we have a discipline created by Freud and for Freud; it is a cultural force that is detached from Freud's person but that still, in its methodology and ethic, reflects his character. The following important quote tells it all:

In culture it is always the example that survives; the person is the immortal idea. Psychoanalysis was the perfect vehicle for Freud's intellectual character. When, at last, Freud found himself, having searched systematically but in vain in various disciplines, he established a new discipline, first of all for himself.

Later, as psychoanalysis became more adaptable, the hidden force of Freud's character began to be effective through the discipline, detached from his person. Psychoanalysis became a transferable art, and therefore a cultural force.[21]

Freud was the chief architect and exemplar of the analytic attitude and the "analytic ethic" applied to the arena of human affairs. It is upon this analytic attitude and ethic that psychoanalysis as a therapeutic art depends. Each man has his heroes, and Moses, Hannibal, and Oliver Cromwell are three of the more important for Freud.[22] The "independency," "cerebral rectitude," and "moral tenacity" shared by these otherwise quite different historical personages express themselves in Freud in an analytic ethics of honesty which he employed with ruthless and uncompromising rigor to himself as well as to others. Many of Freud's specific ideas about dreams, the unconscious, and the importance of infantile sexuality were held as true before his time. But no man before Freud had ever submitted the products of his own dream life to the kind of unsparing and dispassionate analysis in the way Freud did in his greatest book, *The Interpretation of Dreams.* Under the impact of this analytic keenness both the "highest" and the "lowest" in man are shown to have a far more intimate contact with each other than man generally likes to think. In addition, under the sharp eye of analytic scrutiny, neither man's highest moral ideals nor his most primitive instinctual yearnings can be judged very trustworthy. The analytic attitude, as realized by Freud in his life and as practiced in all good psychoanalysis, comes down to this: it teaches (1) an accepting but restrained enjoyment of the transitory pleasures of life, (2) an accommodating but basically detached relation to the demands of the communal and political good, and finally, (3) a shrewd eye to negotiating small compromises and fleeting states of inner balance in the face of the enduring conflicts between the two regimes of id and superego and the hard face of external reality. Freud, according to Rieff, was neither a romanticist nor an idealist—he was a realist. He held out no hopes for salvation and believed in no cures. He hoped to increase man's sense of well-being, not through cure or not even through happiness, but by decreasing his pain and lowering his suffering.

Psychoanalysis as a Moral Science

There is little doubt that Rieff is right: psychoanalysis is a cultural force today giving large numbers of people their basic self-understanding as well as a technology for self-manipulation. He is also correct in seeing the psychoanalytic movement, especially through its procedures for the training of new therapists, as a bearer of the moral character of Freud himself.

The moral character of Freud as it was reflected in the therapeutic and pedagogical procedures of psychoanalysis gives Rieff a unique vantage point from which to interpret the entire corpus of Freud's writings. Rieff is not a literal-minded man. Starting from where he does leads Rieff to give some astounding new interpretations to certain aspects of Freud's thought which were once believed to be settled beyond question. When viewed from the perspective of Freud's own character and the specific procedures of the psychoanalytic hour itself, all of Freud's theories take on a surprisingly moral tone. In fact, according to Rieff, psychoanalysis becomes a "moral science"; it becomes *the* moral science in the sense that it is the only viable moral wisdom for modern man.

There can be little doubt about the essential rightness of Rieff's interpretation of psychoanalysis as a moral science in the form that it was conceived and practiced by Freud himself. As a moral science, Rieff sees it as a "penultimate" ethic, a "negative" ethic that gives no positive answers yet criticizes all positive answers. Our discomfort with Rieff's interpretation can be stated in the form of two questions which the remainder of this chapter will attempt to illuminate: (1) Because of Rieff's adherence to certain privileged Freudian doctrines, does he see the full potential of psychoanalysis as a moral science? (2) Can he finally maintain his intriguing distinction between "penultimate" and "positive" ethics? The answer to this latter question will determine the validity of everything he has to say about the viability of psychological man and his ethic.

What specific content does Rieff give to his claim that psychoanalysis is a moral science? Near the beginning of his book on Freud, after briefly tracing Freud's early flirtations with neurophysiology, Rieff makes the following summary statement about the shift that had gradually evolved but was fully evident by 1900 in *The Interpretation of Dreams*:

> In the materialist conception, mind is the agent of the body; in the Freudian conception, as it gradually emerged through these early years of uncertainty, the body exists as a symptom of mental demands.[23]

This is the lesson that Freud learned from his study of hysteria and from his discovery that sexual traumas, which he once supposed to be the cause of neurosis, were most often only imagined, in fact, only wished. Not only did the imagined trauma contain a hidden "wish" but the symptom itself was maintained by a "will to forget painful memories" and the patient's "desire to be sick." [24] Rieff points out that the technique of therapy practiced by Breuer "in which cure was effected on a semi-conscious and passive patient, preserved the mechanistic assumption of the disease as an alien entity within the patient." But Freud gradually moved in another direction. For Freud, we are told, "neurosis was no intruder"; rather, it was an "element of character, identical with the patient himself." [25] In addressing psycho-analysis to a moral agent and eliciting his conscious cooperation, Freud "restored an ethical, and therefore a social, conception of human sickness." [26]

Taking for his theme the idea that for the mature Freud "body exists as a symptom of mental demands," Rieff reinterprets and, in fact, exonerates Freud's continuing tendency to use the language of mechanics and the terminology of sexual energetics. Freud had a "heavily metaphoric cast" to his thought; he translated "too easily into metaphors the literally intended concepts of physical psychology." [27] Gradually other metaphoric expressions appeared and reinterpreted the mechanistic ones. His tripartite division of mental regimes was sometimes referred to as a "suite of connecting rooms" or a "trio of inner voices like the good and bad counselors of the old morality plays." [28] The most important of all was the "political" metaphor with its Platonic overtones which sees the mind as a conflict between the masses with their superior strength and their weaker but better or-ganized rulers.[29] Freud once wrote: "Our mind . . . is no peacefully self-contained unity. It is rather to be compared to a modern State in which a mob, eager for enjoyment and destruction, is to be held down forcibly by a prudent superior class." Most striking and yet most ques-tionable is Rieff's tendency to excuse even the most crude of Freud's quantitative language of sexual energetics, such as can be found in his *Three Essays on the Theory of Sexuality*, as a "vast ethical meta-phor" which "bears an oblique 'scientific' plea for greater sexual lati-tude" on the part of the "repressive order" of Victorian society.[30] Finally, Rieff defends Freud against those mathematically oriented psychologists of our day who would look down upon Freud's careless use of metaphorical language: quantification may be more precise, but it is also more distant "from the human subject." [31]

Rieff, more than any other Freudian interpreter, has demonstrated that the neutral, analytic attitude of psychoanalysis constitutes a certain kind of ethic—an ethic of honesty. This ethic, and the larger moral system that it implies, is best illustrated in the psychoanalytic procedure itself, especially in the process of free association. But if psychoanalysis is a moral science, Rieff sees it as a humble one. Moreover, it is the kind of humility that ends up humiliating all else that surrounds it. A humbleness that humiliates; this sums up the content of psychoanalysis as a moral science. Rieff writes, "Freud's is a penultimate ethic tooled to the criticism of ultimates." [32] It cannot provide a positive ethic; in fact, it "is dependent on that which it criticizes—ethics that are positive and ultimate." Rieff himself admits that although psychoanalysis can free us to choose, the problem of choice still remains, and that here "at the critical moment, the Freudian ethic of honesty ceases to be helpful." [33]

However, Rieff believes that there is a place for a negative ethic of honesty. A negative ethic has a role to play for two reasons: (1) In the past all positive ethics have been systems of renunciation induced by repressive authorities. (2) Authority itself is predicated upon an unhealthy manipulation of *love* and *power*. As questionable as they are, it is from the vantage point of these two assumptions that Rieff accepts the efficacy of what he considers Freud's primary mission. Exposing the ambiguity and impurity of Western man's most cherished moral achievements, this "was the moral mission left to the psychologist after philosophy and religion had raised man too high." Rieff writes further:

> According to the Freudian counsel, man must not strain too far the limitations of his instinctual nature. Therefore, knowing, becoming conscious of these limits, is itself a primary ethical act. Consciousness, self-knowledge, interpretative revelation and decision, candor, talking things through—all presume a necessary reduction of ethical aspiration. Without this imperative, Freud's conception of therapy is meaningless. "A little more truthfulness," Freud recommends, instead of the painful old passion for goodness.[34]

It may be true that Western civilization has been built on moral ideals that all too often have been pretentious, authoritarian, renunciatory, and finally rotten to the core with ambiguity. Granting this, however, does not concede to Rieff the correctness of his major assumption—that all positive ethics are built upon systems of renunciation and assume repressive authority. Yet it is on the validity of this assumption, as well as others we will soon review, that Rieff can defend the usefulness of a penultimate ethic, and the validity of restricting psychoanalysis to what might be called the basement step of ethical reflection. Surely, psychoanalysis must have hidden within it a positive ethical vision; no system of criticism can criticize successfully without envisioning an alternative to the object of its attack. It may be that psychoanalysis is not only a moral science, but that it is also far more than simply a penultimate ethic.

The Rieffian Uses of Freud

There are important ways in which Rieff uses the substantive teachings of Freud in developing his concept of psychological man. Yet there is a sense in which Rieff has learned both everything and nothing from Freud. It is finally the person of Freud—his character—that Rieff carries with him. Rieff is sufficiently erudite about the advances of modern psychology to realize that there are many unsatisfactory concepts in Freud's writings. He is especially critical of Freud's geneticism, his failure to develop an adequate theory of perception, his heavy-handed symbolic interpretations, and his reductionistic interpretations of history and art. However, Rieff has the interesting tendency of criticizing the literal content of a Freudian concept and then restating it at a higher, more symbolic level where it can be accepted for what Rieff considers to be its "true" or "genuine" meaning. It is quite clear from the pages of his *The Triumph of the Therapeutic* that in the end Rieff accepts most of Freud's cardinal teachings on the nature of instinct, the role of reason, and the inevitable conflicts between self and society. When Rieff is giving a sociological description of what he considers to be the empirical manifestations of psychological man, his analysis depends *very little* on the body of Freudian doctrine. When he is describing psychological man as an imagined and hoped for character type who might solve the problems of modern existence, Rieff *very much* depends on basic Freudian theory.

Let us examine what Rieff believes he has learned from Freud on the three following subjects: (1) the nature of reason (or the ego), (2) the nature of human instinct, and (3) the inevitable conflict between self and society. In each case, our object will not be to debate the correctness of Rieff's understanding of Freud, but to examine his use of Freud in the development of his concept of psychological man.

We begin with Rieff's concept of reason. To bring economy and focus to our discussion, we will also carry it with us as we examine his concept of instinct and his view of the relation of self and society.

Reason, for Rieff and for the emerging psychological man, is, as always, the capacity for synthesis. But reason, as psychological man will use it and as psychoanalysis understands, is really "technical reason." It is reason operating as a small-time negotiator shrewdly working out modest compromises and partial syntheses with an eye toward a slightly improved standard of emotional well-being. Reason, as Rieff puts it somewhere, "is a bourgeois gentleman." In one place, Rieff distinguishes between two "theories of theory," which of course is the same as distinguishing between two theories of reason. One view sees reason (or theory) as the mind's effort to grasp the "order" and "unity" of the whole of things. The second view sees reason and theory as "power." This latter view does not seek after the meaning or unity of the whole, it simply "uses" what it finds.[35] It is clear that Rieff associates *his* understanding of technical reason with the latter viewpoint and associates with the former all efforts to establish a positive community of social demand.

Freud's theory of the ego implies a similar view of reason as technical. Rieff writes: "To Freud, reason is without content, a technical instrument. Psychoanalytic therapy proposes no substantive program to the ego. . . . Indeed, . . . reason is a mediating aptitude and not an inclusive end." [36] As is well known, for Freud the ego was originally a part of the id, a part which, under the impact of reality, had become differentiated from the id and adapted to the demands of the external world. This means that the ego is weak, has no power of its own, and must use "tricks," be "crafty," and be "sly" in order to gain sufficient power from the id to rule. Therefore the synthesizing, harmonizing, or mediating power of the ego is, as Rieff calls it, strictly a "bureaucratic function." [37] The ego neither aspires to nor needs an all-embracing synthesis, a total identity. The drive for wholeness—a picture of oneself in the total scheme of things—is only a need of the ego when driven into despair by the dictates of a bad conscience. The technical reason of psychological man will make it possible to forget the big problems of meaning and to learn to live with partial answers and incomplete syntheses. He will learn how to exist with "unbelief" and then move along with the important business of good living.

Rieff tends to disparage the efforts of the most respected of Freud's followers (people such as Heinz Hartmann, Anna Freud, and David Rapaport) to "strengthen" the position and function of the ego in the psychic economy. Rieff believes that these efforts on the part of the so-called "ego psychology" tend to overlook the conflictual character of the mind, a view of mental operations as important to Rieff as it was to Freud. At a later time, we will demonstrate how mistaken is Rieff's view of ego psychology and how unfortunate it was for his own thought that he so impatiently rejected its findings.

This brings us to our second topic—Rieff's understanding of the instinctual dimensions of man. The conflictual character of the mind is preserved, in part, for both Freud and Rieff by maintaining a sharp distinction between the manner of functioning of the ego and the id. Although the ego is dependent on the id for its energy and is in many ways its servant, it functions according to the practical, logical, cause-and-effect operations of technical reason. The instincts, for both Freud and Rieff, are different. Rieff does a great deal to refine Freud's theory of instincts, but in the end he holds them in much the same regard as did Freud: man's instincts are chaotic, persistent, blind, stupid, and contain within them the seeds of their own dissatisfactions.

Rieff points out that instinct for Freud must always be understood to mean instinctual "imagination." Rieff believes that "it is not instinct which the Freudian science examines as the root problem, but the *instinctual or natural imagination.*" [38] With the phrase "instinctual or natural imagination" Rieff is asserting that for the mature Freud, instinct is inseparable from man's imagination and his linguisticality. He writes that Freud "studies the body through the language of the mind." This brilliant observation of Rieff's, well in line with the best studies on Freud proceeding from the French phenomenologist Paul Ricoeur and the French psychoanalyst Jacques Lacan, is never carried through to its final meaning.[39] He never successfully investigates what either imagination or perception (he often complains that Freud has no adequate theory of perception) adds to the workings of instinct in man. Instead, he follows Freud very much as he stands without benefit of further clarification. The instincts are finally those timeless urges for pleasure through the reduction of tension. They tend to be quite unaware of the problems of adaptation related to living in a "real" world; and the pleasures they mediate are transitory and self-extinguishing.

The main function of the id—and he believed it to be the same with Freud—is its critical function of protest against the oppressiveness of culture. Rieff admits the confusion that besets the Freudian theory of instincts, but accepts it primarily as a "mythology" to protect the individual from the tyranny of culture. Unconscious instinct, as Freud understood it, is the "individual's defense against a repressive culture." [40] Rieff believes that the Freudian view of instincts establishes the idea of human nature as "a hard core, not easily warped or reshaped by social experience." [41] The issue at stake is a political and cultural one. For Rieff, the Freudian "hard core" of human nature is preferable to the liberalism of such thinkers as John Dewey, Karen Horney, or Harry Stack Sullivan, who tend to "let the idea of the individual be absorbed into the social." [42] It never occurs to Rieff that there may be methods other than through the subpersonal mythology of the instincts to protect the individual from progressivist forces of modern society which would endlessly manipulate and revise human nature.

Certainly, there are ways in which the givenness of instinct protects the individual from the tamperings of social forces and places a clear limitation upon both the perfectibility and the alterability of human nature. The limitation of the view held by both Freud and Rieff is that it fails to take account of the more creative capacities of man's lower biological and instinctual nature. In addition, Rieff's tendency to limit reason to technical reason is supported by his tendency to dissociate completely reason and instinct, ego and id. Recent advances in ego psychology have tended to play down the absolute distinction between ego and id made by Freud; rather, such thinkers as Heinz Hartmann and Robert White see the human personality as a hierarchy of mechanisms of organization and adaptation ranging from lower, more diffuse processes (id) to higher, more differentiated ones (ego). [43] As we shall see in a later chapter, such a view makes it possible to understand why the lower mechanisms of organization are not completely reliable guides to adaptation (because of their diffuse, undifferentiated character) while at the same time helping us to understand how id and instinct can constitute more creative forces than simple blind protest. On the other hand, this view tends to give a relative autonomy to the higher processes of the ego, yet it helps show why they are not completely trustworthy without being fed and informed by lower processes of the ego and the id. The central problem of human reason is to keep the lower and the higher processes in reciprocal contact with one another since neither the low nor the high are completely reliable in themselves. Such a model, then, helps us to recapture a view of what Paul Tillich called "ontological" reason (the whole of reason) in contrast to "technical" reason as advocated by Rieff. It helps restore a vision of reason as related to the entire organism which is man, both his higher and his lower processes.

Rieff seems to denigrate the true character of both the high and the low in man. He fails to give full credit to either the reason that is in the id or the actual relative autonomy of the higher ego processes. Man's higher quest for wholeness and rational symmetry and his lower feelings, hunches, and passions are both deflated by Rieff. This is the metapsychological foundation for the detachment of psychological man. Being able to trust neither the high nor the low in himself, psychological man must resort to the detachments of technical reason and its shrewd negotiations in order to save himself from the possible excesses of both.

Rieff himself seems dissatisfied with certain aspects of Freud's instinct theory, especially as it shows up in his understanding of the nature of play and the creative functions of dreams. Yet he does not seem to understand that the dissatisfactions he holds and the revisions he proposes would greatly affect his own view of human reason and its subsequent working out in his theory of psychological man. Rieff complains that Freud had no adequate theory of play and that he saw little of the playful in either art or dream. For Freud, both art and dreams, although more than catharsis, were little more than useful attempts at self-mastery through repetition. "Utility" was their function and utility meant nothing more than the attempt to restore the mental apparatus to a previous state of balance through repetitive "mastery" over the disturbing experience. Against Freud, Rieff writes, "Dreams arise not only out of tension and distress and unfulfillment, but also out of a spontaneous pleasure in the mind's activity." [44] In another place, Rieff complains, "He did not believe that art—or the play of children—could be the product of superabundance and spontaneity." [45]

Unfortunately, Rieff's efforts to correct this blindness in Freud leads to another excess in a different direction. Play is not simply spontaneity either. In contrast to both Freud and Rieff, the truth is more nearly this: there is no human activity that can be characterized as totally work (mastery) or totally play, totally utilitarian or totally spontaneous. The brilliant work on the nature of play by the great Swiss psychologist Jean Piaget is probably nearer to the truth. His work is increasingly better known to psychoanalytic ego psychology and is rapidly becoming an established part of more recent developments. [46] His categories of "assimilation" and "accommodation" are very helpful in understanding the true nature of play. In mature, conscious human work or labor, man achieves adaptation between himself and the demands of external reality by making his own basic human equipment and needs (what Piaget calls "schemas") conform to the demands of the outer world: this is *accommodation*. In childhood play, art, and dreams, man removes himself from the immediacy of external reality and achieves another kind of adaptation between himself and his world by making the outer world conform more closely to the inclinations of his own basic human equipment and needs: this is *assimilation*.

> The point is that every human action contains within it both the polar elements of assimilation and accommodation. The difference between instances of human action is that in some, accommodation seems to dominate assimilation, while in other instances, assimilation rules over accommodation. When accommodation rules over assimilation we are likely to call such action work. If assimilation to given or previously developed schemes of action appears to predominate over accommodation to external realities, one is likely to call it play. Yet, since all human action contains both the polarities of accommodation and assimilation, all human action contains, in varying proportions, elements of both play and work.[47]

Men are working (employing "adaptive intelligence") in their art and their dreams, but here their work is more like play in that it is more relaxed, more fruitful, and more certain of a specifically human solution. Problems that are too big to solve in reality are often addressed in dreams, art, and children's play by reducing (sometimes even distorting) the problem to more humanly manageable proportions. At least this is the function of good dreams, good art, and happy children's play. Problems playfully dealt with in dreams, art, and children's play are often problems that will later be solved in reality. Reducing or distorting the problem to more manageable proportions, as we do in these three expressions of the human spirit, often restores to us those more active and courageous modalities which make it possible to solve—or at least more adequately address—the problem as it stands in all of its brute force in external reality. Of all the thinkers reviewed in this study, Erikson, more than the others, holds a view of the relationship between play and work most similar to the one put forth by Piaget.

Had Rieff been more consistent in carrying through his dissatisfaction with Freud's failure to account for the play element in dreams and art, it would have forced him to reassess his own limitation of reason to technical reason and his dissociation of reason from the lower, instinctual processes. If there is a playful wisdom in the lower processes, then indeed reason is more than simply technical; reason receives some of its content—some guidelines—from the lower processes themselves. It may well be that reason in man reaches both higher and lower than Rieff imagines. And if psychoanalysis has discovered something about the lower processes, it may be that it has discovered something relevant for the domain of positive ethics as well.

Positive ethics may not be based simply on renunciations demanded by irrational authority and communal demand. Positive ethics are in part the product of the clarification and public articulation of some of our own deepest intuitions about the character of human nature, both that which is the "highest" and that which is the "lowest."

This brings us to the third subject we have promised to review—Rieff's view of the inevitable conflict between self and society. Rieff bases his belief in this inevitable conflict on three sets of ideas: (1) the sharp distinction between instinct and technical reason, (2) the belief that all movement from lower to higher values comes through sublimation and that sublimation always costs something from the individual, and (3) finally, the belief that all authority (the force behind cultural sublimations) represents a victory of tender love over sexuality and instinct. We will quickly review these three sets of ideas before turning to our final delineation of the nature of psychological man.

The sharp distinction made by Rieff between reason and instinct and the limitation of reason to technical reason means simply this for the relation of self and society: all renunciations necessary for the harmonious working of the social order must come about either through external authority and sublimation or through the prudence inspired by psychoanalytic insight. They never come about spontaneously from forces and perceptions internal to the individual.

In contrast to Rieff's position, it should be clear that all social harmony is not based primarily on renunciations. This overlooks the entire range of integrating forces associated with the mutual satisfactions that operate in so many areas of life, best symbolized by the mother-child relationship or the sexual experience itself—both of which afford the possibility of giving while receiving and receiving while giving pleasure to another. The harmonizing effects of these and other primal exchanges will be carefully considered in the chapter on Erikson.

To overlook the harmonizing results of this area of life, as does Rieff, does not, however, invalidate his major point, i.e., that social harmony does require renunciations. Certainly renunciations are necessary. But because of his sharp distinction between reason and instinct, Rieff can never believe that the lower can ever collaborate with the higher in support of their own limitations. Yet it is only too obvious that there are times when a surfeited stomach sends messages to the higher centers of control pleading for a termination of the feast. Children have often been noticed to spontaneously stop eating their favorite snack in willing exchange for another food containing vitamins or minerals which they lack.[48] All renunciation is not brought about by obedience to external authority. There is inevitable conflict between the individual and his social world, but this conflict is wrongly stated when it is based on the idea that all limitation and renunciation comes from the "outside," whereas only need and impulse come from the "inside." [49] The ego does more than simply work its acts of inhibition in response to the pains and threats it perceives as possible from the outside world. It performs its functions of control and self-limitation partially on the basis of the internal messages it receives from its own instinctual depths. There is a more complicated relation between the renunciations that come from within and renunciations imposed from without than Rieff will admit.

The last presupposition behind Rieff's understanding of the conflict between self and society is this: that renunciations are brought about by authorities toward whom we have "tender" feelings. In saying this, Rieff is making an important distinction between "tender feelings," "respect," or "love" on the one hand and "sexuality" on the other. Rieff's thesis, based on a somewhat heretical exegesis of Freud, is that authority exploits feelings of love while, on the other hand, rebellion is based on sexuality. It is our tender feelings of love and respect for the authorities upon whom we depend that lead us to repress our sexuality, the deepest core of our individuality. To reassert our sexuality is to defy or disenchant our respect for authorities.

On the priority of affection to sensuality, Rieff writes the following words:

> Affection or tenderness is not a sublimation of sexuality, as Freud himself sometimes supposed and as his interpreters have invariably presumed; affection, deriving from the infant's gratitude to its all-protecting parents, is the primary form of love, prior to sensual feeling.[50]

This point of view sees authorities manipulating our tender and grateful feelings toward them, thereby causing us to sublimate our sexuality to higher and more neutral goals. But according to both Freud and Rieff, sublimation always "costs" the individual; it necessitates a deliberate repression of bodily pleasure. This is the ground upon which Rieff asserts the inevitable conflict between the individual and the social order.

Although Rieff states this division between affection and sensuality less dialectically than Freud himself conceived it, it is theoretically problematic for reasons other than his divergence from Freud. More than he realizes, it puts him not only outside the circumference of orthodox analytic theory but well within the theoretical circle of neo-Freudians such as Erich Fromm, whom Rieff generally tends to disparage. The major difference between Freudian and neo-Freudian schools of thought has to do precisely with the latter's tendency to handle authority as a nonsensual category. The polarities descriptive of human behavior for the neo-Freudians—Fromm and Horney being the purest examples—are those of independence and dependence. Fromm, for instance, will define the polarities of dependence and independence with no special recourse to a theory of sensuality or libido. The helplessness of infancy and the irrational dependence on authority and adulthood are credited more to anxieties stimulated by cognitive and perceptual ambiguities than to fixated libidinal attachments, as is generally thought to be the case in orthodox psychoanalytic theory.

It is clear that Rieff, in making this distinction between affection and sensuality, has gone farther than he intended. If dependence upon authority is a nonsexual category, then independence is also a nonsexual category. This is to say that sexuality need not be invoked as the central category explaining independence or rebellion. To define helplessness and submission to authorities in nonsexual terms is automatically to place your definition of these phenomena under perceptual and cognitive categories. Children submit themselves to the authority of adults because they sense that the adult sees, knows, and perceives the world in a more masterful way than they do. In addition, people seek freedom from authority when they perceive that their own comprehension and knowledge of the world is as adequate as or superior to that of their leaders. Sensual and sexual gratifications are present at both places—at the pole of dependence upon authority and independence from authority—but if Rieff were consistent, he would have to admit that they take their meaning in relation to perceptual and cognitive judgments.

This brief critique of Rieff's formulation of the conflict between self and society has implications for this theory of psychological man. Psychological man is primarily interested in his own sense of well-being, his own internal satisfactions, his own releasing modalities, and his own sensual and sexual expressivity. Both by inclination and through psychoanalytic insight he has been liberated from affection for and loyalty to authority as well as the renunciations which it imposes. To invest too much in public life, we are told, is obviously to rob oneself of private enjoyments. In the future, psychological man will be apolitical, approving of whatever authorities provide him with a general state of abundance—the social predicate of good living.

The difficulties with this position are manifold. First, it is clear that increased sexuality and sensual expressiveness are not in themselves equivalent to an assertion of political freedom. Instances of sexual and sensual freedom have often been accompanied by the most flagrant examples of blind obedience to totalitarian regimes. This combination stands as a clear possibility in the Orwellian vision of 1984. Furthermore, if modern man has been liberated from the blind transference of infantile dependence to political and religious authorities through psychoanalytic insight (as we hope is the case), this does not mean that he will be less political. It could mean that he will be more political. It could mean that he will now base his trust in authorities on the grounds of rational assessments of competence. Limited as he is to a theory of technical reason, to a low doctrine of man's instinctual life, and to an incompletely worked out theory of perception, Rieff has no way of understanding how man can ever again have positive interests in public life unless he is thoroughly under the spell of blind dependence upon his leaders. Predicting the inevitable demise of such modalities of dependence, he is unable to envision the survival of genuine and autonomous political interests.

Psychological Man

Philip Rieff is a learned and sophisticated student of political theory ready to announce the death of politics. It is not only God who is dead, not simply religion, but politics itself. The death has been long in coming and has not yet occurred, but it is imminent. Economic man with his ascetic individualism and his taste for affluence has for some time been strangling all decent political and public life in the Western world. Psychological man, Rieff believes, will conduct the funeral. Public life, as we have known it in the past, is nearly at an end.

Rieff brings an ambiguous stance to his work. As a sociologist, he simply describes present trends and predicts future possibilities. As an ethicist, he attempts to shape both the present and the future in order to effect his vision of the good. Rieff is more than a student of culture; he clearly aspires to be a maker of culture himself. To this end he evokes images, creates moods, and displays a well-delineated personal style in his discourse. These are the humble materials out of which modern myths are made, and myths are the bearers of culture.

Rieff is trying to project the contours of a new superego for modern man, along with accompanying social institutions, methods of socialization, and ritual celebrations. It will be different from all preceding superego organizations; it will be a superego based on the negative ethic of how to be moral while believing in nothing. To establish such a character type will be "a work of culture." The symbolic that supports the new superego will be the nearest thing to religion that modern man will ever know.

Rieff is not totally in love with psychological man, but then Rieff is not totally in love with man himself. It is a mark of psychological man—and Rieff himself is an example of the species about which he writes—that he does not love or approve or idealize anyone too much. Although psychological man has just been born and is certainly not yet mature, Rieff is clearly fond of what psychological man, may become. Psychological man, Rieff believes, will be no worse and possibly a great deal better than any of his predecessors.

We will now attempt to complete our picture of psychological man. Rieff himself never attempts a systematic description. We will try to give some order to our discussion of psychological man by setting forth his relationship (1) to himself, (2) to his social world, (3) to the experience of time, and (4) to the category of the other.

The most important single thing about psychological man's internal or intrapsychic organization will be the dominance of ego, consciousness, or technical reason. For Rieff, when consciousness is increased, both instinct and superego undergo demystification. Of course, for Rieff, it is not just consciousness; it is consciousness fortified with psychoanalytic insight and the objectifying potency of scientific neutrality. These twin tools help the ego to gain control over the inner life. Psychological man will give a privileged position to the releasing modalities of instinct, but, at the same time, he will bring modest expectations to his pleasures and prudent restraints to his desires.

On the other hand, although his thralldom to his parental and cultural superego will be broken, Rieff believes that psychological man will be a basically honest type, a decent citizen, and a civil friend and neighbor. Rieff writes on one occasion, "Nothing in psychoanalytic therapy encourages immoral behavior." Further on he clarifies this by writing, "This means that psychoanalysis discourages moral behavior on the old, self-defeating grounds—out of what is now called a *sense* of guilt rather than guilt." [51] It is only too clear, I submit, that no psychoanalyst can ever relieve anyone from false guilt without already possessing a standard of true guilt. But this, according to Rieff, lapses over into positive ethics—an area into which technical reason and a penultimate ethic cannot go. The problem with Rieff is his modesty. As we will show later, psychoanalysis, or at least the tradition that is developing from it, may know something about the nature of false guilt simply because it also knows something about the nature of true guilt. Stored in its own unconscious and hidden from public view, it has its own developing positive ethic upon which its penultimate ethic depends. What this larger positive ethic might be, Rieff seems neither to know nor to care. And that it even exists at all, as far as psychoanalysis is concerned, is something Rieff seems to deny persistently.

But psychological man, although primarily interested in his own internality, will have a *social world*. And his world will have some recognizable features—politics, interpersonal relationships, and maybe even something that resembles a religion.

To say that psychological man will be an apolitical type is not to say that he will not participate in politics. Politics, however, will no longer contain its aura of ultimate seriousness. Public life and politics will not be the end of life or the measure of the good. Politics in the future will be devoid of fanaticism; it will also, Rieff hopes, be without that Presbyterian self-righteousness to be found in such political moralizers as Woodrow Wilson and John Foster Dulles. In his review of Freud and Bullitt's disappointing study of Wilson, the most Rieff can say is that it was "yet another symptom of the decline of idealization" characteristic of all modern societies. In addition, he suggests that Freud's dislike for Wilson was really a misdirected dislike of Calvin himself and the Presbyterian style of American politics—the style of the "moral crusade." [52]

As to the apparent revival of political activity on the college campus in the 1960's, Rieff calls it a "mirage." Student protests and demonstrations were really "negative anti-politics." [53] In general, most students were against power and most politicians appeared to them as "Babbitts, phonies, and professional moralizers, lacking culture and sensitivity." The really serious political activists on the college campuses were not main-line Americans at all; they were the first- or second-generation descendants of European, mainly Jewish, intellectuals who have not yet had a chance to become Americanized in their political habits.

These observations about student politics in America, although written in 1961, appear all too true even today. Students during those years primarily practiced an anti-politics. Their massive Vietnam moratoria and their fervent support of figures such as Senator Eugene McCarthy reflected their cynicism about power and their skepticism about political processes. They stand as a living testimony to the sound- ness of Rieff's sociology and the tragic wrongness of his assessment of the prospects for psychological man. Psychological man's detachment from politics may only serve to create the vacuum that will someday produce a regime that will rob him of his own so jealously guarded internal balance. It is possible that psychological man and his pe- nultimate ethic will have no clear criterion for deciding when external circumstances are so bad that he can no longer enjoy the internal freedom and balance that he seeks.

In his review of Hannah Arendt's *The Origins of Totalitarianism*, Rieff speaks with magnificent candor. The Enlightenment principle of equality before the law is nonsense. "Aristocracy still rules the world, even where the slogans are democratic; indeed, especially where the slogans are democratic, as in the Soviet Union and the United States." [54] Here, then, is the tragic flaw in Rieff's thought: the simultaneous proposal of rule by aristocracy coupled with a constituency of fol- lowers who will have neither the criteria nor the power to resist its excesses.

If in the future politics will die as a truly serious form of human endeavor, what will be the place of another domain of the social world—the sphere of interpersonal relationships? The answer is mixed: they will be both more and less important for psychological man. To some extent, the entire locus of social control will move from the hands of fathers and civil authority to the context of mutual confession, mutual openness, and insight mediated through person-to-person re- lationships. "We are, I fear, getting to know one another," Rieff writes in one place. This perfectly expresses his feelings. The hospital and the theater are replacing the church and parliament as our normative institutions.[55] Rieff can imagine the widespread use of psychodrama as a popular therapy. On the other hand, he discredits current uses of group therapy as a return to the use of therapies of communal commit- ment. It is obvious that Rieff might attend a community theater, but he would never be caught dead at an Esalen marathon.

Will psychological man have a religion? The answer is "No" if by the word "religion" one means anything resembling its principal func- tions in the past. In his book on Freud, Rieff was somewhat critical of Freud's interpretation of religion, but in the end he seems to have accepted most of what Freud taught on the subject. Religion dis- tributes the consolations that reward people for the sublimations that high culture demands.[56] But in the future, there will be no high culture, restraint will not be produced by renunciations, sublimations will not occur, and there will certainly be no need for consolations. It is precisely the talent of psychological man, under Freud's tutelage, to live without consolations. Nor will he need totalistic systems of assurances resembling the metaphysical or theological superstructures of the past. The propensities of technical reason do not aspire for wholeness in such grand proportions. He needs no community to give him an identity and no archaic symbolism to give him a sense of being rooted to the whole of things. Rieff ridicules all total communities whether they be the secular religion of communism, the mystical archaism of Jung, or the community of the genitally satisfied of Wilhelm Reich.

Psychological man will experiment with all religions but in the end settle for none. He will reject any particular symbolic for the more sophisticated process of experimenting with the symbolization process itself. The clergy and the church, in an effort to stay alive, will gradually equip themselves to be servants of therapeutic well-being through an endless process of experimentation and manipulation of symbols themselves. At least, this is the best for which Rieff can hope. His real fear, however, is that the church, demoralized psychologists, and misguided intellectuals will all join forces to produce a thoroughgoing remissive culture, devoid of the prudent restraints of psychoanalytic insight and detachment.

And how will psychological man experience time? In a strange way, time for psychological man will be primarily the present. As he does not trust either instinct or reason, neither does he trust either the past or the future. Certainly psychological man has little to learn from the past, be it father, distant ancestor, or primitive civilizations of the ancient world. Psychological man's primary concern with the past is to keep it from "returning." [57] Nor can psychological man expect too much from the future; things do not really get better, either for individual men or for civilizations. At best, one can only *hope* to reduce the pain and mitigate the discontents. There is nothing more to hope for than this. Time, for psychological man, is the prudent present—the sweetness of small enjoyments reasonably guided by the benign directives of insight.

Finally, we must ask, how will psychological man confront the "other"—those who are different, whether it is a man from another country, the stranger from a less modernized culture, or even the child that he may have or the one that may remain in himself. Here, it must be noted, a strange kind of intolerance creeps into Rieff's rhetoric

about psychological man. Psychological man treats the stranger much
as he did the ancestor; both are outside the categories of psychological man. Psychological man has nothing to learn from the stranger.
All the world, Rieff believes, is becoming like the West, yet he makes
no effort to indicate what psychological man should do in the mean-
time until other cultures catch up or what, if anything, should be done
to assure that their evolution toward modernity maintains a modicum
of integrity with their own cultural past. It is clear that psychological
man may be tolerant of differences, but rarely does he actively appreciate them. And last of all, it appears that psychological man has
little, if anything, to learn from his children. Technical reason has
nothing to learn from the regressions of childhood. Just as technical
reason has little to do with instinct, little to do with the archaism of the
past, it has little to learn from the archaism and immaturities of the
child. Strangely, then, raising children will be a process (much like
everything else in Rieff's view of things) that works primarily from
the top down. Bringing up a child will not be a reciprocal educative
process in the fashion envisioned by Erikson; it will be a process of
adults teaching children how to grow up finally to disregard them.

3

NORMAN BROWN

*Dionysian Man and the Resurrection
of the True Christian Body*

Norman Brown, in the introduction to *Life Against Death,* points
to what motivates his intellectual career. He writes, "Inheriting from
the Protestant tradition a conscience which insisted that intellectual
work should be directed toward the relief of man's estate, I, like so
many of my generation, lived through the superannuation of the
political categories which informed liberal thought and action in the
1930's." This sentence points to the paradox in Brown's writings.
Using the vestigial remains of this Protestant conscience, he strives to
relieve man from its curse. Norman Brown has rallied the remnants of
his Apollonian capacity for form and rationality and his Protestant
sense of mission to write, in addition to his earlier books, two intriguing
and highly popular books designed to abolish the very characterological
traits that make the writing of such books possible. Norman Brown is
likely to write fewer books in the future. Thomas B. Morgan says of
Brown: "He is desublimating. He welcomes disorganization in his
control over time and intensely hopes to cultivate a style of living in
the present. He believes he has a richer sense of the possibilities of
life and, conversely, he has lost some of his ability to work. 'My nature
hikes,' he says, 'have become a necessity.'" [1] In view of this trend, a review of his thought may now be in order.

But Brown prefers that his program of desublimation be more than
simply his own private affair. His words are a saving message designed
to take others with him, to create a community of the desublimated—

in short, to save the world. Brown shares an important conviction with Rieff: the problems of mankind are to be located in that which is generally considered to be the highest, the best, the most moral, and the most rational. But after this initial point of agreement, there is a radical divergence between the two thinkers. Rieff would save man from his moral and rational pretensions by failing to take them seriously. For Rieff, culture is costly but necessary. For Brown, culture is deadly and must be dismantled. Rieff advocates a negative community that relativizes and deflates culture through a systematic program of skepticism. Brown preaches not a negative community but a negation of culture, and advocates a new positive community committed to the resurrected body.

It is clear that Philip Rieff would place Norman Brown in the same company as Carl Jung, Wilhelm Reich, and D. H. Lawrence—all prophets of the new faith of modern remissiveness. Rieff saw these men as would-be prophets trying to create positive communities of commitment in service of remissive values. Each has a cure for the evils of modern rationalism. But in place of Jung's confrontation with the Evil God, Reich's democracy of the genitally satisfied, or Lawrence's eroticism of the true Christian family, Brown envisions a desublimation and resurrection of the whole polymorphously perverse body. The new faith can quite correctly be referred to as "Dionysian Christianity," and, as Rieff would have predicted, both Protestant and Catholic theologians have paid no small amount of attention to the concept.

But at the same time, Brown would have his suspicions of Rieff. Rieff would be just one more example of a long list of Apollonian-minded, rationalistic, and culturally adapted Freudians who, like the master himself, labored long and hard to unearth the true depths of man only to bury them again under an avalanche of disembodied psychoanalytic interpretations and verbalizations. For Rieff, one discovers the unconscious to keep it from returning; for Brown, one discovers the unconscious to help it to return. This, in a sentence, states the difference between their understandings of psychoanalysis as a moral science.

Norman Brown has many followers but few articulate defenders. Many of his disciples cannot be very clear about why they believe his work is important. Yet there is something about the general direction of his thought, the intensity of his style, and the totality of his attack upon modernity that evokes deep catharsis and vigorous although diffuse avowals of affirmation from significant numbers of the literary and humanistically oriented scholarly community. Susan

Sontag, speaking for some of this group, believes that Brown, along with Herbert Marcuse in *Eros and Civilization*, rightly understands that "Freud's psychological categories" are indeed "political categories." [2] To this extent, she believes that both Brown and Marcuse have saved psychoanalysis from its academic scholasticism, clinical putterings, and Rieffian accommodationalism; they have set forth, in a way that Freud himself did not have the nerve to do, the radical cultural meaning of psychoanalysis.

Paul Robinson in his *The Freudian Left* and Theodore Roszak in his *The Making of a Counter Culture* agree with the judgment of Sontag.[3] Between the two, Brown is generally conceded to be the more radical. Roszak writes that in the realm of "social criticism, the counter culture begins where Marcuse pulls up short, and where Brown, with no apologies, goes off the deep end." [4] Marcuse, for instance, would use modernity and technology as stepping-stones to the unrepressed society. Brown, however, believes that the path of modernity is too narrow and that, indeed, it is closed. Instead, we must begin the great regression, the new evolution which in reality reverses all evolution and which will take us out of the world of technological mastery and progress and back through the desublimated body, the polymorphous perversity of childish play, on back to the womb, and finally to the nothingness and peace that all men truly seek.

In many ways, Brown's work can be taken as a colossal and brilliant overstatement. Indeed Brown may regard himself as a kind of cultural trickster, a sort of Hermes the Thief attacking the gods of technological reason, capitalism, and war. Brown knows this role well, since most of his early scholarship was spent studying the trickster figure in early Greek civilization.[5] But in contrast to Hermes, who was the god of technology and commerce, Brown, through tricks, aphorism, and exaggeration, wants to take these things away from man once again. "Aphorism is exaggeration, extravagant language; the road of excess which leads to the palace of wisdom." [6] And then later he writes, "Only the exaggerations are true. . . . Aphoristic form is suicide, or self-sacrifice; for truth must die. Intellect is sacrifice of intellect, or fire; which burns up as it gives light." Yet, if there is a tongue in cheek behind the somber words of his 1960 Phi Beta Kappa oration at Columbia University, we have difficulty finding it.

> Mind at the end of its tether. . . . The alternative to mind is certainly madness. . . . Our real choice is between holy and unholy madness: open your eyes and look around you—madness is in the saddle anyhow. Freud is the measure of our unholy madness, as Nietzsche is the prophet

of the holy madness, of Dionysus, the mad truth. Dionysus has returned to his native Thebes; mind—at the end of its tether—is another Pentheus, up a tree. Resisting madness can be the maddest way of being mad.[7]

If some say that it is better to be dead than red, Brown would say it is better to be mad than dead. Or even more specifically, he would say that it is better to be mad on the way to dying, for dying is indeed our common lot. The trick of Dionysian man is knowing how to burn the fires of life brightly, living the fully erotic life, allowing no line to go "unlived," while, all along the way, accepting the inevitability of death as a natural part of living. This is precisely what Apollonian man, in his many forms, cannot do: he can accept neither life nor death and tries desperately to master and thereby escape both. As Susan Sontag and Lionel Abel both point out, there is nothing new in what he says. DeSade and Fourier in France and the "later school of German romanticism" as it took form in the anthropological writings of Theodore Lessing, Ludwig Klages, and Leo Frobenius have all been cited as giving expression to much the same vision.[8] Whatever final judgment must be brought to bear on Brown's writings, it cannot be denied that the writings have helped crystallize the rejection by large numbers of youth and intellectuals of what Daniel Bell has called the "activity principle"—the dominant cultural value of Western life from Protestantism to Marx. It is the principle of actively striving to "conquer nature, and to assert man's primacy and control over the material world. It is this . . . which is being repudiated as a cultural mode." [9]

We will approach Brown as one among many contemporary attempts to recover the archaic foundations of man's mental life. Although Norman Brown's efforts toward this end must finally be rejected, it at least serves the purpose of keeping alive the truth that modern man may have something to learn from the animal, the child, and the primitive in his own collective and individual history. The archaic in man should not be unearthed simply to be more effectively controlled, as Rieff proposes. Rieff's cryptic dictum that "the only difference between symbol and symptom is that between advocacy and analysis" must finally be considered narrow-minded and fundamentally wrong.[10] For adult, twentieth-century Western man to believe that he has nothing of importance to learn from animal, child, primitive, or his own unconscious processes would be the surest sign imaginable of his impending cultural sterility. A great army of modern intellectuals other than Jung, Reich, and Lawrence—those discussed and rejected by Rieff —are attempting, in diverse ways, to recover the archaic foundation of mental life. We can point to Konrad Lorenz and Desmond Morris in the area of ethology; Mircea Eliade, Paul Ricoeur, and Gilbert Durand in the area of phenomenology of religion; Gaston Bachelard and Theodore Thass-Thienemann in the psychoanalysis of language; and Claude Lévi-Strauss in cultural anthropology—to mention only a few of the most prominent. Brown's mistake is that he goes one better than psychoanalysis itself; all thinking, for Brown, is a redirection and a sublimation of mental processes that basically aim for only one thing: a return to the undisturbed equilibrium and nothingness of uterine existence. That is the substance of the archaic, for Brown. Brown believes that all attempts to integrate the archaic into the adult, differentiated consciousness finally perpetuates rather than cures the disease. Rather, it is his desire to dismantle the adult, differentiated consciousness, so that man will no longer fear to return to the archaism he once was so rudely forced to leave. Brown is right to seek the archaic foundations of man, but wrong in the way he does it. To seek for the archaic, one must do so from the position of the adult, dif-ferentiated *cogito*. This adult ego or *cogito* is indeed an embodied *cogito,* and it is the contours of this embodiment that we seek in our quest for the archaic. But to say that the ego is embodied is not to say that the entirety of consciousness is a sublimation of more primitive erotic desires to return to the mother's womb.

The Disease Called Man

There has been precious little careful review of Norman Brown's fundamental ideas. This is lamentable, because there is a basic order and consistency to his thought in both *Life Against Death* and *Love's Body.* His move from the scientific mode of discourse in *Life Against Death* to the poetic and aphoristic utterances of *Love's Body* does not alter the fundamental core of ideas that undergirds his thought as a whole. If Brown's thought were pure poetry and pure prophecy, one could rightly object to any effort to submit his writings to critical analysis. But there is a rational and even *literal* core to his thought which invites analysis. In fact, the heart of Brown's difficulties is that there is too much, rather than too little, literalism about what he has to say.

We will try to review the core of his fundamental ideas of union, play, death, repression, and sublimation. Then we will return for a more critical examination of the most important idea of all, the meaning and function of play in human life. Amid the confusion and

Dionysian excesses of Brown's thought, there is more than a little wisdom. His deficiencies center around his inadequate concept of play and his poorly grounded understanding of man's twofold tendency toward both union and independence, participation and individuation. Brown dimly recognizes that man wants something more than union, but he does not know how to establish man's wish for individuation. Therefore Brown's concept of human play as the real reflection and projection of man's true wishes (his true self) is one-sided. He comprehends the way that play reflects man's desire for union and participation, but fails to acknowledge how human play reflects man's desire for individuation and centeredness as well.

Brown has one point of similarity with Erikson—both settle upon the mother-child relationship as a paradigmatic human phenomenon revelatory of fundamental truths about human nature. More important than father and son, husband and wife, is Madonna and Child. But this point of contact between Erikson and Brown will finally only serve to emphasize their profound differences. Whereas the mother-child relationship for Erikson is a subtle interplay of complex patterns of mutuality involving cognitive, libidinal, economic, and historical elements, for Brown it finally entails only two elements: (1) the fundamental human desire for union and (2) the inevitable fact of separation and the threat of death. The only difference between *Life Against Death* and *Love's Body* is that in the latter book Brown takes these convictions even more seriously and more literally.

Brown corrects the Freudian preoccupation with the Oedipus complex and moves the focus of study to the pre-Oedipal relationship with the mother. In doing this, he emphasizes the later Freud who tended to interpret the castration complex in the light of a more fundamental anxiety over separation from the mother. The logic of Brown's social philosophy is simple enough. Man is basically a creature of erotic desire, a creature in quest of pleasure. But pleasure is itself intermediary to a deeper desire, the desire for union with the mother and with the world (world and mother are equal for Brown). The desire for union expresses itself in the free play of the whole erotic, polymorphously perverse body. But play itself is a phase traversed toward the eventual goal of union and the final peace (release from tension) that union grants. Two factors, (1) the infant's long period of dependence upon his parents and (2) the consequent intensity of the experience of separation from the mother, frustrate the goal of union and set man upon the long detour of repression, history, and culture. All history, all cultural advance, all rationality is really neurosis, a sign of man's self-repression. All of man's cultural pursuits reveal the hidden child-hood wish for playful and erotic union with the world through the mother.

This overview of Brown's thinking needs to be differentiated. Of prime importance is his conviction that union is the essential wish of childhood. In making this assertion, he maximalizes the romantic and existential overtones implicit in the concept of Eros developed by Freud rather late in his career.[11] Brown's task is to go beyond any-thing Freud himself ever considered and attempt to cleanse the con-cept of Eros of any connotations of acquisitiveness and domination clearly present in Freud's earlier theories on sexuality.

Here is how he does it. He writes, "The sexual instinct seeks, over and beyond bodily pleasure, some appropriate form of union with objects in the world."[12] He goes on to tell us that Freud repeatedly asserted that "infantile sexuality . . . exhibits two modes of relating itself or binding itself to objects in the world."[13] The two terms most generally used were "identification" (the desire to be *like* another object) and "object-choice" (the desire to *possess* another object). Identification is often said to apply to the father, and object-choice generally refers to the desire to possess, or to have, the mother.

Brown believes, however, that this distinction does not hold. Freud himself points the way: deeper than the "possessiveness" of object-choice and the "being-like" of identification is the desire for incor-poration, that is to say, union. Brown writes:

> Freud's own analysis of possessive love (object-choice) and its primal model, love of the mother, shows that its erotic aim is not possession but union with the object, a union which is hardly distinguishable from his own category of identification. He derives identification from the de-sire for union with the world in the form of incorporation, after the primal model of the relation of the child to the mother's breast. At the same time he says that incorporation of the object is the aim of normal adult loving, i.e., of object-choice. Thus the distinction between object-choice and identification breaks down, both of them meeting in a project of incorporation or being-one-with-the-world, modeled on the primal relation of the child to the mother's breast. Hence Freud says that "at the very beginning, in the primitive oral phase of the individual's existence, object-cathexis and identification are hardly distinguishable from each other."[14]

The progress of Brown's argument is clear. Both identification and object-choice are grounded in oral incorporation. On the other hand, oral incorporation is cleansed of connotations of possessiveness and domination and gradually, through a subtle process of redefinition, expanded into the larger, more existential-sounding concepts of union and being-one-with-the-world.

One final step is needed before Brown reaches his ontology of the mother-child relationship. He must point out the role of narcissism in man's fundamental relations with the world through the mother. He concludes that "the essence of love of the mother is the need to be loved." [15] Such a love is essentially narcissistic and self-loving; it is fundamentally a desire "for pleasurable activity of one's own body." [16] The essence of all love is the ego's tendency to seek for objects through which it can love itself. Union with objects (especially the mother) in the external world becomes important for the narcissistic ego because the love with which the ego loves itself finally becomes associated with the objects that give the narcissistic ego its pleasure. In this way, the objects of the external world become incorporated with the narcissistic ego; as we first love ourselves, we later come to love the objects that give us pleasure.

Brown, as does Herbert Marcuse, draws a moral meaning from this meditation on the narcissistic love of the infant for the mother. The gratifying qualities of the mother become the paradigm of reality as the infant experiences it and wishes it to be. The accrued feeling of narcissistic pleasure experienced by the infant is never lost. When the cold and frustrating character of reality finally imposes itself upon the child, this quest for union and total bodily pleasure may be repressed but is never eliminated; it lingers as an unconscious wish secretly guiding all the strivings of adulthood. Brown and Marcuse agree that the moral meaning of psychoanalysis rests in the imperative to alter reality and the world so that they may more nearly match this unalterable wish of the pure pleasure ego of childhood. The moral import of psychoanalysis should be to seriously pursue the possibility of a society without repression. "Limitless narcissism" and the "erotic sense of reality"—these are the ultimate goals of life.

In *Love's Body* the emphasis upon the mother-child relationship is not only retained but intensified. In addition, the focus seems to move from the paradigm of breast-feeding to the even more regressive intrauterine situation. Here the writings of both Bachofen and Melanie Klein are invoked. Since *Love's Body* is primarily aphorism, we can do no better than to quote it directly. "The world is our mother: The outside world is 'the mother's body in an extended sense.'" Or again, "To explore is to penetrate; the world is the insides of mother." [17] And, finally, "All walking, or wandering, is from mother, to mother, in mother; it gets us nowhere." [18] This is an intriguing sentence and it invites a paraphrase from the perspective of Erikson's moral psychology. He might say, "All walking, or wandering, is from *old* mother to *new* mother; it gets us somewhere." Not the literal mother but various objects and experiences that participate in motherly modalities of existence are what Erikson writes about. Not so for Brown. Brown speaks of the literal mother. All new mothers, whether they be group, fraternity, science, or politics, are really substitutes for the one and only real mother, the first mother.

However, Brown seems to have a doctrine of the fall—a fall away from the paradisiacal enjoyment of the mother. We might call Brown's doctrine of the fall a doctrine of a necessary and unfortunate fall. This reverses the conception, often found in Christian theology, of the fall as unnecessary (a consequence of man's freedom) but fortunate (it provided man with a chance to grow and to move into union with God from a position of higher levels of individuality).[19] Brown seems to believe man's fall into repression is the result of an inevitable concatenation of circumstances that have to do with the long period of infantile dependency and the peculiar nature of the human family. Although the fall into repression appears to Brown as inevitable, it is in no way fortunate. In contrast to Rieff, Marcuse, and even Freud himself, all of whom believed that man's history of repression was a necessary stage in his evolution to independence and rationality, Brown believes that this history has served no good purpose at all.

Man's long period of infantile dependence under the protection of the human family does two things: (1) It gives the infant an unusually long and free period of erotic enjoyment undisturbed by external necessity, and (2) it leads the child to be unusually dependent upon the parents and needful of their love.[20] Against the background of this long and intense period of erotic freedom experienced by the human infant, the inevitable anxiety of separation from the mother is experienced with proportionate intensity. The human child, in an effort to mitigate the intensity of his anxiety, subdues or represses the intensity of his erotic desire for union. What we have is actually a double repression: both body and the anxiety of death are repressed. In an effort to flee the threat of separation (death as separation anxiety) one also represses the erotic desires for union which are threatened by the possibility of separation. Man, the most erotic of all creatures, is also the one who is not strong enough to face the anxiety of separation from his sources of erotic union. Man is the creature who represses himself.

It is interesting to note that Brown, who feels that most of man's problems are rooted in man's inability to accept his own animality, centers his discussion of man's fall into repression at a point in man's development where he has already evolved into a creature vastly different from the other animals. The human child's long period of dependence is due to the complexity and slowness of development of his cortex, upon which he must rely because of the unstable and imprecise nature of his instinctual equipment. There is a difference between man and the other animals besides that which repression creates. That Brown has not adequately accounted for this difference will become gradually clear as we proceed.

Brown, at least in the beginning in *Life Against Death* although less so in *Love's Body*, considers himself an optimistic thinker. His motivation is therapeutic; he wants to give man reason to hope. Therefore in his earlier book he tries to reconstruct Freud's instinctual dualism (Eros against Thanatos) and replace it with what he calls an instinctual dialectics. In the state of nature, in animals, and in the child before repression occurs, the life and death instincts are in union; they meet in the concept of nirvana and the experience of homeostasis and the release of tension.[21] On this issue, Brown agrees with the early Freud rather than with the later Freud. In his early thought, Freud tended to equate the pleasure principle, the reduction of tension, homeostasis, and nirvana. In Freud's later theory, however, the death instinct was introduced as something distinct from the pleasure principle and homeostasis. Against this position, Brown believes that it is only in man, under the conditions of repression, that the pleasure principle becomes separated and in dialectical tension with nirvana and the death instinct. Brown believes that in animals, the forces of life and the forces of death are in balance in the "static homeostasis principle." But, as Brown writes: "Instinctual repression transforms the static homeostasis principle in animals into the dynamic pleasure principle in man. . . . It is the search for instinctual satisfaction under the conditions of instinctual repression that produces in man the restless quest of the pleasure principle for a quality of experience denied to it under conditions of repression."[22] Brown believes that if man could put an end to his repression, then the restless pleasure principle would return to the nirvana-principle, i.e., the death instinct of the later Freud. Brown concludes by suggesting, "If therefore the nirvana-principle 'belongs to the death-instincts' and the pleasure principle belongs to Eros, their reunification would be the condition of equilibrium or rest of life that is a full life, unrepressed, and therefore satisfied with itself and affirming itself rather than changing itself." [23] Brown believes that this reformulation saves nature, animals, and man from the ontological dualism of Freud's later twofold division of the instincts, and provides a ground for both therapeutic and social hope.

It is the nature of repression to split apart Eros and the death instinct. This further means that both forces, now torn apart, are externalized and projected into the outer world. Eros takes the form of the restless, never-ending search for pleasure and the death instinct takes the form of man's vicious and unmitigated aggression and destructiveness toward both self and others. When man is unrepressed, the instincts of life and death are in balance; the process of living and the process of dying are experienced as one and the same. After repression, when these instincts are torn apart, man develops not only restless desire for pleasure but also an active though unconscious desire to die.

It approaches genius the way Brown combines psychoanalytic and existential categories. Man's twofold wish to fulfill the desires of his body and to escape the threats of death express themselves, as Brown sees it, in an existential project. This existential project, however, is complex; it contains in hidden form both a regressive desire for union with the mother and a regressive desire to die. This existential project creates the peculiar organization of sexuality which Freud discovered. The oral, anal, and genital stages of libidinal development are not, as Freud thought, natural and biologically inevitable stages of sexual development. They are created in response to the existential project to flee separation by forcefully turning to the mother. The concentration of libido in the oral cavity is caused by the child's efforts to regain the mother through the mouth. The concentration of libido in the anal region is even a more active attempt to return to the mother by, in fact, denying one's dependence upon the mother and by becoming a mother to oneself—by giving birth to a baby through the anus. Finally, the genital stage is the most extreme neurotic expression of activity and denial of dependence. Here, the child seeks to cope with his threatened dependence and union with the mother by transforming "passivity into activity with the Oedipal project of having a child by the mother; that is to say, by becoming father of oneself." [24]

The Oedipal project itself is not a natural love for the mother. Biology itself brings about no natural concentration of the libido in the genital area and would not itself lead to incestual fantasies of genital union with the mother. The real wish of man is to unite his entire, polymorphously perverse body with the mother, not just the penis. Brown rewrites the logic of the Freudian theory of symbolism in the light of its later emphasis upon the pre-Oedipal mother. Phallic symbols do not really refer to the penis, and the penis does not really refer to itself. All phallic symbols as well as the penis itself are really symbols, resulting from repression, of the entire erotic body. *Love's Body* is a poetic investigation of these symbolic equivalences. All phallic symbols—king, president, priest, representative—are really repressed expressions of the Oedipal project to be father to oneself; they are blind and unconscious existential projects to overcome the fear of death by becoming God, by becoming one's own cause—Spinoza's *causa sui* or Sartre's *être-en-soi-pour-soi*. But the phallic symbol is a phony; the real referent is the whole body. "The whole person is identified with the penis—the basic equation of body and phallus." [25] Not the penis in the vagina, but the whole body in the womb, in union with the mother—this is the real sexual wish. The Oedipal project to become one's own father and mother and child (in short, to become one's own cause) is a defensive maneuver, a neurotic detour, and a substitute for the real wish to be one with the mother.

The characterological relevance of this vision is important. It puts into question the organization of man's sexuality around genitality and generativity as well as man's higher quest for immortality through his progeny. One must be careful about too quickly calling Brown a nihilist. One should be cautious about statements such as the one of Frederick Crews, "He eliminates our problems by eliminating us." [26] It is clear that Brown was motivated, especially in *Life Against Death,* by the desire to improve the life of man. An interviewer of Brown says he is "proud of his two daughters and two sons" but fears that "they may be unprepared to live in the world if the worst happens (the dropping of the bombs) and they survive." [27] To put it bluntly: Brown is not against having children; nor is he saying that this is the implication of psychoanalysis. What he is saying is this: having children is not the central purpose of life. True regeneration, he believes, does not come about through generativity and genitality. He wants to break the idolatry of the genital, the generative, and the quest for immortality. In addition, he is saying that if children are to be brought into the world, they must learn the true meaning of life, which is to die. To live well is to live fully while dying. There is no good living without good dying. He concludes *Life Against Death* with the sentence, "And perhaps our children will learn to live a full life, and so see what Freud could not see—in the old adversary (*the death instinct*) a friend." [28] Brown's original attempt to be positive about life finally comes to this: people can live well only when they realize that they really would have preferred not to have been born at all.

It is important to state Brown's position properly. Only then can the full dimensions of his modern-day Manichaeism be grasped. In *Love's Body* he goes beyond his earlier understanding of the nature of man's fall into repression. The problem is deeper than man's inability to accept separation after long periods of infantile dependence. The problem is life itself; it is an accident, a disruption in the tension equilibrium of the universe, and an endless detour designed to return to the original state.

> The womb then is a tomb. To be born is to die, and life is really death-in-life. Psychoanalysis is the rediscovery of the Orphic or Oriental vision of life as sleep disturbed by dreams, of life as a disturbance in death. In the philosophy of Freud's *Beyond the Pleasure Principle* and Ferenczi's *Thalassa*, life itself is a catastrophe, or fall, or trauma. The form of the reproductive process repeats the trauma out of which life arose, and at the same time endeavors to undo it. The "uterine regressive trend in the sex act" is an aspect of the universal goal of all organic life—to return to lifeless condition out of which life arose. "The goal of all life is death." In this philosophy life and the main stages in biological evolution (sexual differentiation, adaptation to dry land) are catastrophes excited by external forces: these catastrophes create "tension"; and the aim of life (or of evolutionary adaptation) is to get rid of the tension, and so die. Life is a temporary (accidental) disturbance in a lifeless (and thus peaceful) universe. It is best, then, never to have been born; and second best, quickly to die. Nirvana is release from the cycle of rebirth.[29]

Brown's most conclusive statement on generativity and life is stated soon after the above quotation. He writes:

> And then we shall see that Generation is not the reality but a shadow of the reality: Generation is only an image of Regeneration. The real birth would be birth from the womb of the dream world. The real death is the death we are dead with here and now. Real life can only be life after death, or resurrection: life other than the life whose goal is death, and whose pattern is the repetition-compulsion, karma.[30]

Blake, Ferenczi, Roheim—these are the men who feed Brown's vision of the relation of generativity and life. Man will be less likely to destroy himself prematurely with the bomb when he realizes that from the start death is the goal of life. Mankind will be less inclined to destroy itself with its technology if it does not try to upset the true direction of the universe through idolatrous generativity and striving for immortality. "The 'sin' in the sex act is not that of love but that of parentage. It is the father and the mother, not the lover and the beloved, who disappear from the highest Paradise." [31] And, finally, he quotes Nietzsche: "All that is unripe wants to live, that it may become ripe and joyous and longing—longing for what is farther, higher, brighter. 'I want heirs'—thus speaks all that suffers; 'I want children, I do not want myself.' " [32]

But the weakest point in Brown's thought, and the point toward which we have been working in our analysis, is his understanding of the polarity of individuation in the ontology of man. In *Life Against Death,* Brown seems to acknowledge that there is an individuation process; life seeks more than simply union. Brown knows of a deeper, more healthy drive for individuality than the pseudoactive masculinity of the Oedipal project and its flight from death. Before the fall into repression, when the life instincts and the death instincts are in harmony, the tendency toward individuation and the drive toward union are also in balance. Brown follows the metapsychology of the later Freud to its logical conclusions: the drive for union is rooted in Eros and the tendency for individuation is rooted in the death instinct. Under the conditions of repression when the death instinct is repressed, man also represses his authentic individuality. As Brown says it: "If death gives life individuality and if man is the organism which represses death, then man is the organism which represses his own individuality. Then our proud views of humanity as a species endowed with an individuality denied to lower animals turns out to be wrong." [33] Even the lilies of the field have more individuality than repressed man because living and dying is all the same for them and they "take . . . no thought for the morrow."

The grounding of the drive for individuality in the death instinct presents great problems for Brown's ontology of the human. We are left with important questions that we will later attempt to address more carefully. Can the death instinct carry the full weight of grounding human individuation, the *principium individuationis?* Does the human tendency toward individuation have any real grounding in Brown's vision, or is it only subsumed under the drive toward union? For instance, can one become anxious when one's individuality is threatened, or is anxiety experienced only as a response to the possibility of separation? And, finally, if life is play, does play express both these tendencies of human nature, the drive toward union and the drive toward individuation? It is our contention that Brown neither in his poetry nor in his prose truly understands the nature of the *principium individuationis,* and that this is the fatal mistake which renders his vision bizarre, maybe even absurd.

Character and Modernity:
Apollo and *Homo Economicus*

The heart of our inquiry is the question of the relationship of character and modernity. What kind of man must emerge to cope and live successfully with both the dangers and the possibilities of modernity? Brown's answer to the question is the most radical of all the psychoanalytic moralists we are studying; his hermeneutics of modernity is the most pessimistic and his prescription for the organization of human energy to confront modernity is the most extreme. Brown's answer to the question of character and modernity is supremely clear and simple. Modernity, for Brown, is an extreme expression of the generally neurotic and self-destructive tendencies of history. Modernity is the death instinct gone wild, delirious with autonomy, completely unmitigated by Eros. The problem of modernity comes down to this: how does man get out of it? The good man is the man able to escape modernity; he is the Dionysian man, that is to say, the Dionysian Christian. The Dionysian Christian defeats the autonomous death instinct by being strong enough to face death itself. But before he can be strong enough to die, he must be strong enough to live, to live the life of the resurrected body.

The differences between Rieff and Brown are in their understanding of history—and their interpretations of modernity are many and deep. Rieff writes about the psychoanalytic theory of history, but when he interprets history himself he becomes strangely unpsychoanalytic. Weber, not Freud, is finally the key to history for Rieff. He acknowledges vague rumblings in the historical background of endless Oedipal struggles and timeless returns of the repressed. But on top of this subterranean current are real, creative historical events; often these events are unintended or accidental misunderstandings that gain a life of their own and go on to shape a civilization. The Old Testament prophets, Calvin, Disraeli, Freud himself, are examples of historical events that can never be explained adequately by an exclusively psychoanalytic interpretation of history. Therefore Rieff has no psychoanalytic interpretation of modernity, although he does have a psychoanalytic interpretation of the kind of man—psychological man—that modernity seems to be producing.

Brown, on the other hand, offers a complete and detailed psychoanalytic interpretation of history in general and of modernity in particular. Few subjects remain untouched. In *Life Against Death* we find psychoanalytic interpretations (Brown's version) of religion, money, economics, technology, division of labor, the city, science, work, and much more. In *Love's Body* he extends the list to include government, democracy, kingship, fraternity, sacrifice, and eucharist, to mention only a few. In general, however, modernity is history and mind "at the end of its tether," as he so bleakly puts it in his "Apocalypse." History is created by repression and is marked by man's ceaseless attempt to change himself, to make himself something different. Modernity has brought this frantic activity to improve and change oneself (the unconscious wish to return to the mother) to the end of the line.

We must approach Brown's discussion of history and of modernity from the perspective of our major concern, the psychology of character. We will discuss his psychoanalytic interpretation of history and of modernity from the standpoint of his typology of historical character types. Apollo, *homo economicus,* and Dionysus as character types— these will be our main concern.

For Brown, Apollo is the symbol of what is most sick about man: thought. *Animal symbolicum* is *animal sublimans*.[34] Thought (cognitive activity) itself is disease. Apollo is the god of rational thought, form, aesthetic distance, moderation, and pseudo masculinity.[35] All men, although they may be far from attaining the Apollonian norm, contain within them an Apollonian tendency. This is to be found in the fact that, for Brown, all thought and all symbolic activity is founded upon repression. Brown carries through to its logical conclusion an element of Freud's thought about the nature of thought which Freud himself neither repudiated, corrected, nor followed through to the end. Relying strongly on Freud's major texts on the psychoanalytic theory of thinking, especially his 1925 essay on "Negation," Brown discusses the relationship between repression, thought, and sublimation. The ego, Brown maintains, is not a creation of the reality principle; the ego is created by the inability to "accept reality, specifically the supreme reality of death and separation." [36] The ego protects itself from the threat of separation by negation—it negates or denies the reality of its own libidinal wishes and the reality of the threatened separation. In addition, it hallucinates a fantasied image of the longed-for object. The object now becomes a part of the ego, a hallucinated, fantasied part of the perceptual field of the ego. But the new internalized object has now become desexualized; the truly sexual character of our attachment to the object is denied through negation. This is the nature of sublimation. Sublimation is the desexualization and internalization of objects in the external world with which we formerly had a directly erotic relationship.

The process whereby man desexualizes the world and internalizes it

into the self gives man a "soul," a fantasied, dreamlike world of substitute gratification. This is the origin of the Greek mind-body dualism,
the beginning of philosophy and science, the foundation of all cognitive thought. Brown writes, "The starting point for the human form of
cognitive activity is loss of a loved reality." [37] All thought, as well as
all symbols, is finally the effort to recapture the fullness of the repressed body in erotic union with the world.

The search for the lost body of childhood is the key to *homo
economicus*. Economic man is repressed man anxiously searching for
the sacred body. In contrast to the theories of classical economics,
homo economicus is not motivated by the desire for rational exchange
or the utilitarian motives to improve one's standard of living. The
motivations of economic man are basically religious; they are founded
upon the desire to recapture the lost body of infancy, which, under
the conditions of repression, is experienced as sacred—something both
wholly other, feared, yet highly desired.[38]

But to understand fully the character of economic man, one must
understand the symbolic equivalence between money and feces. After
the ego represses, desexualizes, and internalizes its erotic relationship
with objects in the world, it then, once again, projects its desexualized
fantasy back into the external world. The consequence of this new
projection is the search for the lost body in the world of desexualized
and inanimate things—in the world of death. When this is understood,
it becomes easier to comprehend Brown's explanation (something of
an improvement, it seems to me, over the standard psychoanalytic one)
of how money and feces invariably become symbolic equivalents.
What, to begin with, are feces? Are they a part of the external inanimate world or a part of the body? It is just this status of ambiguity
which gives feces their privileged position in the world of inanimate,
dead objects for the reception of the projections of the repressed
body. As we saw earlier, just as the oral and the genital regions can
be the centers of the wish for union of the whole body, so can the
anal region and its products.[39] But also, as we learned earlier, the
wish projected on the anal region is the universal wish to recapture
the erotic union of the lost body by becoming father and mother to
oneself—feces as symbolic child. Saving things, saving money, saving
property—in short, the prudential, calculating character of *homo
economicus* has its origin in the impulse to save or hold on to the feces
as a substitute for the lost child, the sacred body of infancy. Of
course, under the conditions of repression, to attempt to find or save or
hold on to the lost body is actually to hold on to a repressed body, and
a repressed body is a dead body. Dead also are feces and money.

We cannot take the time to follow Brown's amazing journey through history, from primitive man on up, and his attempt to account for the facts of economic life with his various dialectical themes on the concepts of sublimation and the search for the sacred body. The list of thinkers, philosophers, anthropologists, and economists whom he addresses seems endless—John Maynard Keynes, Marx, Hegel, Eliade, Marcel Mauss, Claude Lévi-Strauss, Adam Smith, Durkheim, and many more. In his dialogue with these men, Brown is very much in control; some are rejected, but most are reconstructed and pressed into the support of Brown's campaign to subjugate economic history to his theory of the anal complex.

In some ways, the theory is not so amazing as one would first think. Who can deny that history is indeed riddled with symbolic associations between anal imagery, money, property, and interest (increment, the child of excrement)? Even the logic of Brown's theory of anal symbolism is more complicated than the orthodox psychoanalytic view. Anal imagery is never really the ultimate referent in any association between money, property, capital, and the anal region. Always, for Brown, both feces and money are symbolic of another referent—the body, and the whole body at that. What finally constitutes the problem with his analysis, beyond whatever sins in historical method he may commit, is the ontology of the body upon which the entire edifice is built.

In fact, if Brown's fundamental understanding of the meaning of the body (which is to say, his understanding of the nature of the quest for life) were more trustworthy, what Brown has to say about Protestantism and its relationship to *homo economicus* might be more convincing. There is little question that there is an intimate relationship in Luther—however it is finally to be interpreted—between anality, the devil, sin, bondage to the world, and capitalism. The facts are simply too obvious and demand interpretation. Not only Brown but Erikson and Fromm as well (Rieff is the only exception) attempt to account for these facts, all employing different metapsychological assumptions.

Not to be ignored either is Brown's perceptive portrayal of the deep paradox in Luther's simultaneous condemnation of capitalism as the work of the devil and his tacit acceptance of it in his doctrine of vocation (calling, *Beruf*) with its affirmation of secular vocations as the arena where salvation is to be won.[40] He chides Weber (and implicitly Rieff) for not understanding the full significance of the role of Luther's *theologia crucis* in bringing about Protestantism's ambivalent but effective support of capitalism. Certainly Weber understood the importance of Luther's critique of monastic, nonworldly vocations, but Brown believes he failed to understand that Protestant Christians were called by Luther to occupy their secular, often capitalistically oriented vocations as a "cross," as a way of taking "upon oneself . . . the hate of the Devil, of the world, of the flesh, of sins and of death." According to Brown, Weber misses the way in which "the Protestant surrender to calling and to capitalism is a mode of surrender to the Devil and to death." [41]

Hence, Brown leads us to the conclusion that there is nothing in the modern world—nothing specifically associated with modernity—that is exempt from repression and sublimation and the regressive destructiveness of the death instinct torn asunder from Eros. Capitalism, science, technology, the city, even government—nothing is exempt. Democracy itself is the work of repression. The fraternity of democracy presupposes rebellion against the father, and, of course, rebellion against the father is really the project to become father to oneself.[42] All is death and destruction; there is no way through it. Marcuse is wrong, Brown tells us, and does not see that "revolution is a slate wiped clean." [43] Brown wants none of the partial incorporations of history and modernity, none of the bland images of modern alienation expressed in ideas of "participation," "fellowship," or "interaction." Brown wants total incorporation and fusion. "Total incorporation, or fusion, is combustion in fire. . . . The real prayer is to see this world go up in flames." [44]

The Dionysian Christian

It is extremely difficult to write about Norman Brown's eschatological vision and the primal figure around which it is built—the Dionysian Christian. It is pure vision and pure ultimacy; there is nothing proximate and penultimate about it. Brown is completely devoid of an interim ethic. It never occurs to him to tell us how we get from here to there—how we get from the repressed body to the resurrected body. His task, as he conceives it in *Love's Body,* is to erect the poetic vision. He bypasses the programmatic problems of political procedure. In fact, for him, politics has become irrelevant; the problem is a cultural one, a matter of man's self-understanding. It is man's self-understanding that he is trying to change; poetry, not politics, is the ultimate instrument of change. Once again, let us impose an order on Brown's development of the idea of the Dionysian Christian that Brown himself might resist; let us discuss the Dionysian Christian from the perspective of his relationship to himself, his sense of time, his relationship to the world, and his relationship to the "other."

Brown is attempting primarily to effect a revolution in man's relationship to himself, that is, his self-understanding. One cannot understand Brown's intellectual career unless one grasps that Brown is addressing first of all the intellectual, academic community of which he is a part, and, secondly, *homo economicus* which he believes to be the dominant personality type in Western culture. Brown does not yet know Rieff's "psychological man" or David Riesman's "other-directed man." Were he to meet them and get to know them, he would find in them essentially nothing new. Brown wants to *strengthen* man's ego. He writes: "The path to ultimate reunification of the ego and body is not a dissolution but a strengthening of the human ego. The human ego would have to become strong enough to die." [45] Brown, like Rieff, is finally in the business of peddling insight; the difference between them is that Rieff is still peddling Apollonian insight and Brown wants to peddle Dionysian insight. Brown finds a Dionysian and Christian eschatology buried deep within the Apollonian consciousness of psychoanalysis. After psychoanalysis has finally done a psychoanalysis upon itself and uncovered these riches, it must then be turned loose on mankind as a whole; "the general consciousness of mankind needs to appropriate psychoanalysis, the science of neurosis." [46] Finally, Brown does not want to destroy consciousness, just as he does not want to destroy the *principium individuationis*. The fact that his inadequate ontology of individuation and his poetics of individual nihilation suggest otherwise should not lead us to become confused. Brown does not want to annihilate consciousness; he wants to replace the linear, abstracting, distancing, form-dominated Apollonian consciousness of his academic colleagues and the prudential, calculating, hoarding, and grasping consciousness of *homo economicus* with the playful, boundary-breaking and death-accepting eroticism of Dionysian consciousness. Near the end of *Love's Body* he says it as clearly as he can:

> The unconscious to be made conscious; a secret disclosed; a veil to be rent, a seal to be broke open; the seal which Freud called repression. Not a gradual process, but a sudden breakthrough. A reversal of meaning; the symbolism suddenly understood. The key to the cipher: the sudden sight of the real Israel, the true bread, the real lamb.[47]

Poetry and symbolism, then, are the key to the new "ego strength" and the new consciousness of the Dionysian Christian.

It is through poetry and through symbolism that Brown wants to reintegrate (recapitulate) back into time, back into the life of the conscious ego, the ultimate goal of life—the harmony of life and death in its goal toward union with the mother. "To make it new is to make it recur. In fulfillment is recurrence, recapitulation. Fulfillment gathers up the past into the present in the form of a recapitulation: that in the dispensation of times there might be a recapitulation of all things in Christ." [48] This panegyric in the name of poetry is continued in two later essays. In "From Politics to Metapolitics," delivered at Harvard University in 1967, he writes in the style of poetry:

> Beyond the reality-principle is poetry
> > taking metaphors seriously
> > (metaphors and analogies)
> > that way madness lies.[49]

Even more recently, in an essay entitled "Daphne, or Metamorphosis," he writes: "Saying makes it so. Poetry, the archetypal fiat; or creative act." [50] When one understands from this perspective, one can see that Brown is not recommending an immediate and violent end to the world. Nor is he advocating a massive, literal rush to return to the womb. It should not even be necessary to point this out, but unfortunately it is; too many responsible critics have already understood him to be saying just this.[51]

Through poetry and aphorism, Norman Brown wants to break the literalist Protestant mind and the scientific mind of the modern academy and the modern world. His image of the Dionysian Christian is not a goal to be reached tomorrow, but a symbol to open the modern consciousness to the depths of its own being. *But the difficulty with Brown is that he too is a literalist.* He substitutes for the literalism of the modern mind an even cruder literalism of a psychoanalytic variety. The referent of the symbol of the Dionysian Christian is still the infant in the mother's arms, at her breast, or even more specifically, in the womb. This is the literal referent behind all of Brown's mystical-scientific-poetic vision; because this is true, all of his secondary symbols and concepts—play, erotic union, spiritual body— retain a peculiarly restricted and narrow meaning.

Poetry and symbolism generally involve a double meaning. Brown believes this too; but for him, the double meaning of poetry means saying one thing and *always* meaning another specific thing. In Brown, the double meaning degenerates to *double-talk*. Brown's theory of symbolism is subject to the criticism that John Needleman, following the insights of Ludwig Binswanger, leveled against Freud's reductionism. Needleman tells us that the Freudian theory sees the symbol as always an "effect-sign" of a hidden and repressed sexual meaning.[52] Needleman quotes Ernest Jones to make his point.

> As energy flows from them [the primary interests] and never to them, and as they constitute the most repressed part of the mind, it is comprehensible that symbolism should take place in one direction only. Only what is repressed is symbolized; only what is repressed needs to be symbolized.[53]

In Freud's view and in Brown's there is actually no reciprocity between symbol and referent, no common element to which both refer that permits them to mutually qualify one another, as is the case when language reaches the level of true symbolism.[54] As Paul Ricoeur has shown, the symbol does indeed have a double meaning; it contains both a regressive and a progressive meaning.[55] For Brown, however, the symbol has finally only one meaning—the regressive meaning. This is why poetry for Brown is not double meaning, but double-talk; it reduces the world of language to a rigid system of signs with only one, quite literal meaning.

Because Brown has no real ontology of individuation, he can envision no other union besides a regressive one; it excludes union with the world, with one's fellowman, or with God. It is a union that is none other than what he says it is—"incest." The way of symbolism is the way of silence and "the way of silence is not only death but incest." [56]

That Brown gives us a literal consciousness (a literal-mindedness) with only one referent can clearly be seen in his understanding of time. For Brown, the past and the future are a result of repression. If repression did not exist, there would be only the present, only eternity. Yet it is not the controlled and prudential present that Rieff gives us; it is an ecstatic, eternal present. As Brown writes, "The war against death takes the form of a preoccupation with the past and the future, and the present tense, the tense of life, is lost." [57] When man has repressed his life he is always trying to recapture it in the future or he is always nostalgically remembering it from the past. Brown tells us that "only repressed life is in time, and unrepressed life would be timeless or in eternity." [58] Yet, from the perspective of where we actually are as historical, repressed beings (according to Brown), it is clear that man has only one truly valid category of time—and this is the *past*. As we saw above, "fulfillment gathers up the past into the present in the form of a recapitulation." [59]

But what can be said about the relation of the Dionysian Christian with the social world, i.e., with other people, with the world of politics, with the family, with wife, and with children? Unfortunately, very little. We are not quite clear whether for the Dionysian Christian business would go on as usual with one's children, one's wife, one's government, or not. We can only assume that if he marries, he will know that he really marries his mother. If he procreates, he will do so only out of a sense of exuberance and never as a way to have heirs, or as a way to leave a mark on the world, or as a way to provide for the continuation of the race. If he has a government, we assume that the Dionysian will look at it in a somewhat Lutheran fashion; governments are doubtless necessary to control people under the state of sin (that is, repression) but contribute nothing to the real fulfillment of man. Under the conditions of fulfillment, governments, of course, would vanish.[60]

As for the stranger—the other—there is a sense in which he does not exist. All men, deep down in their hearts, are Dionysian Christians. All symbols, all faiths, all religions, are really, as far as Brown is concerned, a disguise for the true religion—Dionysian Christianity.[61] Hence, the Dionysian Christian believes, in the end, that all strangers are his brothers. But beyond this we cannot go. It is really not Brown's concern to ask the more puzzling question, which is this: In this world where some people take their differences very seriously, where some may resist being called a Dionysian Christian and being referred to as brother in this sense, how does the Dionysian Christian approach the "other"? The Dionysian Christian sees all religious particularity as a result of repression. The difference between Dionysian Christianity and all other religions is the difference between the resurrected body and the body of repression and death. In this world the Dionysian Christian is separated from all others not of his faith by the thick wall of worldly sublimation and neuroses.

4

THE EGO, PLAY, AND INDIVIDUATION

The purpose of this chapter is to restore to man the so-called "high" in his nature. And we want to do this within the circumference of psychoanalytic energetics. Reason, imagination, awareness—these are the dimensions of man that both Rieff and Brown, in their respective ways, have taken away. In doing this, both are faithful to their mentor, Freud. Yet only after we raise the "high" in man to its proper dignity can we submit it to a balanced moral critique. Both modern character and modern society indeed do suffer from a misdirected use of that which is perennially associated with the best and highest in man.

The major problem with both Rieff and Brown is their respective conceptions of the role in human life of those central organizing functions generally referred to as the "ego." Neither of them properly understands either the functions of the ego or how to go about grounding it metapsychologically. Because of this failure, Rieff and Brown commit tragic errors both in their understanding of the nature of the good man and in their interpretation of modernity.

Neither Rieff nor Brown has any respect for the advances that have been made by psychoanalytic ego psychology. Both of them dismiss these more recent developments as misguided ventures from which psychoanalysis should return as quickly as possible. Neither of them seems to be aware of the clinical usefulness of the contributions of Heinz Hartmann, Ernst Kris, David Rapaport, Robert White, and Erik Erikson. Hence, their respective efforts to set forth the moral meaning of psychoanalysis stop short of saying anything at all positive about this aspect of the psychoanalytic tradition which is for all practical purposes now considered to be normative in clinical psychoanalytic circles.

We have already said a great deal about how both Rieff and Brown misconceive these central organizing processes called the ego. What is even more interesting than the specifics of their errors is witnessing the diverse directions in which their fundamental mistakes permit them to go.

Neither of them believes that it is *natural* for the human ego to be either structurally or energetically independent from the id. It is fair to say that for both Brown and Rieff it is in some sense *unnatural* for the ego (these central organizing processes) to be differentiated from the id. Of course, Norman Brown explicitly states that the ego emerges via the unhappy road of sublimation and negation. Clearly, Rieff believes the same; he follows Freud in the belief that the ego has no energy or power of its own and that it rules only because it is "sly" and "cunning" and knows how to trick the id into prudent delays and temporary restraints. The difference between them is that Brown calls the differentiated and sublimated ego an unfortunate and unnecessary disease, whereas Rieff would call it the fortunate and inevitable grounds upon which culture is established.

This difference in interpretative psychology leads to a different programmatic. Brown wants to strengthen the sublimated ego to face and accept its own desublimation and final dissolution. This is the paradox of Brown's program—how to make the ego (which by definition must be a result of sublimation and repression) strong enough to accept into consciousness the deeper desire to *lose consciousness,* to return to the primordial darkness, and to die. Rieff's program is vastly different. He wants to place the controlling and inhibiting functions of the ego on new grounds—not the grounds of sublimation and superego prohibitions but the grounds of psychoanalytic insight and modern stoic prudence.

Their respective views of the ego strongly influence their interpretations of modernity. Rieff, as we have pointed out, gains his view of the forces producing modernity from a variety of sources, but his understanding of the nature and the role of the human ego strongly affects his view of the way that human energies should be organized in the context of modernity. Man must learn how to live *without belief* and without involvement in communities of commitment. The ego has no fundamental need for wholeness anyway. The ego is a technician (technical reason) in the service of the id. Men, according to Rieff, do not need *meaning* or *positive moralities;* they need *pleasure* and *control.* Positive ethics and communities of commitment once gave men control, not meaning or direction as is often thought. And since neither positive ethics nor positive communities are any longer a possibility, man must give up the quest for meaning and establish his control on a new basis, the basis of insight. Insight does not give meaning or interpretation; it gives a *new kind* of control, self-limitation, and restraint.

Brown's understanding of the ego as a consequence of sublimation and repression leads his interpretation of modernity in another direction. It means that human thought itself and virtually all its expressions are, for Brown, a result of sublimation and repression. All science, all technology, and all economics, in their modern rationalized forms, is evidence of the ego's sublimated status.

It has been our thesis that Rieff's inadequate psychology of the ego leads to his narrow view of *reason.* We have claimed that Rieff comprehends neither the true depths nor the true heights of reason. On the other hand, it is Brown's concept of *play* that we find so disappointing. It is disappointing because the category of play is truly important for the understanding of human behavior. We agree with Brown and with Freud: through play, man projects much of what he really wants and much of what is truly human about himself. This we cannot doubt. Furthermore, it is play that helps us to understand so much about human behavior, especially man's larger cultural and religious pursuits. But, for Brown, as was the case with Freud, play is free release of energy on the way toward union. The goal of all play is to end play and to find union. In other words, play, for Brown, reveals nothing about man's desire for individuation, just as reason (we might add), for Rieff, reveals nothing about man's desire for wholeness and meaning. The category of individuation, in Brown, is very difficult to understand and seems almost indistinguishable from union itself. In this, Brown is faithful to the orthodox psychoanalytic tradition which, in the race to amplify its basic discoveries, never succeeded in adequately explaining an entire range of human behavior related to the *principium individuationis* in man, i.e., the fact that man grows, that he explores the world, that he thinks, and that he apparently does all these things, at times, because he both needs to and wants to. Brown's position on the nature of human individuation appears to be contradictory. On the one hand, he explicitly affirms that there is a kind of unrepressed principle of individuation. On the other hand, he seems to believe that the only kind of anxiety that exists is *separation anxiety*. Anxiety occurs when separation from the mother appears as a possibility. Or to put it differently, anxiety occurs when the wish for union seems threatened. Yet if Brown is serious about the polarity of individuation, there should be another kind of wish (as we suggested earlier) and another kind of anxiety when that wish is threatened. If there is an authentic thrust toward individuation (one more fundamental than that which appears under the conditions of repression), then there indeed should be a *wish* for individuation and an accompanying anxiety when that wish appears threatened. But of this second category of wish and of this second type of anxiety we hear nothing.

The views of the human ego held by Rieff and Brown are variations of the orthodox Freudian position on the subject. In the next paragraphs we will summarize some of the pertinent developments in Freud's theory of the ego and certain later developments to be found in the seminal thought of Heinz Hartmann and of Robert White. At certain points in our discussion we will relate this short historical survey to both Rieff's view of reason and Brown's ontology of play and individuation. Our goal is to witness how psychoanalytic ego psychology has gone about restoring the so-called "high" in man. Reason, thought, individuation—these qualities in man are not simply a result of disease.

The Ego and the Principle of Constancy in Freud

To understand Freud's final position on the nature of the human ego, one must understand how Freud attempted to account for the development of the ego within the purview of his theory of constancy. Even in his earliest attempts to establish a rigorous psychology of man in his "Project for a Scientific Psychology," Freud worked with the constancy principle as the sole foundation of motivation.[1] This principle, which in some form stayed with Freud the rest of his life, meant that the basic tendency of every organism is to rest in a state of equilibrium. Action (or the change of energy states) is the result of internal or external stimuli—either internal deficiencies or external disruptions. If action is a factor in individuation, then it is clear that organisms (including the human organism) do not move, do not change, do not act, in short, do not grow unless they are frustrated into it.

This principle was explicitly applied to the nature of thought itself in his important 1911 essay entitled "Formulations Regarding the Two Principles in Mental Functioning." In this short piece, thought appears as a response to a lost object. The first mental response (the primary process response) is consistent with the pleasure-pain principle and attempts to restate, as quickly as possible, a state of equilibrium. This first response, then, will be a hallucinated response, a hallucination of a satisfaction that, in fact, has not occurred. Freud tells us, however, that "it was only the non-occurrence of the expected satisfaction, the disappointment experienced, that led to the abandonment of this attempt at satisfaction by means of hallucination." [2] At this point, a new principle of mental functioning is introduced, and "what was presented in the mind was no longer what was agreeable but what was real, even if it happened to be disagreeable." [3] This second principle of mental functioning is the celebrated "reality principle" of Freudian psychology.

From our perspective, what is important to note is that the capacity to perceive and relate to objects "realistically" appears to be born out of frustration. And frustration always means separation from the loved object. It is just this frustration and this separation which provokes the human infant toward all the qualities one associates with individuation: action, reality-oriented thought, and relative independence from the maternal matrix. Without this frustration and forced separation the child would not act, would not think, and would not leave its mother.

Freud used the word "ego" (ich) to refer to that concatenation of forces which protect the organism from dangers in the external world. His mature theory of the ego can be found in his 1923 volume entitled *The Ego and the Id*. Here he emphasizes again that the ego "is that part of the id which has been modified by the direct influence of the external world . . . [and which] seeks to bring the influence of the external world to bear upon the id and its tendencies, and endeavours to substitute the reality principle for the pleasure principle which reigns unrestrictedly in the id." [4] This emphasis on the ego's protective role in relation to the outside world is consistent with his emphasis in the 1911 article. Before the 1911 statement, Freud had tended to neglect theoretical work on the nature of the ego. As far back as his early work on hysteria, the functions of the ego had been understood largely to be limited to that of defense against painful memories. The major interest of Freud in the intervening years had been the charting of the vicissitudes of the sexual instincts and the complexities of the unconscious.

In *The Ego and the Id* the renewed interest in the ego expresses itself in several distinct advances which are summarized in this volume.[5]
Under the impact of his discoveries concerning melancholia and narcissism,[6] Freud's early theory of motivation, which made a distinction
between sexual instincts and ego (the instincts of self-preservation),
has now been revised. He now sees the ego as being formed out of
the residue of abandoned object-cathexis; the image of the lost object
is now set up in the ego and the libidinal cathexis once attached to
the external object is now transferred to the ego and its image of the
lost object. The practical result of this revision was to make the ego
even more dependent upon the id. The ego no longer has energies of
its own (energies for self-preservation); the very energy of the ego now
comes directly from the id, since the id now cathects the ego and the
images of abandoned objects that it contains. This energy cathexis of
the ego is called "secondary narcissism." [7] Freud assumes that the
energy comes from the id, but that at the same time, there occurs a
process of desexualization. He writes, "the transformation [of erotic
libido] into ego-libido of course involves an abandonment of sexual
aims, a desexualization." [8] In turn, Freud assumes that this desexualized
ego-libido can now be used by the ego to join forces with either the
erotic or the destructive instincts, the two grand classes of instincts
forging up from the id. "We have reckoned as though there existed
in the mind . . . a displaceable energy, which neutral in itself, can
be added to a qualitatively differentiated erotic or destructive impulse,
and augment its total cathexis." [9] This is the beginning of Freud's celebrated concept of desexualized ego energies, a concept to which we
will return very quickly.

On the other hand, new trends in Freud's thought which seem to
give the ego greater prerogatives and powers become crystallized in
this volume. The so-called structural view of personality that divides
the psyche into ego, superego, and id replaces the older topographical
system with its division between unconscious, preconscious, and conscious. Now we are told that significant parts of the ego itself are
unconscious and that these are the parts most distinctively associated
with its repressing functions. Freud was forced to this view of the
unconscious ego in order to explain the unconscious resistances so
evident in a patient's free association. Freud tells us: "There can be
no question but that this resistance emanates from his ego and belongs
to it. . . . We have come upon something in the ego itself which is
also unconscious, which behaves exactly like the repressed—that is,
which . . . produces powerful effects without itself being conscious." [10]

Not only does Freud assign the ego's powers of repression to this unconscious sphere, he also speaks of positive mental functions or thoughts occurring with the quality of unconsciousness. There is evidence, he believes, that "difficult intellectual operations which ordinarily require strenuous concentration can equally be carried out preconsciously and without coming into consciousness." [11]

Hence Freud's formulation of the ego contains an ambivalence—one that is never solved. On the one hand, the ego is completely dependent upon libidinal cathexis for its energy. On the other hand, it has surprising unconscious power to repress libidinal impulses. On the whole, however, the importance of the ego grows in Freud's writings. In his outstanding 1926 volume entitled *Inhibitions, Symptoms, and Anxiety* he reverses his earlier theory of anxiety which explained it as being a result of dammed up libidinal energy.[12] Now anxiety is seen to be the cause of repression, not its result. And, of course, the organ that signals anxiety is the ego. However, it is in this volume that we learn that all anxiety is basically separation anxiety—anxiety over the possibility of losing (becoming separated from) the gratifying object (the mother). Here Brown follows Freud very closely. Closely, too, does he follow Freud when Freud insists that the castration threat is really an anxiety over losing the instrument through which union with the mother can be effected.[13]

At the end of his career, Freud leaves us a view of the ego that sees it as part of the id, that gains its energy from the id, but that has the power to repress the id ruthlessly.[14] It is like a police force that is weaker by far than the mass it governs but that stays in power simply because it is better organized. He never moved beyond his concept of neutralization and desexualization of libidinal energies as the source of energy for the ego. He never posited the idea, as is now fashionable in ego psychology, that the ego might have sources of energy independent of the erotic energies of the id. He did, however, at various times, both very early and very late in his career, assume that the ego was composed of certain apparatuses or structures which were not basically a part of the id. We must thank Heinz Hartmann for calling our attention to two very important passages.[15] As early as 1905 in *Three Essays on the Theory of Sexuality* he suggests that there must be a constitutional tendency to inhibit sexuality. He writes, "But in reality this development [of sexual inhibitions] is organically determined, and fixed by heredity and it can occasionally occur without any help at all from education." [16] Toward the end of his career, in his important essay entitled "Analysis Terminable and Interminable," he wrote, "It does not imply a mystical overvaluation of heredity as we think it credible that, even before the ego exists, its subsequent lines of development, tendencies and reaction are already determined." [17] This is commonly interpreted to mean that Freud believed that the ego was determined, in part, by its own constitutional givens. The energy of the ego was that of the id, but the structures and apparatuses of the ego, we are told, may be somewhat independent of the id.

This progression in Freud's thinking about the ego (certainly a most ambivalent progression) was not detected by many of his followers. Many of them still assumed that all interest in the external world was still aroused under conditions of frustration and need. Hence, Fenichel could write in a 1937 article designed to summarize what was then known about the ego that "the first 'affirmation' of the world is an intermediate aim on the way to its 'negation.' " [18] This assumes that the first tendency of the organism (both ego and id) is to sink back into a state of quiescence as soon as possible, forgetting the external world until the next moment that need is aroused. This, of course, is the view held by Brown. This is why he sees the ego and its work as basically driven by the anxiety of separation, as basically sublimation, and, finally, as basically unnatural. It is also, strangely enough, at the foundation of Rieff's view that the id and the external reality are, for Rieff, always robbing the id of its peace.

The Ego in the Writings of Heinz Hartmann: The Fuller Vision

The important work of Heinz Hartmann is in many ways quite consistent with the later thought of Freud on the nature and functions of the ego. However, Hartmann does put psychoanalytic ego psychology into a new framework; he shifts the emphasis from a study of defensive functions of the ego to a study of its adaptive functions. In addition to this shift of emphasis, Hartmann makes some important theoretical contributions either not found in Freud or only unsystematically developed. Even Anna Freud's brilliant 1936 study of *The Ego and the Mechanisms of Defense* continues her father's preoccupation with the defensive functions of the ego.[19] Only a portion of Hartmann's rich thinking is relevant to our discussion here—namely, his concept of the "conflict-free ego sphere," his theory of the "average expectable environment" (so important for the thought of Erikson), his contributions to the theory of neutralization, and his restatement of the relationship of the ego and the id.

Near the beginning of his great 1939 work entitled *Ego Psychology and the Problem of Adaptation*, Hartmann wrote:

> We must recognize that though the ego certainly does grow on conflicts, these are not the only roots of ego development. Many of us expect psychoanalysis to become a general *developmental psychology:* to do so, it must encompass these other roots of ego development, by reanalyzing from its own point of view and with its own methods the results obtained in these areas of nonanalytic psychology. This naturally gives new importance to the direct observation of developmental processes by psychoanalysts (first of all the direct observation of children).[20]

When Hartmann asserts that there are ego functions that do not grow directly out of conflict, he has something very specific in mind. He means "conflict" to refer to what psychoanalysts have always meant by that word—a conflict between an instinctual impulse and an external threat, danger, or frustration. He is not saying, as many interpreters believe, that there are ego functions subject to no conflict at all. He does not rule out the possibility of other kinds of conflict besides one involving instinctual id impulses. Nor is he denying that sometimes conflict-free ego spheres become implicated in instinctual conflicts. He is simply saying that the entire growth of the ego cannot be accounted for by recourse to conflicts between the id and its environment. In the following quotation he lists some of the ego functions not directly the result of this conflict:

> Not every adaptation to the environment, or every learning and maturation process, is a conflict. I refer to the development *outside of conflict* of perception, intention, object comprehension, thinking, language, recall-phenomena, productivity, to well-known phases of motor development, grasping, crawling, walking, and to the maturation and learning processes implicit in all these and many others. . . . I propose that we adapt the provisional term *conflict-free ego sphere* for the ensemble of functions which at any given time exert their effect outside the region of mental conflicts.[21]

The importance of these words for the redirection of psychoanalytic thought is still not fully comprehended. And, of course, the implications for Brown's understanding of psychoanalysis are enormous. Perception, intention, thinking, memory plus a wide variety of motor capacities are the result of constitutional givens which develop out of a combination of maturation and learning. They are not the result of conflict, defense, or repression; in fact, defense and repression *presuppose* these structures and capacities. Hartmann pointed this out in a 1956 article entitled "Notes on the Reality Principle." Here Hartmann demonstrates that Freud's theory of the transition from the pleasure principle to the reality principle contains important implicit assumptions. The capacity to postpone a pleasure to the future cannot be explained by instinctual frustration alone. He writes:

> The postponement of control to discharge is one of the essential features of the human ego from its beginnings; it is probably an essential feature already of its forerunners, before the ego as a system of personality has been fully established. We should consider what is, I think, a necessary assumption that the child is born with a certain degree of preadaptiveness; that it is to say, the apparatus of perception, memory, motility, etc., which help us to deal with reality are, in a primitive form, already present at birth; later they will mature and develop in constant interaction, of course, with experience; the very system to which we attribute these functions, the ego, is also our organ of learning. What I have said is to the point here, because it means that *some preparedness for dealing with reality precedes those experiences Freud referred to.*[22]

The ego's capacity for postponement precedes frustration; it is not created by it. And this capacity depends on certain constitutional givens present at birth.

The ego, then, is not just epiphenomenal, nor simply an internalization of the external world. Hartmann tells us that "the ego as a regulative agency too has constitutional roots. In the course of psychoanalysis, ego constitution (just like drive constitution) appears . . . as a limit to the explanation of a behavior by environmental influences." [23] *In contrast to both Rieff and Brown, who see the id as the only effective constitutional given that can resist environmental determination, Hartmann is assigning this role, at least in part, to the ego.* Robert White and Erik Erikson will go farther in this direction. Hartmann himself, however, goes so far as to give to the ego almost equal constitutional primordiality. This is what he means when he writes, "In some cases it will be advisable to assume that both the instinctual drive processes and the ego mechanisms arise from a common root prior to differentiation of the ego and the id; though after they have structuralized, they may secondarily enter into the most varied connections with each other." [24]

Hence, from the perspective of Hartmann, the ego is not just a product of the frustrations of the external world. As the central control agency of the organism, it both protects the organism from the pressures of the external world and guides it toward positive adaptation with the external environment. The ego does this, in part, because it possesses certain basic mechanisms that are "preadapted" to an "average expectable environment." "Strictly speaking," Hartmann tells us, "the normal, newborn human and his average expectable environment are adapted to each other from the very first moment." [25] The concept of average expectable environment, so important for the thought of Erikson, suggests that the constitutional givens, both at the level of the id and of the ego, are preadapted to "fit" into a range of average environments. Some environments, clearly, are beyond this range; others are not. Men (and animals) adapt to some environments *alloplastically*—they change the environment to "fit" their preadapted capacities. At other times, man adapts *autoplastically*—he changes himself (within the limits of his constitutional givens). There are limits to both alloplastic and autoplastic adaptation. But it is interesting to read Hartmann's remarks about alloplastic adaptation, which has certainly been man's preferred modality of adaptation, especially during the modern period. "Learning to act alloplastically," he writes, "is certainly one of the outstanding tasks of human development; yet alloplastic action is actually not always adaptive, nor is autoplastic action always unadaptive." [26] Adaptation in its most successful forms is always a mutual process wherein both the environment and the human organism mutually qualify each other. "Thus, adaptation is primarily a reciprocal relationship between the organism and its environment." [27] This is a basic condition for life. Later we will see how Erikson refers to this process of reciprocity between organism and environment, between self and society, and between man and nature as a process of "mutual activation and regulation."

In spite of Hartmann's insistence on the constitutional given of the ego apparatus and the increased emphasis he assigns it in the processes of adaptation, he still feels obliged to explain the *energy* of the ego with Freud's concept of neutralization. He makes one important advance over Freud, however. He believes that ego structures are empowered by a neutralization of both the sexual and the aggressive drives of the id. Freud, as we know, applied the concept of neutralization to only the sexual drives. In his 1939 essay, Hartmann anticipates the direction his concept of neutralization will take. In discussing the importance of both the synthesizing and differentiating functions of the ego, he seems to explain the former as a manifestation in the ego of Eros (the sexual libido) and the latter of Thanatos (the aggressive instincts). He writes, "Since we somehow connect the synthetic function of the ego with the libido (our conception of this relationship is unimportant here), it is plausible to assume an analogous relationship between differentiation and destruction." [28] Hartmann clearly states this extension of the theory of neutralization in a 1946 article that he wrote with Ernst Kris and Rudolph M. Loewenstein.[29] In the introduction of his *Essays on Ego Psychology* he states this advance simply when he writes: "Freud has repeatedly stated that the ego works with desexualized energy. It seemed reasonable, to me as to other analysts, to broaden this statement to include also energies derived from aggression which, through the mediation of the ego, can be modified in a way analogous to desexualization." [30]

Of course, as we have pointed out in our discussion of Brown, this is not far from the way he grounded the principle of union and the principle of individuation; union was grounded in the erotic instincts and the individuation was grounded in the destructive instincts. In spite of Hartmann's advances in the theory of the ego, it is finally faithful to Freud's basic theory of instincts; to this extent, his thought is afflicted with the same kinds of strange contradictions that can, if one remains faithful to them, take one in the direction of the nihilism of Brown or the skepticism of Rieff.

However, it should be noted (because of its importance for our later argument) that neutralization, for Hartmann, does not mean that the ego and the reality principle are without their pleasures. In fact, we are told, "The pleasure potentialities afforded at the various levels of development by the ego, its functions, and its aparatuses, are of great significance for the stability of ego organization, its effectiveness, and the kind and extent of its functioning (synthesis, defense, assimilation, learning, ability, etc.)." [31] This observation, consistent with the concept of "function pleasure" put forth earlier by Karl Bühler in 1929, will be carried on by Robert White and given a new theoretical context with his concept of "independent ego energies." When the concept of function pleasure is applied to the operations of the ego, we begin to see the contours of a new idea: thinking, perception, memory, motility rather than being the results of a defense against pleasure (a result of repression) have their *own* pleasures which are realized in the very functioning of these capacities. If the higher ego functions indeed have their own pleasures, one cannot write off their cultural expressions in thought, science, or philosophy, as, by definition and under all cases, the result of repression and sublimation.

Before we leave Hartmann, a final word about his view of the relationship between the ego and the id seems in order. That the ego and the id somehow shade into each other is certainly a principle dimly visible in the work of Freud. In the thought of Hartmann, however, this concept takes on a different valence. In many ways, the id in his thought becomes more like the ego than the reverse. This is to say that the id is seen to have some of the regulatory capacities of the ego. He points out that animals probably have "a sort of ego" too. In fact, instincts in animals contain much of the regulatory character that is found in the ego at the human level. "Instinctual drives" (the English translation of the psychoanalytic concept of *Trieb*) are different from animal instinct (*Instinkt*) in that instinctual drives have far less regulatory capacity. There is, then, in man a much "sharper differentiation of the ego and the id—a more precise division of labor between them." [32] In contrast to Norman Brown's mythology of the animal, Hartmann writes, "The assumption that lower organisms are regulated only by the pleasure principle (or the nirvana principle) is—in the form in which it is usually stated—certainly untenable." [33] Although there is a greater differentiation between ego and the id in man, we cannot assume that this division of labor in man is absolute. The id still contains some regulatory functions: "We cannot assume that the regulating factors and their relation to the external world begin to function only when the ego is fully developed. . . . Ego development is a differentiation, in which these primitive regulating factors are increasingly replaced or supplemented by more effective ego regulations." [34]

This is why Hartmann can speak of two approaches to adaptation— one *progressive* and one *regressive*. Progressive adaptations which follow the advances of ego development are sometimes not sufficient for all adaptive purposes. Regressive adaptations, although sometimes destructive, are often more successful than an exclusive reliance on progressive measures. Hartmann tells us that "there are adaptations— successful ones, and not mere unsuccessful attempts—which use pathways of regression." [35] The reason why regression is important for adaptation is simply that all the regulatory mechanisms of the total organism are not found in the higher ego processes.

> The reason for this is that the function of the most highly differentiated organ of reality adaptation cannot alone guarantee an optimal total adaptation of the organism. . . . There is, for example, the detour through fantasy. Though fantasy is always rooted in the past, it can, by connecting past and future, become the basis for realistic goals. There are the symbolic images familiar in productive scientific thinking; and there are poetry and all the other forms of artistic activity and experience.[36]

And of course Hartmann could have added *religion*. But we can conclude from this, against the biases of both Rieff and Brown, that the lower processes are not discontinuous with the higher. Reason, it seems, depends on the lower as well as the higher. The differentiation between the rational (in the sense of higher adaptive processes) and the irrational may be more pronounced in man, but it is not categorical —a mistake that both Brown and Rieff, with different consequences, unfortunately make. Indeed, there is wisdom to be gained from "regression in the service of the ego," to use Ernst Kris's well-known phrase.[37]

These last remarks carry farther our assertion made in the chapter on Rieff; recent developments in psychoanalysis no longer support either Freud's or Rieff's narrow understanding of the role and function of the ego in human life. Hartmann's hierarchical view of the relationship of the ego to the id clearly broadens the psychoanalytic view of the ego. The emerging psychoanalytic view of the ego no longer implies a view of technical reason that sees it as a spiritless servant calculating the safety margin between pleasure and external frustrations or dangers. Reason, in man, must be thought of as the totality of regulating functions relating man's internal needs to the external environment. It includes the highest process of abstraction and conceptualization as well as the lowest mechanisms of regulation sometimes identified with the id. Reason in man is primarily an adaptive process. It serves the total process of living. What Heinz Hartmann has to say about the ego can now be considered representative of the major implications of psychoanalysis for the issue of the nature of human reason. It can be considered a definitive answer to the distortions of such thinkers as Rieff and Brown, and it is an answer from within the psychoanalytic tradition, in fact, an answer from its most respected and widely acknowledged theoretician. The view of reason emerging here may have more affinities with ancient philosophical views than even the most philosophically astute psychoanalysts might be willing to admit.[38] In fact, it does no real injustice to Hartmann's view to suggest that it is nicely captured by the characterization of reason found in Alfred North Whitehead's famous book entitled *The Function of Reason*. There he once wrote, "The function of Reason is to promote the art of life." [39] No single statement could be truer to Hartmann's understanding of the role and function of the ego in man.

Play and Individuation
in the Thought of Robert White

We must now concentrate our attention on the ideas of play and individuation. We have said that play, for Brown, reveals nothing about man's desires for individuation. We said further that if Brown really took individuation seriously, he would posit an anxiety about loss of individuation just as he posits an anxiety as a response to the possibility of separation. In the thought of Robert White we see psychoanalytic theory taking a definite turn that results in placing the ideas of play, individuation, and anxiety in a new foundation.

In 1963 Robert White, a professor of psychology at Harvard University, issued a monograph entitled *Ego and Reality in Psychoanalytic Theory: A Proposal Regarding Independent Ego Energies.* In this essay he attempts to bury for good, with due respects, the widely held psychoanalytic assumption that the ego operates on neutralized energies from the id. White proposes, instead, the idea that the ego and its structures, although often under certain circumstances claimed (energized) by the instinctual drives of the id, have their own independent source of energy. White, as Hartmann before him, hopes to make psychoanalysis into a general psychology. He also, as did Hartmann, broadens the range of data and information that he will press into the job of clarifying and amplifying psychoanalytic theory. He makes especially effective use of important new advances coming from experimental work with animals and with children as well as new theoretical breakthroughs coming from physiological psychology.

For our purposes it is sufficient to consider only a few concepts out of his many rich and careful reformulations of some of the central conceptions of psychoanalytic theory, namely, his concept of effectance, his view of play, his theory of mothering, and his reformulation of the concept of anxiety.

White believes there is considerable evidence to support his belief that the ego has sources of energy independent of the two primary instinctual drives, the erotic and the destructive, postulated by Freud. In saying this, he does not want to convey the idea that independent ego energies are somehow secondary or nonbiological. He believes, rather, that "independent ego energies are as basic as anything in human nature, and that they have a clear significance for survival." [40] What kind of data and what set of experiences lead White to posit independent ego energies? It is primarily the phenomenon of play, in both animals and humans. According to both classic psychoanalytic theory and classic learning theory in academic psychology, the animal or the child acts, learns, and becomes interested in his environment only under the pressures of deprivation and need at the level of primary drives (hunger, thirst, sex, pain). When satiation develops, the organisms should, theoretically, return to a state of quiescence. The facts are, however, that this does not happen. Rather than sinking back into inactivity, both animals and humans, after need reduction, often play;

in fact, that is when they are most likely to play. And when they play, they seem primarily interested in causing effects, making a difference in the external world and enjoying the consequences of their actions. Hence, White calls the energies behind the behavior of play "effectance" energies. And he calls the experience that accompanies this activity "a feeling of efficacy." He writes, "It might be described as a feeling of doing something, of being active or effective, of having an influence on something." [41] But this feeling does not necessarily need to be connected with particular intended results. The activity of play is satisfying "in itself, not for specific consequences." As White points out, it is close to what Karl Groos has called the "joy of being a cause." [42]

But do animals really play? They certainly seem to, both in their natural environments and in experimental situations. Konrad Lorenz's beautiful description of the playful antics of jackdaws in high winds and Gavin Maxwell's account of the "perpetual play" of otters are two striking examples. And who hasn't seen puppies playfully wrestling or a cat striking at a ball after feeding and adequate sleep? More controlled experimental observations seem to eliminate the possibility that some obscure primary drive, or the need to reduce anxiety, or some kind of secondary reinforcement may explain these phenomena. When rats in a maze learn to explore and investigate passages that lead away from home, food, rest, or even sex, we wonder if they do not have other interests besides these basic drives for which one must account.[43] Something similar must be concluded when we learn that, according to the well-known experiments of Butler and Harlow, monkeys can be taught complex skills with nothing more as a reward than the opening of a window so that the animal can look out at the day-to-day activities of the laboratory in which their cage is located.[44] We could multiply indefinitely the number of experiments performed in recent years in which well-fed, comfortable, and sexually satisfied or inactive animals seek out new experiences or try to create novel effects, often with surprising persistence and eagerness. Many animals seem to be highly attracted by new objects introduced to their environment and spend varying lengths of time playing, hitting, kicking, moving, or manipulating them. The time they spend in this activity is generally in direct proportion to the size, color, or complexity of the object. And quite often, the introduction of novel experiences or opportunities for exploration and investigation can stand as rewards for the learning of complex tasks. Hence, doing "something to the environment, producing effects upon it and changes in it, seem to stand . . . as rewards in their own right." [45]

When one turns to human beings and the play of children, it seems almost to be laboring the obvious. But in the light of the theoretical blindness of early psychoanalysis, it is precisely the obvious that must be labored. Ethology, for some time now, has known that all animals have exploratory urges. But from the standpoint of the ethologists, man is the most exploratory animal of them all. Desmond Morris calls this urge *neophilia* (love of the new) and notices that in children the urge is so strong that "parental restraint is necessary." [46] The play of a child seems to have much to do with gaining novel experience and producing novel effects. Certainly, many of the early activities of the child— his crying, his searching for the mother's breast, his expressions of discomfort—have to do with the imperatives of his primary drives. But there is a growing list of researchers who insist that visual exploratory behavior unrelated to primary need fulfillment can be observed in infants as early as a few days after birth, and certainly by the end of the first month of life. Who has failed to see little infants, after they have been fed and while they are still quite comfortable, staring at lights, windows, and bright objects? A few weeks later, the child gains great delight from kicking, grasping, rolling from side to side, and making sounds with his voice. Gesell and Ilg describe in detail what parents see daily in their children at six months of age; when given a small object such as a clothespin, they will pull it, twist it, drop it, put it in their mouth, bang it, pick it up, etc.[47] White seems most impressed by the observation made by Jean Piaget of his own son, Laurent. At three months he accidentally moves a rattle (while sucking his finger). He removes the finger from his mouth and then begins moving the rattle, gradually more vigorously until he is laughing uproariously at the results. Or later, at eleven months, Laurent is observed dropping his toys almost systematically from various heights and positions, apparently observing the different effects of the fall. Such incidents could be multiplied endlessly from both informal and systematic observation.

The point is that standard tension reduction models of the operations of primary drives can never explain this playful behavior. The pleasure found in these activities cannot be assimilated to a tension reduction model. The difference is that these activities seem to have no clear consummatory aim and are far less phasic in the rise and fall of their drive pattern. As White points out, "It does not conform to the pattern of a drive with respect to such features as somatic source, preferred objects, and consummatory aim." [48] Or again, "It is clear that in some circumstances satisfaction is correlated with increases of arousal or tension." [49]

It is important to point out that, for White, effectance and a sense of efficacy do not explain the complexities of adult behavior. The more mature and complex forms of these phenomena, at the adult level, White calls *competence* and *sense of competence*. Competence is the accumulative "capacity to interact effectively" with one's environment.[50] Both learning and innate capacity play a part in the development of competence, and learning can be motivated by the need for both effectance and instinctual pressure. In addition to the accumulative history of effectance called competence, White also speaks of a "sense of competence" and defines it as the subjective experience of one's actual competence. Needless to say, White believes that competence and a sense of competence, understood in a broad and general way, are the concepts to be offered to psychiatry around which to build a new criterion for the nature of health.

It is through effectance and its accumulated results that a child gradually builds up his sense of reality, develops a stable sense of the objects and relations in the external world, and learns to distinguish himself from the external world. All of this is accomplished through the internalization of a sense of one's own action and its consequences in the external world. As the child plays, each of his actions causes him to make a rudimentary observation about its consequence. In this way, he is building up a sense of reality which, at other moments of physiological need or danger, equips him with highly valuable information which he can then use in the pursuit of his goals. Traditional psychoanalytic theory—with its clumsy conceptual baggage of neutralized energies, bound cathexis, and counter cathexis—has great difficulty in explaining all these phenomena.

It is more important, for our purposes, to move on and examine White's conception of the role of the mother in producing early deviations in ego development. Here we learn that the fear of separation from the mother is not the only cause of sickness, and although it is certainly a factor in many forms of illness, it is so for reasons somewhat different than traditional psychoanalysis (or, for that matter, Norman Brown) would lead us to believe. When separation anxiety is a factor in mental disturbances, it is not solely because the child does not receive enough love, enough sensual maternal affirmation, enough basic supplies, or because the mother's absence is really all that threatening. All these factors *can be* traumatic to the growing child. But the real destructiveness of anxiety over separation or deprivation is due to the fact that when the child is worried, anxious, or deprived, he may not have enough energy *left over* for the free play during which he can exercise his ego capacities and build up a sense of reality.

Therefore his ego is "swamped" with instinctual needs or anxiety and he literally does not feel the security or well-being necessary for *independent* play and exploration.[51] The real importance of separation anxiety is that it "inhibits" the tendency toward more individuated play and experimentation with reality.

But we must not get the idea that the more maternal protection, the more maternal satisfaction—in short, the more complete the union between mother and child—then the more independently will the child play and explore. Clearly, this is not the case. A close symbiotic relationship with the mother can inhibit exploration away from the mother's side just as can separation anxiety or physical deprivation.[52] So White states the situation boldly when he writes:

> Effectance, leading as it does to increased competence in dealing with the environment, can be conceived of as inherently an urge away from the necessity for being mothered. When a child undertakes to be independent, to do something in his own way or to achieve some goal without adult help, he is acting in opposition to mothering impulses.[53]

White makes it clear that independence behavior—even the negativism of the two- or three-year-old—is not simply externalized "aggressive or destructive" behavior, as Brown most likely would like to interpret it. It is a part of a generalized move toward autonomy. "The process of separation-individuation," White contends, "can be conceived of as one which the mother can allow to happen or which she can largely prevent from happening." [54] But it is not something that she can *make happen*. Nor is it a result of an anxiety over separation, a fear over death, or a result of repression. There are, of course, examples of behavior overdetermined toward individuation and autonomy that may indeed involve elements of separation anxiety and repression. But these special cases are not what Brown has in mind. He is speaking of a general condition of man wherein all examples of autonomy, exploration, and manipulation are a result of separation anxiety. This, of course, simply proves to be untrue.

Hence, separation anxiety is not the only kind of anxiety. Or to say it differently, what appears to be separation anxiety can often be interpreted from another perspective. Anxiety is a response to a threat that can render us helpless. We can be made helpless by being prematurely torn away from a natural matrix; or we can be made helpless by having our own independent regulatory capacities destroyed or made ineffective. Often the two are difficult to distinguish. White refers to the work of Kurt Goldstein with brain-injured soldiers to make the point that anxiety in some instances can clearly result from a threat to our powers of autonomy and self-regulation.

The problem can be clarified if we start from the idea that anxiety and competence stand in reciprocal relation. The point has been sharply made by Goldstein (1940), who conceives of anxiety as the subjective aspect of a threat, that ordered adequate behavior will break down and turn into catastrophic behavior. . . . Threat is not solely a quality of the stimulus; it lies rather in the relation between the stimulus and our ability to deal with it.[55]

Hence, the drive toward autonomy seems to be a fundamental element in the energetics that motivate life. It is not, as Brown maintains, grounded in the death or aggressive instincts. For instance, the psychoanalytic contention that the thought processes are somewhat divided up between neutralized libido and neutralized aggression is untenable. We saw in Hartmann the idea that the integrating or synthetic functions of the ego are empowered by neutralized libido and that the differentiating or analytic thought processes are empowered by neutralized aggressive forces. With reference to differentiating thought processes to be found in play and exploratory behavior, White writes the following:

Difficulties have resulted from the attempt to interpret all play and exploratory behavior as a manifestation of erotic or aggressive instinctual energies. Since erotic and aggressive aims are by no means regularly apparent, it becomes necessary to stretch the meaning of the two energies to such generalities as binding things together or pulling things apart. This analysis is fatal to an understanding of the meaning of exploratory acts. *Joining and separating occur in lightning alternation in manipulative behavior,* for example, but pointing out this superficial fact obscures the real meaning of the behavior, which is to find out what can be done with objects. On this point effectance and efficacy yield a more penetrating analysis than instinctual drives.[56]

It is, in fact, now clear that the entire structure of Freud's later instinctual dualism is crumbling. This demise is equally ominous for Brown's instinctual dialectics. The idea that there are two basic classes of instinctual energy which flow through the system, activating its various parts, now seems completely out-of-date when seen from the perspective of new advances in neural physiology. And it makes little difference whether these two sets of energies are seen to be dualistically or dialectically related to each other. The truth is, the nervous system is not a set of relatively dead wires that are energized by larger categories of energy which flow through the system like electricity through a telephone line. Rather, the organism and its nervous system is now seen as alive throughout, composed of structures and cells that contain their own characteristic kinds and qualities of energy. Hence, the difference between sexual, aggressive, or the less vivid but quite persistent ego experiences is more of a matter of the activation of the energies resident in particular organs and structures related to sexual, aggressive, or ego activities.

> Seen in this light, an instinctual drive does not function with its own kind of energy, but with neural energies released in particular *places* (centers) and organized in particular *patterns.* Energy can be called sexual, for instance, only by virtue of the fact that certain somatic sources or hormonal conditions activate certain nerve centers which in their turn activate a characteristic pattern of excitations in skin, genitals, and elsewhere. . . . Aggressive energy is differentiated from sexual by the places and patterns that are central in the excitation. An ego interest, such as learning the skills necessary for an occupation, is neutral in the sense that its places and patterns are not those of either eroticism or aggression.[57]

Of course, energies activated from one center can "irradiate" to other centers and structures. Ego interests *can be* sexualized or aggressivized. But ego interests—thought, exploration, inquiry, analysis, skills, etc.— are not, to begin with, simply the result of neutralized, sublimated, desexualized, or deaggressivized energies of the id.

Why, now, have we labored so long to save, so to speak, the "high" in man? And why have we done this at the level of energetics? These questions are important. In fact, later, we will put ourselves in the apparently contradictory situation of saying that energetics are not sufficient to accomplish the total task of moral interpretation. We insist, rather, that energetics serve only as indices of the range of possible meanings that a phenomenon can have for man. Energetics help us toward an understanding of the "archeology of the subject," to use a fortunate phrase suggested by Paul Ricoeur.[58] It does not tell us how the archaic potentialities of man are and can be elaborated in particular situations. What we have done here is to demonstrate that there are powerful arguments, within the psychoanalytic tradition itself, which indicate that individuation, thought, exploration, manipulation—in short, all the things that are so often identified as the chief characteristics of modern man—themselves have "archaic" status in the life of man. They are not a part of man's quest for death; they are a part of his quest for life. *Only when they are endowed with their proper dignity can we then submit them to their proper critique.*

And submit them to their proper critique we shall do. Because later, in our discussion of modern man, we will contend that the problem of modern man has much (although not everything) to do with an overreliance on the higher aspects of his ego processes. The problem of modern man is a problem of reason; it is a problem internal to his own ego processes. It is not that the higher processes are simply a result of sublimation, as Brown contends, or that only technical reason is real, as Rieff contends. It is rather that reason consists of higher and lower processes of the ego (and possibly we should include the higher regulatory processes of the id). Modern man has identified too completely with the higher; there no longer is a sufficient dialogue between the higher and the lower. Modern man no longer lives, as he must, out of the fullness of reason. It is precisely the concept of generative man that may be closer, as long as we remain within the confines of psychoanalytic theory, to an adequate statement of the true relationship between the high and the low in man.

In the work of such men as Heinz Hartmann and Robert White, psychoanalysis is evolving a new image of man; it is an image of man no longer ruled by the pleasure-pain principle in any simplistic sense. It is a vision of man that portrays him with a crucial need to influence his environment. Man has the need to exercise his powers and achieve a sense of mastery with respect to an environment that he activates as it activates him. Effectance, competence, influence, mastery, the exercise of potentialities—whatever one calls it—this appears to be a crucial need which must be realized to some degree if man is to feel and to be human. Both Fromm and Erikson extend this theme. In fact, it is in the light of this understanding of man that they render their somewhat negative evaluation and interpretation of modernity. The facts are, they insist, that in modern societies, man's drive for effectance, mastery, and power has gone astray and has created an environment that both distorts and frustrates the very thing which man needs most. Effectance, mastery, and power in the sense that ego psychology speaks of it, i.e., as mutual activation and mutual regulation between man and his social and natural environment, has nearly been lost. In its place have come a thousand hideous demons. But Fromm and Erikson, to whom we turn next, will tell us a slightly different story about how it happened, what it means, and what must be done to correct it.

To follow them, however, is to steer a course between certain features of the emerging regressive counter culture that can champion the thought of such men as Brown and the core of detached urban-technological elite who can celebrate the thought of men such as Rieff. Neither a skeptical negative community proposed by some nor an instinctual utopianism advocated by others will carry us through the narrow gates of survival.

5

ERICH FROMM

*The Productive Personality and
the Coming of the Messianic Time*

Erich Fromm is at the same time one of the most widely read and
most severely criticized and misunderstood authors of our day. He
must at least have the satisfaction, however, of knowing that most
criticisms of his thought are so poorly conceived that they merit little
serious consideration themselves.[1] His work is marked by a combination of genuine courage and Olympian detachment from some of the
taboos of scholarly discourse.

Consequently, Erich Fromm is never quite in step with the fashions
of his time. Orthodox Freudians have always been skeptical of Fromm
because of his rejection of classical psychoanalytic instinct theory.[2]
Neo-orthodox theologians, while appreciating aspects of his analysis
of contemporary culture, found it fashionable to attack his allegedly
optimistic and progressivistic anthropology as well as his utopian
eschatology.[3] Sociologists of the so-called structural-functional school
such as Winston White have classified him as an "intellectual ideolo-
gist" along with other thinkers as diverse as Herbert Marcuse, William
Whyte, C. W. Mills, John Kenneth Galbraith, and Hannah Arendt.[4]
Reviewers of his works in the popular press have become increasingly
irritated with his Marxist humanism.[5] Marxists themselves, while applauding his leadership in introducing Marxist thought to a larger
American public in his three books *Marx's Concept of Man, Beyond the
Chains of Illusion,* and *Socialist Humanism,* are critical of Fromm's
tendency to emphasize the humanistic elements in the early Marx
rather than his later ideas on revolutionary class struggle.[6]

Even though the student movement in the United States is articulating ideas that at one time were closely associated with Fromm's name (his criticism of the capitalistic, consumer-oriented, technological and managerial elements in Western society, as well as his persistent call for a return to participatory democracy), many students are more likely to ground these ideas in the instinctual utopianism of Herbert Marcuse than in the more idealistic-sounding thought of Fromm.[7] Marcuse himself admits that his analysis of contemporary culture and society has strong affinities with Fromm, but he accuses Fromm of mutilating Freud's instinct theory (the true ground for the "Great Refusal"), of "spiritualizing" freedom and happiness, of succumbing to the style of the "Power of Positive Thinking," and finally of playing into the hands of those who would perpetuate the consumer and performance-oriented society of which Fromm himself is so critical.[8]

In order to interpret Fromm and his concept of the productive personality, one must, first of all, locate him in the context of all the different intellectual interests and methodological procedures that characterize his writings. This variety alone lends to the confusion which has marred most attempts to interpret his thought. Fromm's writings extend over a period of forty years. He has a Ph.D. in philosophy from the University of Heidelberg and received his training in psychoanalysis from the Berlin Psychoanalytic Institute. He has lived and taught respectively in Germany, in the United States, and in Mexico. In addition to his writings in psychoanalysis, sociology, ethics, and the psychology of religion, his *May Man Prevail* was an ambitious probe into the area of international politics. He has been one of the most energetic and successful initiators of the dialogue between Western thought and Eastern religion (especially Zen Buddhism). He has also been a significant stimulus to the international dialogue on Marxist humanism.

His blunt, uncomplicated, and readable style has contributed immensely to his enormous popular success, but it has also served to give a tone of pedestrian simplicity to his writing that makes his hurried historical judgments only too obvious while often obscuring the overall wisdom, force, and occasional brilliance of his formulations. However, it is for the very reason of his methodological richness and the variety of subjects he has touched that Erich Fromm is a man to be taken seriously. Many writers say some of the things that Erich Fromm has been saying these last forty years better than he does himself. But in many instances, Fromm said them first, and, taken as a whole, his thought constitutes one of the most commanding moral interpretations of Western civilization presently available.

History will probably grant that Fromm is indeed a wise man. But it will also record that he was a man very much in a hurry. Somewhere in the middle of his career Fromm undoubtedly made the decision to sacrifice methodological elegance and academic specialization for breadth of scope and singleness of purpose. Boiling below the surface of his calm and deliberate prose is a deep but well-directed sense of panic about the present human situation. It has been only since the middle of the 1960's that this kind of emergency mentality began to grip large portions of the academic community in the United States. Fromm has felt it for over thirty years. In retrospect, Fromm no longer seems like an alarmist.

His analysis of Western civilization—capitalism, bureaucracy, scientism, and technology—has been both sober and somber. But it has not been cynical, nor has it been nihilistic. He has used both psychoanalytic and Marxist concepts to unmask our ideologies, false consciousness, and false ideals. But whereas Rieff uses psychoanalytic concepts to show that all ideals are false, Fromm uses psychoanalysis to expose the motivational and characterological distortions that render valid ideals debased. In addition, although Rieff seems undisturbed over the present direction of corporate capitalism, scientism, and technology and, in fact, attempts to evolve an accommodational penultimate ethic in its support, Fromm's analysis of these movements almost matches that of Brown in the depths of its despair. But whereas Brown proposes to save us with a utopia of regression, Fromm has the audacity to propose a utopia of progression and advance. For Brown, the way out is *back;* for Fromm, the way out is *up.*

The remarkable fact of our times is that more intellectuals and young people are willing to believe that the way out is indeed back rather than up. Rieff has discussed this remissive faith which reigns in our day with his characteristic brilliance. In contrast to the way up or the way back, Rieff has proposed a lateral move—a side step, so to speak— into psychoanalytic detachment. What Rieff cannot understand is that there are other ways to get out by going up besides the way up that man has used in Western Protestant civilization for the last three or four hundred years. This is the essence of Fromm's intellectual commitment: to find a new solution to the approaching catastrophe toward which man is moving by redefining and reestablishing the utopian vision which forms Western man's consciousness. Fromm's error is that he does not fully understand that in our time the way up must also be accompanied by a way down and a way back. Modern man and modern civilization will be humanized when the way up incorporates the archaic foundations of human existence as both a support and a limitation. Fromm in some ways knows that this is true, but he does not know it deeply enough. His problem is primarily one of style.

In the course of a single work, one may find Erich Fromm following any one of the following methodological styles: psychoanalytic energetics and metapsychology, sociology and the social psychology of character, a rather loose but often perceptive kind of philosophical and phenomenological eidetics, an uneven but frequently insightful hermeneutical appropriation of religious and mythological symbols, and, finally, a daring although often naïve program of ethical prescription at both an individual and a social level. Who attempts more than this? And who approaches these tasks with the kind of unguarded directness displayed by Fromm?

His most lasting academic contribution has come in the area of the social psychology of character. David Riesman acknowledges that Fromm's concept of the "marketing" character was a major inspiration and source for his own portrait of the "other-directed man" in his classic *The Lonely Crowd*,[9] a book of such importance in sociological circles that it was able to inspire, eleven years after its publication, the massive symposium entitled *Culture and Social Character*, edited by Seymour Lipset and Leo Lowenthal.[10] Yet Fromm has not spent a lifetime refining his social psychology of character. Much of the honor for Fromm's early insights has been awarded to Riesman. Wider horizons have commanded Fromm's attention and pressed him to grander though less elegant tasks.

What is probably most confusing to many psychoanalytically sensitive readers and many young people impressed with the instinctual utopianism of such men as Brown and Marcuse is the combination of scientific-sounding explanatory concepts on the one hand and phenomenological or eidetic concepts on the other. For instance, it is quite evident in Fromm's earliest major work, *Escape from Freedom*, that he had rejected traditional psychoanalytic libido theory. Of course, for many readers, to reject or restate psychoanalytic libido theory is to reject the body itself as fundamental to behavior. Fromm never intended to do this and, in fact, did not do it. In place of classical libido theory Fromm substituted a larger concept of bodily energy that included, but was not confined to, the classical tension reduction model of sexual libido. But more important than that, Fromm was making use of the concepts of organic individuation and integration put forth by Jean Piaget[11] and Kurt Goldstein.[12] These more organismic theories of development are body-oriented as much as—if not more than—the classical psychoanalytic theory of the libido. They assume that the organism has an internal drive to grow and a positive interest in the world outside itself, an interest that transcends simple survival. Furthermore, this position assumes that the organism contains tendencies both toward higher levels of independence and toward higher levels of relatedness; it holds that growth proceeds simultaneously through a process of internal *differentiation* of the various parts of the organism and successively higher levels of integration of these parts.

These insights Fromm quickly incorporated into his thought and moved on to his wider interests. He did not follow the long and tedious path of the more systematic and conscientious ego theorists such as Heinz Hartmann, David Rapaport, Ernst Kris, and Rudolph M. Loewenstein, who have struggled to remain faithful to basic psychoanalytic theory by explaining these progressivistic forces within the organism in terms of *neutralization* of libidinal energies.[13] Consequently, it was only in the late 1950's and the early and mid-1960's that psychoanalytic ego psychology in the works of Robert White, Robert Holt, and Peter Wolff began to take account of and incorporate the careful scientific advances to be found in the works of not only Jean Piaget and Kurt Goldstein but such men as Heinz Werner as well. In other words, it was only then that psychoanalytic ego psychology arrived, certainly in a more systematic and rigorous way, where Fromm was during the early 1940's. Psychoanalytic ego psychology stands today as both a confirmation and a correction of the neo-Freudian formulations such as those of Erich Fromm. Psychoanalytic ego psychology has now demonstrated that there are other ways to talk about human emotionality such as joy, happiness, pleasure, and love than the classical tension reduction model of orthodox psychoanalysis or early American experimental psychology such as that of Clark Hull.

The mediating figure between Fromm's work and the psychoanalytic ego psychologists was Ernest Schachtel and his brilliant theoretical formulations, especially his work *Metamorphosis*.[14] Schachtel is himself a longtime friend and colleague of Fromm at the William Alanson White Institute of Psychiatry. In the foreword to *Metamorphosis*, Schachtel gives special thanks to Erich Fromm "from whom I have learned a great deal and whose friendly interest has contributed much to the development of my thinking." Much of what Fromm once said from a phenomenological and philosophical perspective about the more idealistic-sounding effects of joy, happiness, love, and hope, Schachtel has restated from a more scientifically convincing ontogenetic point of view, acknowledging at almost every step his fundamental agreement with Fromm. In turn, Fromm in his later writings relies

more and more on the work of Schachtel, especially for the development of his theory of memory, his theory of the unconscious, and his
theory of the important concepts of *activeness* and *passiveness,* which
are so fundamental to his understanding of the productive personality.

Had Fromm stayed in closer contact with the developments of
psychoanalytic ego psychology, he would now be able to state more
convincingly the energetic and metapsychological grounds for some
of his more philosophically and phenomenologically derived concepts.
As an example, we can point to his crucial belief that man has certain
"powers" which must be exercised if he is to remain truly human. This
concept, which is at the heart of his vision of the productive personality, resonates very well with the concept of "efficacy" and the
theory of independent ego structures and ego energies developed by
Robert White which we reviewed in the last chapter. Fromm, however, especially in *Man for Himself* where he first systematically sets
forth his theory of the productive orientation, gives credit to a wide
variety of thinkers for helping him with his formulation—Bergson,
James, Brentano, Husserl's analysis of the public "act," Aristotle,
Spinoza, and Goethe, to mention only a few. Nowhere does he mention a psychoanalytic thinker except Freud. Of Freud's concept of the
genital character, which as we will see later does indeed greatly influence Fromm's thinking, he says this, "The description of the genital
character does not go far beyond the statement that it is the character
structure of an individual who is capable of functioning well sexually
and socially." [15] Fromm knew what Heinz Hartmann,[16] Philip Rieff,
and Freud himself well knew—that psychoanalysis as it left the hands
of Freud cannot project a positive ethical vision. Or to say it more
concretely, it cannot clarify on the basis of its own concepts the positive ethical vision that it indeed implicitly holds.

It would be possible for Fromm to restate his understanding of
productive "power" in the light of recent developments of psychoanalytic ego psychology. This would not gain him much but it would
gain him something. We have already stated our agreement with the
position of French and German phenomenology, especially the work
of Paul Ricoeur: the fundamental structures of man's psychic life need
to be stated from the perspective of the embodied *cogito* and its situation of relatedness to the world. But we also, as Ricoeur has suggested,
believe it is profitable to use objective and scientific categories in a
diagnostic way, as a method of revealing the depth of human experience
that phenomenological analysis may not fully grasp, always taking
care, as a final step, to restate the diagnostic findings in terms of their

relationship to the embodied *cogito*.[17] This is the value of Fromm's early use of the scientific categories of Piaget, Goldstein, and, later, Schachtel. Their discoveries serve as a diagnostic resource uncovering deeper intentionalities of the organism that provide a possibility for man's more mature emotions such as love, hope, and joy. Were he to use the advances of psychoanalytic ego psychology, his empirical diagnostics might be more convincing to psychoanalysts themselves, psychoanalytically oriented political theorists, as well as instinctual utopians such as Brown, Marcuse, and their followers. Without some attention to metapsychological questions of energy and structure, no purely phenomenologically oriented thinker can ever be certain that his eidetic essences are anything more than sublimations, reaction formations, or projections. If Freud's early theory of psychological energies is correct, Norman Brown's view of the goal of mental life and his interpretation of the real meaning of symbols is basically correct. The fact that it can be demonstrated, as we did in the last chapter, that the totality of psychic energy does not operate on the basic tension reduction model is in itself diagnostic evidence that all of man's growth-oriented intentionalities are not simply sublimations.

But actually, for Fromm's purpose, his rather hurried use of selected scientific material which substantiates the growth-oriented character of both the body and its mental life is justified. Fromm is fully aware that a metapsychology of energy and structure cannot in itself reveal the essential structures—the eidetics—of man's relation to his world. Only a psychology that also operates at a phenomenological and existential level can accomplish this. It is the very fact that Fromm took this step that simultaneously renders his formulations less elegant but finally wiser and more trustworthy than those of most of his detractors.

Although Fromm is constantly correlating scientific and explanatory concepts with broader phenomenological and philosophical concepts, he takes still another step. He attempts to incorporate the symbolic material of the religions of the world, most specifically of Zen Buddhism and the symbolism of the "messianic time" found in Judaism and Christianity. All these various sources—scientific explanation, philosophical and phenomenological anthropology, and religious myth and symbol—are brought together to form an ontology from which Fromm derives both the best and the worst in man. It is also from these various sources that Fromm constructs both an individual and a social-ethical vision, which is indeed worth serious consideration.

It is Fromm's phenomenological description of the characteristics of the productive personality—love, reason, work—that leads Herbert

Marcuse to charge Fromm with a moral idealism which supports the domination and repression of Western capitalist society. This charge is all the more startling in view of the general similarity, in many respects, of their systems of thought. Fromm's concept of the "marketing" society is similar in spirit to Marcuse's idea of the "performance principle." Both Fromm and Marcuse have attempted to effect a synthesis between psychoanalysis and Marxist humanism. Both are Germans who were exposed to some of the same philosophical currents —Heidegger, Hegel, Marx—moving through Germany between the two wars. Yet, in spite of this general similarity in their intellectual concerns and backgrounds, they consider themselves enemies, as their bitter exchange in *Dissent* during 1955 and 1956 so clearly demonstrates.[18]

The premise of Marcuse's synthesis of Freud and the early Marx is his severe attack on neo-Freudianism which was set forth in the epilogue of *Eros and Civilization*.[19] Although Karen Horney and Harry Stack Sullivan were both roundly criticized in this piece, Fromm is clearly the center of attack. But even in the introduction to *Eros and Civilization* he feels compelled to write, "Freud's 'biologism' is a social theory in a depth dimension that has been consistently flattened out by the neo-Freudian schools." [20] It seems that it was necessary, even before Marcuse could begin his book, to dissociate himself from Erich Fromm, whose project was so near and yet so far from his own.

It is good, then, to note this similarity between Marcuse and Fromm rather than the more often observed complementarity between Marcuse and Brown. Certainly both Marcuse and Brown are important figures in creating the consciousness of the contemporary counter culture, as Theodore Roszak has so correctly demonstrated.[21] Yet there are many differences between Marcuse and Brown that are important to remember. Marcuse is interested in political reform through revolution, whereas Brown is interested only in a revolution of cultural consciousness.[22] Although both Marcuse and Brown ground their thought in the instinct theory of Freud (specifically Eros and Thanatos), each comes out with a very different vision of the final relation that can exist between instinct and culture. For Brown, instinct (as it was for Freud) is inevitably in conflict with culture. He makes no special effort to envision a society in which instinct would have a freer play. His thought ends in a mysticism of regression that seems to remove the human project from any particular historical or social expression. Marcuse, on the other hand, believes in the possibility of a nonrepressive civilization. Such a civilization would be built on the rather contradictory idea of "non-repressive sublimation." [23] In the present culture, dominated as it is by the "surplus repression" of the performance principle, expressions of sexual libido have been narrowed to specifically genital experience. The new culture that Marcuse portrays will be predicated upon the affluence amassed by the performance principle of the present industrial and technological society. But the affluent society should make it possible, he believes, to repudiate the repressive and narrowing consequences of the performance principle, thereby permitting a wider expression of man's libidinal energies to objects other than those appropriate to genital activity.

The heart of the confusion in Marcuse's thought, from a metapsychological point of view, is his persistent tendency to equate libido, sexuality, and Eros. This was certainly a problem for the later Freud, who introduced the idea of Eros as a general life instinct without reconstructing his libido theory in the light of this broader concept.[24] Marcuse is probably correct in saying that there are other erotic impulses (sensual impulses) in the human organism besides the strictly genital ones. But it does not follow that these other sensual impulses should be called sexual or libidinal, as he persists in doing. As we have learned from Robert White, the need of the ego for efficacy is indeed a sensual need; it is based on its own energy and experiences its own particular kind of pleasure. But the pleasure and sensuality of the ego and its need for playful efficacy is significantly different from the sensuality and pleasure of the id and its libidinal energies. Libidinal energies are phasic, consummatory, and seek for tension reduction. The energies of the ego are less phasic, nonconsummatory, and seem to enjoy variation in tension rather than simple tension reduction.

We have already pointed out that White's conception of the ego's tendency for playful efficacy and his theory of independent ego energy can constitute a metapsychological foundation for Fromm's belief that the productive personality needs to exercise its powers and potentialities. To be productive, in Fromm's sense of the word, does not imply the repression of the erotic and sensual dimensions of man. The ego and its capacities have their pleasure, and they are neither antagonistic to nor identical with the pleasures of the libido. But if man needs the pleasures of the ego's efficacious and playful participation in a responsive world more than the pleasures of the libido, then one's understanding of both man and society are likely to be different from what Marcuse would lead us to believe. The problem of modern man becomes somewhat different than that depicted in Marcuse's more recent and widely appreciated (among the radical young) *One-Dimen-*

sional Man and *Soviet Marxism*.[25] *It is not that the performance principle dominates Western man by repressing his sexuality (no matter how widely sexuality is defined). It is, rather, that the performance principle dominates man by defeating the pleasures of his sense of efficacy.* This is the metapsychological ground for the analyses to which both Fromm and Erikson will lead us. For Fromm, modern society breaks down man's capacity to exercise his power, his potentialities, his experience of participating in a world by influencing and shaping it. For Erikson, modern society thwarts man's sense of mastery. For Erikson, mastery is always a sense of active wholeness, a sense of mutual activation and regulation between man and his environment. It is fair to see the pleasure of efficacy as a dimension of both Fromm's idea of power and Erikson's concept of mastery. At the same time, the two ideas (power and mastery) contain, at the hands of their respective authors, phenomenological and existential dimensions that go beyond any discussion of energetics, no matter how it might be conceived.

It will gradually become clear, I hope, that no metapsychology built on the tension reduction model, which neither Brown nor Marcuse ever overcomes, can be adequate to appropriate conceptualization of modern man or of modern society. And for the moment, let it be said that, as a guide to a possible synthesis between psychoanalysis and Marxist humanism, doubtless one is better off with Erich Fromm than with Herbert Marcuse.

The Human Situation

Before we can examine Fromm's concept of the productive character, we must look at his view of the human situation. The productive man is precisely the man who best answers the problematic of the human situation.

Fromm made a forceful interpretation of the human situation in *Man for Himself*—so forceful, in fact, that he repeats it nearly word for word in *Psychoanalysis and Religion* and *The Sane Society*. His description is basically a synthesis between scientific-evolutionary concepts and an almost Heideggerian phenomenological-existential analysis.

A scientific view of human evolution is fundamental to Fromm's understanding of the human situation. As we will see later, it is also fundamental to his ethical and normative thinking. Fromm shares a fundamental assumption with Freud: there is a parallelism between the ontogenetic development of the individual and the phylogenetic development of the race. But there is an important difference between the two men. For Freud, the parallelism of ontogeny and phylogeny is the Oedipus drama between father and son and its endless cycle of rebellion, threat, repression, and sublimation. For Fromm, however, the parallelism consists of a common evolutionary path shared by both the individual and the race. This common path is the movement, through a process of individuation and differentiation, from relative solidarity with the rest of nature to a position of relative transcendence. As the child differentiates from his mother, so the race differentiates from nature. Fromm believes that the Oedipal struggle is not the key to this process for either the child or the race. Rather, the explanation rests in an evolutionary shift that causes man partially to lose the instinctual regulatory capacities possessed by the other animals and to develop and depend instead upon his higher brain centers and his gradually evolving capacities for awareness, reason, and imagination.[26]

From a more phenomenological and existential point of view, Fromm sees the essence of the human situation as man's experience as a *contradiction*. Fromm writes:

Self-awareness, reason, and imagination have disrupted the "harmony" which characterizes animal existence. Their emergence has made man into an anomaly, into the freak of the universe. He is part of nature, subject to her physical laws and unable to change them, yet he transcends the rest of nature. He is set apart while being a part; he is homeless, yet chained to the home he shares with all creatures. Cast into this world at an accidental place and time, he is forced out of it, again accidentally. Being aware of himself, he realizes his powerlessness and the limitations of his existence. He visualizes his own end: death. Never is he free from the dichotomy of his existence: he cannot rid himself of his mind, even if he should want to; he cannot rid himself of his body as long as he is alive—and his body makes him want to be alive.

Reason, man's blessing, is also his curse; it forces him to cope everlastingly with the task of solving an insoluble dichotomy. Human existence is different in this respect from that of all other organisms; it is in a state of constant and unavoidable disequilibrium.[27]

This contradiction, disequilibrium, or mélange of human existence leaves men with at least two insolvable *existential* dichotomies. One is the fact of death; it confronts all men and cannot be escaped. Man's mortality leads to another dichotomy—the fact that no man can ever realize the totality of human capacities in the span of a single life.[28] Commentators who charge Fromm with glib utopianism and perfectionism generally forget to interpret his utopianism in the light of these fundamental limitations which he places upon the possibilities of human existence. There is no solution to these existential dichotomies, but there are better and worse ways of handling them. In addition, Fromm makes a sharp distinction between these existential dichotomies and those he calls historical contradictions. Historical contradictions in "individual and social life . . . are not a necessary part of human existence but are man made and soluble." [29] As we will see, Fromm's utopian vision of the productive personality is a vision of the man who can creatively live with (but not solve) the existential dichotomies while at the same time energetically solving (and not accepting) the historical contradictions. Only the most pessimistic can deny that between the two sets of contradictions there does remain the possibility of progress and melioration. It is in the margin between the two that we must locate Fromm's eschatology and the vocational field for the productive personality.

This broad understanding of the human situation (derived from what Fromm himself calls an "anthropologico-philosophical" analysis and what others might call an existential-phenomenological analysis) leads us to make two sets of observations. First, it clearly puts him in the company of certain existentialist approaches to the human situation, especially that of such thinkers as Søren Kierkegaard, Paul Tillich, Reinhold Niebuhr, and, more recently, Paul Ricoeur. All these men believe that the essence of man centers around an existential contradiction and disequilibrium or, as Paul Ricoeur puts it, a "disproportion" or "mélange." Common to each of these thinkers is the vision that man is stretched between two poles of existence—one being his rootedness in nature and the other being his transcendence mediated by awareness, imagination, reason, and the capacity for signification. For each of these men, this existential contradiction constitutes the possibility of a fall into evil that man invariably but unnecessarily takes. These thinkers further agree that the structure of evil is man's attempt to find security by overemphasizing one or the other side of this polarity —either his finitude and rootedness or his drive toward transcendence.

Fromm differs from these thinkers in several respects. On the one hand, Fromm holds out for the possibility that man can learn to live creatively with the tension of this contradiction without succumbing to the fall into one or the other side of the polarity. He believes that although the contradiction itself is insolvable, the fall into evil is neither necessary nor inevitable. Fromm entertains this possibility, at least, on the theoretical level. On the level of practical history, Fromm is only too aware that man has perennially chosen the path of evil. In addition, most of these thinkers equate evil with either the flight into transcendence or the flight into finitude, although evil as flight into transcendence is often emphasized more. This explains the great preoccupation, especially among theologians such as Reinhold Niebuhr, with the category of pride. Fromm, on the other hand, is likely to emphasize evil as the regressive fall into finitude—incest, narcissism, death or the premature return to nature. The difference, however, is primarily a matter of style and sensibility rather than conceptuality as such. Theologians such as Niebuhr and Kierkegaard, who pay more attention than does Fromm to evil as flight into transcendence, admit that this flight is primarily a matter of "boasting" or "glorifying" in the "flesh" (Niebuhr)[30] or a matter of "absolutizing" the "relative" and the "finite" (Kierkegaard).[31] Fromm, on the other hand, although primarily emphasizing evil as regression, is fully aware that it takes a variety of transcendental and Promethean forms in sadism, irrational authoritarianism, scientism, and exploitation.

Our second observation deals with the relationship between Brown and Fromm and their perceptions of the human situation. Both Fromm and Brown would admit that some form of union is the goal of life. They would further agree that anxiety and the possibility of death which it signals is man's primary problem. But from here the differences become massive. For Fromm, union must take place from a situation of individuation; individuation and the loneliness it brings are for him irreducible parts of the human situation and ontological givens in the *telos* of human existence. Reason, awareness, imagination, and the drive toward individuation that comes with their exercise are not, for Fromm, the result of repression, as they are for Brown. Whereas for Brown the threat of death creates repression which in turn creates reason, awareness, and imagination, for Fromm the situation is just the reverse. Fromm would contend that it is because man already has evolved the capacity for awareness, reason, and imagination that he can perceive anxiety and death and attempt through various irrational flights, to secure himself against them. For Brown, man's play projects only his desire for union. For Fromm, man's play projects both his desire for union and his desire for individuation, which is to say his desire for a higher union which includes and respects his individuality. This is why, for Fromm, the desire for union has a distinctively progressive meaning; it is an act of the will which builds on the organism's deeper natural tendency toward both union and individuation but which *synthesizes* these two tendencies with artistic discipline. Dionysian man finds union through play, and play is always a matter of release and regression. The productive personality also finds union through play, but play is always a matter of artistic discipline and self-creation, a self-creation whereby the deeper urges of the organism toward both union and individuation are actively transformed and synthesized into ever higher states of balance through a centered act of the will.

Fromm's emphasis upon the givenness of man's reason, awareness, and imagination means that in his thought the concept of *union* is always irreducibly both cognitive and affective. Union is never just a matter of the affections, the feelings, and the body; it is always a perceptual-cognitive matter as well as an affective desire. Man never simply wants affective, bodily union with the world; this wish, or desire, is always strained or filtered through a need for cognitive orientation as well. Hence, for Fromm, the major concepts that he uses with a particularly Freudian sound—union, desire, play, narcissism, sadism, masochism—all receive a peculiarly Frommian redefinition in view of the fact of the irreducibility of both the cognitive and the affective dimensions of life in his thought.

Character and History:
The Social Psychology of Modernity

The best-known, and possibly the most abiding, of Fromm's contributions is his psychological analysis of the major character types that have dominated modern Western history. Erich Fromm was the first psychoanalyst of eminence to broaden psychoanalytic characterology to include a social psychology of historical character types. His characterology parallels, in a loose way, the classic character types of Freud—the oral, anal, and genital types. But there is a major difference: he reverses diametrically the Freudian logic of fixation. Whereas the classical Freudian view asserts that patterns of child training produce the character types of a given culture, Fromm maintains that it is the nature and demands of the social structure of a given culture which create, through the agency of the parents, the kind of character type it needs to support that particular social system. Child-training methods do not by themselves create the adult character and social systems of a given civilization; rather, the adult social system creates and forms the methods of child training necessary to produce and fix in its young the kind of character orientations that it needs.[32] As Fromm writes, "In order that any society may function well, its members must acquire the kind of character which makes them *want* to act in the way they *have* to act as members of the society or of a special class within it." [33]

But there is another important difference between the characterology of Freud and Fromm. For Freud, character was a deep-seated pattern of organization or compromise formation between a man's instinctual desires and the prohibitions of culture. For Fromm, character is also a deep-seated pattern of organization resulting from a conflict. Character, even for him, is a compromise formation. But the conflict is not between the id and the prohibitions of culture; it is between man's situation of rootedness in nature and his irreducible transcendence over nature. Character, then, for Fromm, has to do with the peculiar way a person or culture goes about coping with the problem of existential separateness and finding a modicum of union with nature and his fellowman.

On the other hand, Fromm's concept of character has been strongly influenced by Freud. Fromm shares with Freud the convictions that character underlies and is more fundamental than behavior, that it is the unconscious dimension of the personality, and that character as a whole, rather than specific character traits, is the important determinant of behavior.[34] Fromm also came to believe, as did Freud, that the character orientations associated with the pregenital stages of development are somehow inferior to the constellation of character patterns associated with what Freud called the genital stage of development.[35]

But Fromm's central preoccupation has not been the study of the character of individuals; rather, he has concerned himself primarily with the study of social character, the character traits held in common by the members of a given society. A single civilization may exhibit a predominant character type. This predominant type is formed by the common experiences that shape and pattern the life of the people in this society. The most important of these common experiences is the shared experience of *work*.

This interest of Fromm's in the psychology of social character does not lead him, he claims, to a sociological reduction. Often Fromm's analysis of a given historical phenomenon such as primitive Christianity, the Protestant era, or Nazi Germany, begins with an analysis of the major occupational patterns that exist in the situation he is studying. He then infers the major characterological patterns and conflicts. He ends with an analysis of the relevant ideas and ideals which both order and exploit these characterological trends. Social character is created by social existence, but it can in turn shape both social existence and cultural ideas. The crucial intermediary role that Fromm attributes

to social character in the entire historical process distinguishes him
from the social determinism of the pseudo Marxists, the psychologism
of orthodox psychoanalysis, and the so-called "idealist" position of Max
Weber.[36] He grants an interdependence and a relative autonomy to
all these causal factors—structural and economic existence, social character, and cultural ideals. His concentration on the specific variable of
social character is a strategic though not an exclusive preoccupation.

Fromm's classification of character orientations is organized according to two sets of distinctions. First, he makes a distinction between
productive and nonproductive orientations. Then he makes a distinction
between two types of relations with the world: (1) relations of assimilation which involve the acquiring of *things* and (2) relations of
socialization which involve our interpersonal relationships with *people*.[37] The former distinction between productive and nonproductive
orientations is somewhat analogous to Freud's distinction between
genital and pregenital character types. The second distinction between
assimilation of *things* and socialization with *people* serves much the
same function in Fromm's thought as does the distinction between
I-It and I-Thou in the thought of one of Fromm's former teachers,
Martin Buber.

But underneath and more fundamental than either of these distinctions is the one between passive and active modalities of relating to
the world. At one point Fromm discusses this distinction with the
words "reproductive" (passive) and "generative" (active).[38] A reproductive response to experience simply tends to absorb it without contributing a creative response in return. The generative response is an
active, potent response that gives something in return, that enriches the
experience and the world with a new perspective and a new charge of
energy. The generative response to experience attempts to give more
than it receives. This is the key to the meaning of activeness and
productivity in the thought of Fromm. The weakness and near-tragedy
of his thought is that he chose to develop his positive characterology
around the word "productive" (with all of its resonance with the
terminology and ethos of productionism and the performance principle
of bourgeois, capitalistic society), rather than the word "generativity"
(with its more species-relevant implications for the creative renewal
of the human race). In addition, a better choice of words might have
helped him avoid his overstatement of the normative role of activeness
in human life and helped him to express more accurately the proper
role of these active modalities in the context of the inescapable and
fundamental passivities in the truly generative life.

A brief summary of Fromm's thinking on the nonproductive orientations will help us, by contrast, to understand the productive orientation. The nonproductive orientations, regardless of their differences, share one thing in common: beneath their various behavioral manifestations they conceal a common proclivity toward passivity and regression. The nonproductive orientations of acquiring and assimilating the world of things are *receiving, exploiting, hoarding,* and *marketing.* Parallel to these orientations of assimilating things are four orientations descriptive of our relationships to people: *masochistic loyalty, sadistic authority, destructive assertiveness,* and *indifferent fairness.*[39] We can illustrate the flavor of these orientations by discussing briefly the orientations of assimilation which, in general, are more firmly and convincingly portrayed. The receptive character believes that all good comes from the outside and that he has only to *accept* it passively. The exploitative character also believes that the good comes from the outside but feels that he must *take* it, possibly even with force. The hoarding character, on the other hand, feels that the outside world is hostile, and that the good is inside and he must *preserve* it. The marketing character is a modern phenomenon, a product of market capitalism of the twentieth century. The marketing character experiences himself as somewhat like a salable commodity who molds himself to conform to the desires of others. He *exchanges* a malleable and likable personality for the approval and acceptance of the market.[40]

To understand how Fromm relates his typology of character to history and finally to an understanding of the modern period, several things must be understood. First, Fromm, in contrast to Freud, does not believe that there is a chronological succession, either ontogenetic or phylogenetic, from receptive orientations on up to productive orientations. The receptive is not necessarily earlier and the hoarding or marketing is not necessarily later. Secondly, Fromm does make the startling claim that his orientations are exhaustive: man must relate to the world either nonproductively—by accepting (receiving), taking (exploiting), preserving (hoarding), exchanging (marketing)— or productively.[41]

Fromm makes no real effort to apply his typologies before the modern period, and even here he does it illustratively rather than exhaustively. The modern period has seen all these types of personality. Fromm's evolutionary view of the individuation process leads him to believe that modern man does indeed enjoy more freedom; he is more individuated from nature and from other men than was primitive and archaic man. As Fromm often says, modernity brought more freedom "from" but less freedom "to." This absence of a positive concept of freedom and a positive social vision left modern man more and more alone and anxious. Receptive orientations were sometimes resorted to as solutions and can be seen, according to Fromm, in the masochistic loyalty encouraged by Calvinism and Lutheranism as well as by Nazi Germany in more recent times. The exploiting, or taking, orientation can be seen in the "pariah" and "adventure" capitalists of the nineteenth century.[42] The preserving, or hoarding, orientation existed alongside the exploiting orientation during the nineteenth century and constituted a more conservative and methodical approach to economic pursuits.[43]

The distinctive product of modernity and its institutions is a character type never before seen in the history of man; the evolution from individual to corporate capitalism has brought about the so-called marketing character. Freed from control by overt authority, modern man has now succumbed to the subtle and silent control of the market, of the demands of the corporation, and of the abstract principles of production and management characteristic of an advanced technological society. Alienated from himself as a center of productive power, conforming to the expectation of silent authorities, and manipulated to develop an insatiable desire to consume the products of modern industry, the marketing character is only a short step away from the passivity of the so-called "receiving" character type. The marketing character is also *homo consumens* dedicated primarily to "the satisfaction of consuming and 'taking in'; commodities, sights, food, drinks, cigarettes, people, lectures, books, movies—all are consumed, swallowed." [44]

Fromm extends his concept of the marketing character to a variety of modern phenomena—the drug culture, computerization, and, finally, a growing modern preoccupation with death ("necrophilia"). The passivity of the marketing personality leads him both to conform to and to depend upon anything that promises instant ease. His desire to "take in" instant happiness may lead him to turn either to drugs or to the effortless existence of a computerized world. Behind the behavior of both the addict and the technocrat is a deep-seated passivity and alienation from oneself as a center of creative power. Finally, however, Fromm sees in the desire for oblivion in the drug culture and the fascination with inanimate machines in the technocrat a hidden preoccupation with death and the possible birth of a fifth type on nonproductive character—the *"necrophiliac."* [45]

Fromm's interpretation of modern existence must be viewed at two levels. At one level, modernity is simply a more advanced degree of individual and social individuation. At another level, modernity is corporate and state capitalism (e.g., Russia) with its endless circle of production and consumption and an increasingly numerous marketing personality to fill its needs. It is Fromm's central conviction that these two meanings of modernity cannot coexist. Modernity as an inevitable process of social individuation is ambivalent; to survive it, mankind must produce highly mature people who can learn to relate to the world while at the same time affirming and accepting their individuality and separateness. Fromm clearly believes that modernity in the second sense will destroy the positive possibilities of modernity in the first sense. The marketing personality—the characterological issue of corporate and state capitalism—simply does not possess the strengths to live up to the challenges of a highly individuated and differentiated social world. It is from this perspective that we must view Fromm's pessimism about modern man, a pessimism that sociologists such as Winston White have so much difficulty comprehending. Modern Western man, especially of the middle class, may indeed have many virtues; but his virtues and strengths match neither the challenges nor the opportunities that he faces.

It is tempting to put oneself in the shoes of Erich Fromm and imagine Fromm's response to Rieff's concept of the psychological man and Brown's concept of Dionysian man. Certainly, Fromm would consider both of them as predictable variations of his concept of the marketing character. Psychological man, as Philip Rieff depicts him, is man dedicated to the high art of refined consumption, a consumption mitigated and controlled only by the application of psychoanalytic insight. Psychological man indeed knows that consumption is the end of life, but this end should be humbled—as should all the goals and ends of life—by the healthy skepticism of analytic wisdom. Dionysian man would most likely be seen by Fromm as the final receptive and regressive expression of the marketing character; Dionysian man would be passivity taken to its final regressive goal of union with the all-providing mother and with death. Passive release is the modality common to both psychological man and Dionysian man; the difference is only that psychological man submits his releasing modalities to analytic restraint. Both Rieff and Brown believe that repression and release are the major choices that have always confronted man.

Fromm, on the other hand, presents a completely different set of categories for comprehending the major human choices. *Activeness or passiveness, not repression or release—these are the fundamental al-*

ternatives for Fromm. He would say that the psychological, Dionysian, and marketing character types have in common their shared decision for passivity.

According to Fromm, psychoanalysis, in the hands of such men as Rieff and Brown, has continued along the road that it began to take even before it left the hands of Freud. In *Sigmund Freud's Mission,* Fromm claims that psychoanalysis was basically a conservative social movement from the beginning; it offered an inner balance and a quasi-religious frame of reference for middle-class urban intellectuals who had neither the energy nor the will to make a more radical analysis of the ills of Western civilization or to develop a more profound and constructive alternative.[46] The destiny of psychoanalysis has been to become, through advertising and the mass media, a powerful tool of propaganda supporting the dynamic of corporate capitalism. There is little doubt at all that Fromm would be willing to apply this analysis of the sociological impact of psychoanalysis to Rieff's concept of psychological man. He would also venture the guess that, in spite of Brown's original intentions, the fate of his concept of Dionysian man will be very much the same; it too will become entangled with the passive and releasing modalities of the ethos of corporate capitalism and its normative character type—*homo consumens.*

Psychology and the Science of Ethics

Fromm derives his concept of the productive character partially on the basis of a broad philosophical psychology which he sometimes calls a philosophical anthropology. However, he also amplifies and enriches it through a highly selective and somewhat rigid interpretation of both Eastern and Western religious symbols. His first and chief method, the use of psychology and psychoanalysis for a rational analysis of the normative human character type, is a radical departure from the modern tradition of careful separation of psychology as a science from ethical and philosophical concerns.

For Fromm, ethics has to do with the nature of human character; it attempts to discover the optimal organization (the optimal character) of human energies and the conditions necessary to bring it about. He resurrects an ancient tradition, one that both Rieff and Brown try to bury, when he writes, "Humanistic ethics is the applied science of the 'art of living' based upon the theoretical 'science of man.'" [47] In addition, Fromm claims that "ethics as an applied science depends on . . . psychology as a theoretical science." [48] By psychology, Fromm does not mean the more experimental and empiristic psychologies modeled after the natural sciences.[49] The psychology he has in mind is indeed empirical and scientific but in a larger sense than is generally considered acceptable in most scientific circles today. In fact, Fromm's psychology becomes so broad that it gradually shades into what he calls "philosophical anthropology." Psychology for Fromm is rational reflection upon and ordering of the internal life, both conscious and unconscious, of man.

Fromm holds a more elevated vision than does Philip Rieff of psychology and psychoanalysis as moral sciences. He is fully aware of the penultimate significance of psychoanalysis and its capacity to "unmask" and humiliate the rationalizations behind our moral pretensions.[50] In other words, Fromm simply acknowledges and generally approves of the level of ethical significance of psychoanalysis about which Rieff writes. But he aspires to go farther than either Freud or Rieff is willing to go. Fromm believes that psychoanalysis discovered the modern science of characterology. It has provided us with an initial typology of nonproductive character orientations. But more than that, in its uncertain vision of the genital personality, psychoanalysis has provided us with a positive characterology that Fromm himself attempts to elaborate further in his idea of the productive character. In the hands of Fromm, psychoanalysis becomes extended into a general philosophical psychology and moves from a penultimate to a positive ethic. Fromm aspires to develop an objective ethic, an objective and rationally articulated vision of what man is to become. This ethic is properly comprehended when it is understood that Fromm is indeed trying to project a new vision for what Philip Rieff derisively calls a community of positive "social obligation." In the thought of Fromm—in contrast to most interpretations of his position—we will see how an ethics of community wins out over an ethics of individualism. Fromm destroys false authority in order to restore competent and rational authority. He attacks economic individualism in order to restore true freedom and individuality in community. His good society would lessen everyone's "freedom from" in order to increase their "freedom to."

Authority and community are not antagonistic to individual fulfillment in the thought of Fromm as they are for Rieff. Rational authority and rational ethics have for their purpose the fulfillment of man at both the generic and the individual levels. The good of all men and the good of the individual can be kept in balance only if some distinction can be drawn between the real and the false needs of man. And it must be further demonstrated that the real needs of man, while personally fulfilling and satisfying the individual, are at the same time relevant and serviceable to the fulfillment of the race.

The Anthropology of Productive Man

Let us follow chronologically the development of Fromm's ideas on the nature of the productive personality. We will omit Fromm's discussion in *Escape from Freedom* of the concept of "spontaneous activity." We need only observe that spontaneous activity, for Fromm, is a centered act which integrates the total personality into acts of work and love.[51] These acts of work and love overcome man's loneliness by bringing him back into union with himself, his society, and nature.[52]

In *Man for Himself*, Fromm replaces the concept of spontaneous activity with the concept of the productive character. Here the loose affinity of Fromm's vision with Freud's concept of genital man is acknowledged. For Fromm, the key to the affinity has to do with a controlling analogy or "symbol" which genitality suggests to him (although probably not to Freud). Genitality is symbolic of productiveness—the production of new life through the "union of sperm and the egg." [53] This generative and species-relevant view of productiveness constitutes a controlling image which dominates all of Fromm's writing on the nature of productiveness, robbing it, one must note, of its occasional individualistic meaning.

Although generativity at the biological level provides a model for Fromm's concept of productiveness, the productive orientation, as he understands it, is a broader concept and "refers to a fundamental attitude, a mode of relatedness in all realms of human experience. It covers mental, emotional, and sensory responses to others, to oneself, and to things." [54] "Productiveness," as Fromm defines it, "is man's ability to use his powers and to realize the potentialities inherent in him." [55] In addition, Fromm, following Aristotle, believes that productiveness relates to the realization of those "capacities" or "potencies" *unique* to man.

But what are the capacities unique to man? Productive thinking (reason), love, and work—this is Fromm's answer to the question. In *Man for Himself* he sets forth a phenomenological description of the nature of reason, or, as he calls it, "productive thinking." He lists the characteristics of productive thinking: (1) the capacity to think of ends as well as of means, (2) the capacity to discern the basic or essential features of its object, (3) the capacity for both involved interest in the object and objective respect for the object, and, finally, (4) the capacity for perceiving objects holisticly in relation to their contexts.[56] These phenomenologically derived characteristics of productive thinking are recognizable as a description of thinking free from deficiency and scarcity motivations. Less believable when phenomenologically derived, at least to the scientifically-minded, what Fromm said in 1947 on this subject is now generally accepted as correct, especially after the more scientific descriptions of mature thinking developed by Jean Piaget, Robert White, Ernest Schachtel, Jerome Bruner, and others. Reason, in the grand sense of the word, is really not so difficult to believe in as Freud, Rieff, and even Brown have believed it to be.

Fromm's theory of the productive character is carried farther in his stunningly popular book *The Art of Loving*, published in 1956. Of the three coordinates of the productive personality—reason, love, and work—this book develops the concept of love, and, in fact, gives it a position of predominant importance. Creative work unites us with nature and with objects, but only productive love answers the deepest of all needs—union with other people. And, finally, love itself is the key to the proper use of reason.

Love is characterized as an "art" requiring "knowledge and effort." In depicting truly human love as an art, Fromm immediately warns us to remove from our minds all images of love as a simple, passive release of nature's goodness. Love, as was earlier the case with "spontaneous activity," is a centered activity requiring discipline and artistic synthesis. However, love, although a specifically existential phenomenon, recapitulates at this higher level a distinctively natural phenomenon—the act of generation.

Fromm is constantly juxtaposing phenomenological and existential descriptions of productive love with biological descriptions of generativity. In doing this, he is not reducing the higher to the lower; rather, he is saying that the lower reveals a paradigm of how life is created, a paradigm that is analogically restated at successively higher levels. At the existential level he says: "Giving is the highest expression of potency. In the very act of giving, I experience my strength, my wealth, my power." [57] In all the nonproductive orientations, giving is experienced as impoverishment, as a matter of "giving up." But for the productive person, giving is experienced as a way of expressing one's richness. Not he who "has" but he who "gives" is the one who is rich.

This phenomenology of productiveness as giving can be illustrated at the level of sexual love between man and woman. Beneath this is a deeper paradigm in the interaction of sperm and ovum. From the more archaic and elemental levels, one can ascend again and comprehend the meaning of productivity and giving as a total existential orientation. With regard to productivity and giving at the level of sexual relations Fromm writes:

> The culmination of the male sexual function lies in the act of giving; the man gives himself, his sexual organ, to the woman. At the moment of orgasm he gives his semen to her. He cannot help giving it if he is potent. If he cannot give, he is impotent. For the woman the process is not different, although somewhat more complex. She gives herself too; she opens the gates to her feminine center; in the act of receiving, she gives. If she is incapable of this act of giving, if she can only receive, she is frigid.[58]

In this process of mutual giving and receiving, creativity occurs, a creativity analogous to the union of sperm and ovum. Fromm reminds us "that the union of sperm and ovum is the basis for the birth of a child. But in the purely psychic realm it is not different; in the love between man and woman, each of them is reborn." [59]

But at a higher level of one's total existential relationship to the world, the productive giving at the biological and sexual levels is recapitulated. But here it is neither sperm nor ovum, neither penis nor vagina that is given and received, although they may indeed be a portion of the totality of what is given. In addition, one gives "of his joy, of his interest, of his understanding, of his knowledge, of his humor, of his sadness—of all expressions and manifestations of that which is alive in him." [60] In giving to the other person, he creates a new sense of liveness in the other, a sense of aliveness that cannot help rebounding to enrich the life of the giver. "In the act of giving something is born, and both persons involved are grateful for the life that is born for both of them." [61]

Beyond the element of giving, love contains four elements, all of which further illustrate the active character of love. The four elements are *care, responsibility, respect,* and *knowledge. Care* involves an attitude of active concern for the "life and growth" of both our object of love and that which is born out of this love.[62] *Responsibility* is not so much duty as it is a voluntary responsiveness to the "needs, expressed and unexpressed, of another human being." [63] *Respect* (derived from *respicere,* "to look at") refers to the ability to see "a person as he is, to be aware of his unique individuality." [64]

Finally, love must include *knowledge* of the other person. Here, however, Fromm makes an important distinction between two kinds of knowledge, a distinction that has great implications for the proper positioning of man's entire capacity for reason and knowledge in the context of the total life process. On the one hand there is ordinary knowledge, knowledge by thought. Psychological knowledge is rooted in this kind. In addition, however, there is a deeper kind of knowledge that is rooted in participation or love itself and in which abstract, objective knowledge is finally grounded. For Fromm, true knowledge and reason are in the service of the one grand project of life: the project of finding participation through giving, that is, the project of finding union through creating new life.

One of the most intriguing features of Fromm's understanding of the productive man is the synthesis he makes between psychoanalysis and Marxist thought, especially the early Marx. In the end, it may be that Fromm actually draws more from the early Marx than he does from Freud. What is so startling, however, is to hear how similar, at some points, these giants of modern thought can sound. Fromm believes the early Marx was thoroughly influenced by Hegel's idea that a man's potentialities are manifested through a dialectical process, a dialectical process of "active movement" whereby one's potentialities are activated by contact with the outside world.[65] It is through active relationships with people and objects that one manifests concretely in existence one's "natural essence," one's "species-being." The sexual relationship itself provides the best available index for assessing the level of man's actualization. Marx once wrote:

> From this relationship man's whole level of development can be assessed. It follows from the character of this relationship how far man has become, and has understood himself as, a species-being, a human being. The relation of man to woman is the most natural relation of human being to human being. It indicates, therefore, how far man's natural behavior has become human, and how far his human essence has become a natural essence for him, how far his human nature has become nature for him.[66]

In another quotation, we can see Marx's early theory of the relationship between the active individual and the life of the species, a view that I believe Fromm holds. The following quotation from Marx appears no fewer than three different times in Fromm's written and edited works, attesting, I believe, to its importance for his own thinking. It addresses the weaknesses of alienated, piecemeal, specialized labor of modern industrial capitalism.

Since alienated labor: 1) alienates nature from man; and 2) alienates man from himself, from his own active function, his life activity; so it alienates him from the species. It makes species-life into a means of individual life. In the first place it alienates species-life and individual life, and secondly, it turns the latter, as an abstraction, into the purpose of the former, also in its abstract and alienated form. For labor, *life activity, productive life,* now appear to man only as means for the satisfaction of a need, the need to maintain his physical existence. *Productive life is, however, species-life. It is life creating life. In the type of life activity resides the whole character of a species, its species-character; and free, conscious activity is the species-character of human beings.* Life itself appears only as a *means of life.*[67]

This species-character of man, this free and conscious activity which is the very essence of man, this life for which mere biological existence is only a means, seems very close to what Robert White calls effectance needs, what Maslow calls "growth needs" (as opposed to deficiency needs), or what Schachtel calls allocentric (as opposed to autocentric) modes of perception. The specifically human level of enjoying and relating to the world has been attained when, as Marx says, "need and enjoyment have thus lost their egoistic character, and nature has lost its mere *utility.*" Then, and only then, has "its utilization become human utilization." [68]

Although activeness is close to the essence of productive man, Fromm does give some recognition to the place of the more passive and regressive dimensions of human existence. Fromm believes that the nonproductive orientations (which are the equivalent of regressiveness and passiveness) are negative and destructive only when they are "dominant in the character structure." [69] But when the productive orientation is dominant, then all the nonproductive orientations take on a constructive meaning.[70] As we will see later, it is Fromm's evolutionary thinking, not his general anthropology, that leads him to the unfortunate identification of activeness with virtue.

In his *Revolution of Hope,* Fromm extends his concept of the productive character to include a discussion of productive hope. Hope is a central element of the productive character. It is basically a poetic experience and is best grasped in music, poem, and symbol.[71] Fromm attempts a phenomenological description, but the full grasping of the nature of hope requires an appropriation of symbolic expressions, especially the eschatological symbols of man's religious myths. Hope, then, is the bridge between Fromm's attempt to give a rational description of the productive character and his attempt, to which we will soon turn, to distill it from man's religious myths and symbols.

Fromm describes hope as the capacity to "see and cherish all signs of new life." It is "a state of being" and "inner readiness . . . of intense but not-yet-spent activeness." [72] Hope has an orientation toward the future, but an orientation clearly based on giving birth to potentialities active in the present. This kind of hope Fromm clearly distinguishes from the kind of hope that passively waits on deliverance from the future or the kind of pseudorevolutionary hope that tries violently to force changes which are grounded in no present possibilities. Hope is strongly related to faith, and faith is defined as a "certainty about the reality" of present possibilities. Hope also involves fortitude, the capacity "to resist the temptation to compromise hope and faith by transforming them—and thus destroying them—into empty optimism or into irrational faith." [73]

Hope and the Messianic Time

At a time when it was still fashionable for psychoanalysts to classify religion as a compulsion neurosis on a mass scale, Fromm proposed a psychoanalytic interpretation of religion that saw it as constructive for the human enterprise. As early as *The Dogma of Christ*, written while he still considered himself an orthodox analyst, Fromm began to break out of the standard analytic treatment of religion. Religion, for Fromm, is man's most global and inclusive project of overcoming the existential dichotomies and finding union. All religion, whether theistic or non-theistic, is a "system of thought and action shared by a group which gives the individual a frame of orientation and an object of devotion." [74] Although religion often restricts itself primarily to superego functions (authoritarian religion), Fromm recognized that religion also includes, in varying degrees, adaptive, creative, and even *playful* attempts to find orientation amid life's existential and historical dichotomies. [75] Fromm can, with Brown, call religion play, but he means it much more in the sense used by Johan Huizinga or Adolf Jensen. Healthy religion, constructive religion, projects both man's desire for independence and his desire for union. However, Fromm admits that there have been and can be regressive religions—religions that seek union without freedom.

Fromm believes there is a clear continuity between his vision of the productive character and the ethical core of the great world religions. [76] All the great world faiths—Judaism, Christianity, Taoism, Buddhism, Zen—celebrate the values of love, reason, and productive work. Fromm moves through the world's religions somewhat like a butcher, cutting out the good pieces and throwing the rest in the dump heap of history. If there are variations in the ways these different religions handle these ideals (and, of course, there are), Fromm tends to ignore them. Fromm follows Feuerbach in the belief that man's image of God is a projection of the highest values that men in various ages hold for themselves. Belief in a god is a sign of man's alienation from himself, his projection onto God of that which is an unrealized possibility for men.[77] The love, justice, and reason in terms of which men sometimes portray God are actually projections of man's productive possibilities.

Fromm holds that the dogmas, propositions, and theological orthodoxies in which most religions are wrapped are quite secondary to the inner ethical experience which these doctrines intend to convey. He proposes his own program of demythologization, a study of the inner religious experience (the "X experience") behind various theological formulations. Fromm wants to study what Bultmannians might call the structure of experience behind and beneath religious myth and symbol. His program, however, would include not only Christianity (as it does for Bultmann, and his school) or Western religious experience (as it does for Paul Ricoeur). It would include all the religions of the world, especially the great world religions emerging from what Karl Jaspers has called the axial age. It is Fromm's uncomplicated expectation that they would all reveal a structure of existence, an orientation, similar to the one that he has summarized in his concept of the productive character—an expectation, one might venture to guess, that would cause most historians of religion to shudder.

Fromm's tendency to appropriate those aspects of religion which confirm his vision of the productive character and discard the remainder has gained him little favor among the world's students of religion. Liberal laymen and ministers trained by an older liberal theology of the 1920's and 1930's have often read his thoughts on religion with enthusiasm, but younger theologues trained under the aegis of neoorthodoxy and professional students of religion only smile, if not sneer.

To write off Fromm's view of religion too quickly is to overlook the moral meaning of his position. During a period of historical relativism and general skepticism, Fromm, the psychoanalyst, was holding forth the vision of a universal structure to man that reflects itself in universally acknowledged values and truths. Such an idea seems more believable today than it did twenty years ago when Fromm first put it in writing. The widely acclaimed generative linguistics of Noam Chomsky[78] and the authoritative cross-cultural studies in moral development by Lawrence Kohlberg[79] both suggest a universally shared common structure of the human mind that expresses itself in widely recognized common principles about the nature of the good and the true. It is precisely Fromm's contention that these universal principles are implicit in the symbolism of the great world religions.

There is little doubt, however, that Fromm fails to comprehend the significance of many religious expressions. His tendency to see religious development in analogy to his general theory of ontogenetic and phylogenetic evolution has led Fromm to make serious errors in his interpretation of primitive and archaic religious forms. For Fromm, the history of religions is the history of man's development from incestuous to productive orientations.[80] By "incestuous," Fromm means those orientations to life's existential dichotomies which find union through passive attachment to the primary ties of mother, home, tribe, land, or blood.[81] It can hardly be denied that there is a tendency in Fromm to say that in the ontogenetically and phylogenetically *late* there are, indeed, actualized more strictly human values. The result of this kind of thinking is to say that there is more reason and more love in modern man than there was in primitive and archaic man. Certainly, this elevation of the late at the expense of the early is indeed out of fashion with the spirit of leading students of religion such as Mircea Eliade, Claude Lévi-Strauss, Adolf Jensen, and others who seem to be primarily interested in showing either the continuity or the superiority of primitive man to modern, individuated existence.

But this bias of associating the primitive and the archaic with the incestuous and the passive should not become an obstacle to a proper hearing of Fromm's central message. The historical dichotomies of the modern world when added to the age-old existential dichotomies of human existence require a higher strategy of union than modern man seems capable of exhibiting. This higher strategy Fromm has summarized in his concept of the productive character. Of all the religious symbols Fromm appeals to, the one that best gives the concept of the productive character vital poetic and symbolic expression is the Old Testament symbol of the "messianic time."

Vital self-experiences are most fully comprehended and expressed in symbolic language. This conviction leads Fromm to turn time and time again to the religions of the world, especially to Judaism, the faith in which he himself was nourished as a child. For Fromm, the Old Testament is a story of man's emergence from a primitive union with nature and man. It is a story of man's gradual evolution, through struggle, repentance, and hope, to the higher union of the messianic time. Fromm writes that the two ages, paradise and the messianic time,

are the same, inasmuch as they are a state of harmony. They are different, inasmuch as the first state of harmony existed only by virtue of man's *not yet* having been born, while the new state of harmony exists as a result of man's having been fully born.[82]

The messianic time, and the new innocence and harmony that it represents, comes from going *forward*, not *backward*. In fact, it comes at the end of a long struggle against idolatrous attempts to find union and security in the things of the created world, in the work of one's hands—in short, in the past. For Fromm, the Biblical concept of idolatry corresponds with his definition of incest. It is a cognitive and affective dependence "on the past and a hindrance to full development." [83]

Fromm believes that in the prophetic literature of the Old Testament and in the Talmud, the messianic time is political, this-worldly, and historical. It is "horizontal" rather than "vertical" or "other-worldly" as it was in Daniel and in other Jewish apocalyptic literature. The messianic time is often associated with the appearance of a specific messianic figure, sometimes a leader, sometimes an anointed king, but often in the form of God or the Lord himself. But the messianic figure is more the "sign" of the messianic time than the "savior" or the one who actually ushers in the messianic time.[84]

The vision of "peace" is the central mark of the messianic time. It will be time of peace and harmony between man and man as well as between man and nature.[85] There will also be harmony between the nations and a renunciation of all weapons of force.[86] But this higher harmony comes only as a result of man's own gradual attainment of freedom, responsibility, and love.

In this view, man becomes the agent responsible for ushering in the messianic time. This view of the order of initiatives bringing forth the higher harmony puts Judaism into the greatest conflict with Christianity, a conflict that reveals itself throughout Fromm's writing. But his vestigial Jewishness and his psychoanalytic sensibilities (and probably in that order) render Fromm antagonistic to the idea that the messianic time (or the Kingdom of God) comes as an act of grace on the part of God. To Fromm, this would lead man back toward the inactiveness and idolatry which are at the very heart of the human tragedy.

Fromm quotes the famous Jewish scholar Leo Baeck and asserts that in the "prophetic literature the messianic vision rested upon the tension between what existed and was still there and that which was becoming and was yet to be." [87] Of course, this tension is precisely the tension of activeness which Fromm ascribes to the productive character. This kind of tension between possibilities partially present but yet to be fully realized gives birth to what Fromm calls "dynamic hope," the theme of his later book entitled *The Revolution of Hope*. It is clear that Fromm believes that man himself *activates* the messianic time.

Productive Man: A Summary

We must now state what we have learned about productive man in terms of his relationship to himself, his experience of time, his relationship to his social world, and his relationship to the "other." We stated earlier that Fromm's solution to the problems of modernity is an *undialectical progressivist* solution. We mean by this that Fromm wants to meet modernity with a progressive advance, but an advance that does not sufficiently incorporate within it the so-called low in man—in short, his ontogenetic and phylogenetic history. However, I have not made this charge against Fromm categorically. Fromm is not as progressivistic, not as blindly perfectionistic, and not as wildly utopian as many contemporary apologists for the *status quo* make him out to be. In general, I see productive man as an ally of generative man; they are of the same piece, so to speak, fighting for much the same thing. I believe that it is important to state the progressivist dimensions of Fromm's thought as accurately as possible; only then can one honestly state the ways in which his thought is indeed *not sufficiently* dialectical, *not sufficiently* complex to meet the needs of modernity. However, in many important ways, Fromm depreciates the ontogenetic and phylogenetic early and fails to give a complete account of how man's maturity must include the early and the low.

It is not possible to portray directly productive man's relationship to himself. Productive man always discovers himself indirectly through the world of his action; he does not know his own potentialities until he sees them reflected back from the world upon which he acts. Once this is acknowledged, however, it is possible to speak of productive man's relationship to himself. From this perspective, the first thing to note is that productive man experiences himself as an instability, as a tension or mixture between his progressive capacities for reason, conscience, and imagination and his potentially regressive desires for union and security.

As we have already seen, in his portrait of productive man's relation to himself, there are certain ways in which Fromm does take account of that which is ontogenetically and phylogenetically early. We have seen that productiveness as a progressive advance includes within it man's primitive desire for union. Productiveness also includes, as we have noted, the so-called nonproductive orientations; when the passive nonproductive orientations are organized and guided by the productive orientation, they take on a new and positive meaning. Finally, we have seen that productiveness recapitulates at historical and existential levels of existence the fundamental urge to produce new life.

What, then, has Fromm left out? Why do we still suspect that Fromm has a bias toward the high and the progressive? Why do we continue to distrust his efforts to incorporate the archaic into productivity? Our suspicions indeed have reasons. It is one thing to say that the phylogenetically and ontogenetically low has value when stated in the context of productivity. This Fromm often does. *It is something else, however, to state that meaning of the ontogenetically and phylogenetically low in terms of their meaning for themselves.* This Fromm does not do at all. We can see this first in his typology of character. This typology of character is modeled, in part, on the basis of Freud's developmental psychology. Therefore it suggests a scheme of ontogenetic growth as well as an ideal typology of historically discernible character types. But if this is the case, we are left with the impression that all the stages of growth prior to maturity and productivity are predominantly *passive*. And, of course, this is absurd. The infant and the child have their form of activeness just as has the mature adult.

The truth is that Fromm has no developmental psychology. He reformulates Freud's in order to create a typology of historical character types. This failure, which has been no small problem to the practicing psychologist who is otherwise attracted to Fromm's thought, betrays a bias. Nowhere does Fromm explicitly pay attention to children. Those remarks about children which can be found are likely to be tainted with his typology of character which tends to see everything that is not productive as passive. One cannot resist the thought that, for Fromm, children are a bore. Doubtless it is true that he also finds somewhat tedious the child in the man—the infantile residues in every mature adult. One gains the impression from Fromm that each child's development is something of a straight line moving from passive receptiveness and mother love through a somewhat more active and demanding kind of father love until finally the child reaches a fully active and productive maturity, where, fortunately, he can then give more than he receives.

What Fromm lacks, then, is a well-articulated epigenetic principle. It is precisely the epigenetic principle which states that all the elements of the high and the mature are found in an undeveloped form in the early, the low—the very beginning. The reverse is also the case; true maturity must contain, at a more differentiated level, all the components of the beginning. Erikson uses this principle primarily with his theory of ontogenetic development. Yet it is also present in his attitude toward primitive and archaic man; implicitly it is for Erikson a phylogenetic principle as well.

Fromm's failure to state adequately something like an epigenetic principle can be seen more dramatically in relation to what he says about the superego in man. Fromm acknowledges that the superego and the authority of the father have played an important role in the development of the race. But when it comes to the present, he believes that we are at the place in historical development where it is no longer necessary for the child to have a superego, with all its inevitable rigidity, no matter how kindly or lovingly it has been imposed. He writes, "I do not believe that with regard to the child, in a non-authoritarian society, the authoritarian conscience has to exist as a precondition for the formation of humanistic conscience." [88] If this means that children can grow up without a superego to support them during the period before the archaic and ever-present structures of the ego (the true seat of mature conscience) become stabilized, then I think Fromm is very much mistaken. To say that each man needs something of a superego during his childhood and youth is to say nothing derogatory about his eventual capacity for self-direction. In fact, I would assert, on the basis of the epigenetic principle, that the rudiments of conscience and reason (the marks of adult, humanistic ethics) are present from the beginning. But it is the nature of man that desire and imagination are, in the beginning of life, poorly balanced by perception, conscience, and reason. Although the rudimentary forms of conscience and reason are present from the beginning of life, they need to be supported by the gentle promptings of a healthy superego.

But there is a deeper problem in Fromm's willingness to dispose of the superego so easily. This willingness is part of his unbridled drive toward universality—a universality that does not take into consideration the relative moralities of other people or of oneself. There are no completely universal men devoid of those provincial moralities which occur simply because each man lives in a particular place and pursues a particular vocation utilizing special techniques under unique conditions. Every man (and certainly every child) must have a morality to cover the special and unique about his life. He should also have a grasp of certain universal principles common to all men and all places. But in addition, he must have an ideology and a personal identity that brings the two together. It is precisely this which Fromm does not have and it is this which he cannot appreciate in others. He wants to make each man too quickly into the universal man—into the productive man that is a universal man. We have the feeling that he forgets the particularity of each man; he overlooks, we fear, that each man, in addition to having been at one time a child, is also a man of a particular country and class and may be a fireman, a doctor, a fisherman, or a hunter and, because of these particularities, must have special moralities and customs to guide him in these spheres. At best, there will be a dialogue between his universal conscience and his morality; and possibly his universal conscience can learn to know and affirm what his morality at one time blindly dictated. But that he can live without his special moralities or grow up without a superego is an illusion that we must challenge.

This drive toward universality leads to another reason why we distrust Fromm. We wonder if finally all is reduced to consciousness and lucidity in productive man. This feeling is akin to another that we cannot fail to raise: Does not Fromm have more answers about more things than most men should have? His desire for a science of man (a true psychology) upon which to ground an ethics is certainly an idea to be taken seriously. If man develops a new humanism which commands worldwide attention, such a science will doubtless play a part. But would not such a science, unsupplemented by other measures, do exactly what Fromm's elimination of the superego and man's provincial moralities have done? Would it not reduce all of life too quickly to the universal and deny the particular? If such a science develops (and we believe that it must), it must progress in the context of a personal and cultural dialogue—a hermeneutical dialogue that attempts to comprehend not only the universal but the particular about the symbols and values of each man and each group. To take seriously the particularity in either oneself or other people is to confront mysterious elements of life that are not easily reduced to the categories of a science, not even the broad kind of philosophical anthropology suggested by Fromm. The dictum to make all things conscious suggests that neither the unconscious nor the particular is viewed by Fromm as very deep, very profound, or very complex. Regression in the service of the ego, it should be noted, does not mean bringing all things into consciousness. It means, rather, relaxing the boundaries of the more controlled sectors of the ego so that they can descend into the deeper regulatory functions of the ego and the id, not in order to reduce these denser areas to the clear light of consciousness, but to be nourished and re-created by forces and patterns that the conscious ego can only partially comprehend or understand.

We see the same tendency in Fromm's concept of time. Productive man's eye seems almost totally cast in the direction of the future. In addition, productive man believes that the future must be *made* to occur. Very little comes to man from the future; man must bring, must force, must usher it in himself. But why is this the case? The answer is clear. Productive man must actively form the future because in reality he does not experience receiving very much from the past. Fromm speaks about the passivities of life—those things we receive, and, in part, receive from the past. But he does not believe in very deeply or trust very profoundly these passivities. Shouldn't every psychiatrist know that he who can receive little from the past will also expect to receive little from the future? So we feel a lack of continuity in productive man's experience of time, a lack of organicity which marks the truly gracious life.

Yet we must take very seriously Fromm's remarks about the dynamic character of hope. Productive man does have an active quality about his ego; generative man, as Erikson speaks of him, also has this active quality. Both of these character types truly feel that there is much in life and in the future that they must form themselves. But generative man does not, as does productive man, simply capitalize on present potentialities. He has the experience of being nourished by and co-operating with past and present forces which *blend* with his own activeness to form the future. As we will see, the principle of *reciprocity* is more marked with generative man than with productive man. And this is because Erikson knows better than does Fromm that men act partially out of their own energies but also partially because they have been acted upon; just as he knows that a man's giving is partially guided by his own will but is also very much a product of the spontaneous gratitude that comes from having received. Therefore, Erikson knows, in ways which escape Fromm, that the final demarcation between the passive and the active in man is very difficult to draw. There may be more of a place in life for *grace* than Fromm would like to admit.

What have we learned about productive man's relationships with his social world? We have learned that he is a man of love and that he can give of himself even more than he receives. We have learned that through his productive giving he activates his social world just as he in turn is activated in the process of his giving. Productive man is very much a political man. His political interests exceed by far those of psychological man, Dionysian man, and even perhaps those of generative man. Psychological man is political only to the degree necessary to maintain the abundance that makes his psychological comfort possible. His only great political virtue is his distrust of all true believers. Dionysian man, of course, believes that politics is the realm of death; strangely, he can accept death but he cannot accept politics.

Fromm grounds the political activity of productive man in his self-interest and self-love. Love, as Fromm understands it, applies to oneself as well as to others. Genuine self-love and self-interest are the cornerstones of the productive character and his ethic. The difficulty with modern society has not been its doctrine of self-interest; rather, the problem has been with the serious "deterioration of the meaning of self-interest." [89] The concept of self-interest has been narrowed so that it includes only economic interests. Fromm, on the other hand, believes that one's self-love and self-interest must serve the actualization of the "real self" and its real needs. And, as we have seen, one's real needs are not antagonistic to the interests of the community simply because real needs, according to Fromm, are species relevant.

In his ambitious *The Sane Society*, Fromm sets forth his vision of "communitarian socialism," his theory of the good society in which productive man would live. On the one hand, it is a society whose goal is the unfolding of the "human powers" of its individual members, where every member is an "end in himself" and never a "means toward another's end." On the other hand, it would also be a society where "opportunism" is considered asocial, where social concerns become "personal matters," where "private" pursuits do not interfere with "human solidarity," and where "responsible" participation is both permitted and encouraged.[90]

When Fromm becomes more concrete we hear him speak of a society where the "workers" control (although not necessarily own) the means of production. Workers would be individually activated by sharing in the definition and direction of the productive activity that constitutes their occupation. In this vision of things, the portion of their individual powers which would be actualized is that part relevant to the meaning and direction of the corporate enterprise of which they are a part. In the end, Fromm envisions a world of more centralization rather than less, but a centralization balanced by a kind of decentralization designed to stimulate "participation and responsibility" in centralized decisions. Fromm's new society would be a veritable beehive of active participation in community affairs. The entire population would be divided into groups of five hundred persons for the purpose of debating and directly influencing centralized decisions—a nation of town meetings. Clearly, under such a system the individual powers to be actualized are only those relevant to the responsible influence and direction of the whole.

One is inclined to believe that productive man is more than political —he is hyperpolitical. He exercises his powers by making decisions about everything—at his work, in his neighborhood, in his community, in his state, in his nation—with regard to all the world. Productive man is interested in everything, is informed about all, is willing to debate each new issue, and exercises his franchise in every sphere that touches his life. Productive man is active man; he exercises his powers over far more areas of life than is the case with most contemporary men. He attempts to influence with conscious intentionality all spheres of life to the very end of the horizon of his consciousness.

Productive man is influencing, controlling, and guiding everything around him. But the reverse is also true. Because all his neighbors are also productive men, he too is controlled and influenced by them. Hence, the social and political world of productive man is indeed a communitarian society. It will be a tighter, in some ways more restrictive, society than has been the case for the last one hundred years. Productive man in the new active society will have far more "freedom to" and far less "freedom from" than Western bourgeois man has known in the past.

Participatory democracy, the small group, the face-to-face encounter, the small unit within the larger unit—this is the nature of the shape of things to come. In contrast to Rieff's new world, the small group, the face-to-face encounter, has a political rather than a specifically therapeutic meaning for Fromm. People will come together in small gatherings not to make each other comfortable but to stimulate each other in the responsible use of their powers as human beings. The new communitarian society that Fromm envisions can indeed include the therapeutic vision put forth by Rieff, but the reverse is not the case. There is no place for productive man in the world of psychological man, just as there is no room for an ethic of positive community within a penultimate ethic of negative community. But it is certainly true that the positive communitarian ethic of productive man can embrace some of the therapeutic aims of psychological man. Men in the new communitarian society will indeed be more comfortable (have more inner well-being), but it will come as a consequence of their increased productivity and not as an end in itself.

Will there be religion in the new communitarian society, the new active society? The answer is yes; it will be a grand public and civil religion, a general religion that *celebrates* and *ritualizes* the new positive ethic of productive man. Fromm believes in religion—what he calls humanistic religion. All men have the need for "a system of thought and action . . . which gives the individual a frame of orientation and an object of devotion." [91] If man needs "systems of action" and "objects of devotion," then it follows that man needs ritual. Fromm speaks of ritual as "collective art." [92] It is a "shared" activity that attempts to investigate and give expression to the great themes of life that are often lost in the routinization of everyday affairs. The kind of ritual art about which Fromm speaks is vastly different from the individualistic art that marks most modern expressions. Modern societies are without collective art. Instead, we consume the art of others in an effort to give expression to our desire for some transcendence over the deadening grind of our mechanized existence. We "drink in," as Fromm says, the "movies, crime reports, the liquor, the fun."

Once again, productive man and generative man (as we will soon see) have in common this great regard for ritual. But a close examination shows that there is a significant difference. The ritual that Fromm seems to have in mind is the grand ritual, the total ritual that every great religious tradition and every grand community always develops. He speaks of Greek drama, medieval passion plays, the Indian dance, and Hindu, Jewish, and Christian religious rituals. What does he omit? And why is the omission so important?

Fromm omits the rituals of everyday life. He omits the organic patterns of mutual regulation, that kind of adaptive settledness which comes when individuals and communities have discovered, almost without knowing, a reciprocal pattern for relating to one another that is creative, fulfilling, and regulatory for all involved. *What Fromm misses is the continuity between the little, everyday rituals and the grand, collective rituals.*

This, then, is what gives his thought its lack of organicity. This is why we fear that all will be reduced to consciousness, planning, activeness, debate, discussion—a world of meettings, committees, memos, canned collective art, contrived collective experience. This is why productive man will strike us, in comparison to generative man, as so hyperpolitical. Can any man take all of that? Each man must take some of it. There is little doubt of that. And men in the future must be able to manage more of this kind of activity than in the past. But there must be a limit. Relationships cannot multiply endlessly. There must be a limit to one's active participation; certainly one cannot take responsible action in all these spheres of life.

Generative man, as we will see, is a creative ritualizer. He is willing and able to actively evolve the new, to take conscious responsibility in wide areas of life, to exercise decision as both a duty and a way to fulfillment. But he has the capacity to ritualize life at the level of both its grand and its small expressions. He has the gift to join with others in the creation of new patterns of mutual regulation, patterns that will doubtless find expression in grand community rituals but apply to life's most mundane and unspectacular activities as well. Generative man is content to permit some of life to have a certain quality of unconscious organicity. When old rituals break up and need revision, he will be able to confront this task; but when new rituals gain a certain workability to them, he will not resist their gaining a new sedimentation. For rituals are somewhat like the beds of rivers—they provide an avenue, a direction, and a secure limit through which life's energies and needs can flow.

Finally, what should be said about how productive man will meet the "other," the "stranger"? To answer this question, we must ask another. What does the flight into premature universality do to the other whom we confront? Fromm, as did Brown, can affirm all men as his brothers. Whereas Brown believes that all men have the same regressive wishes, Fromm believes that all men have the same progressive wishes. Or, more accurately stated, he believes that all the great expressions of the human spirit throughout all time amount to very much the same thing. So he can say, "The human reality . . . underlying the teachings of Buddha, Isaiah, Christ, Socrates, or Spinoza is essentially the same." [93] To Fromm they all advocate the same ideals, the same great values of love, reason, and truth. Is Fromm mistaken in this uncomplicated assertion? Probably not. It is probably true that one can abstract from the world's great spiritual expressions a quite similar basic ethical vision. But this does not really help us very much. For abstract ethical vision can mean very different things when placed in the context of the specific moralities of different cultures. Man in the context of the conflicts of pluralism, which will mark modernity in the future, must do more than affirm what all men have in common. *He must understand the differences that surround their commonness.* He must understand how universality is embodied in particular styles and he must comprehend how particular styles can give birth to that which is universal. We will see soon how generative man attends to both the universal and the particular in the stranger and that he does this because he first attends and takes with equal seriousness both the universal and the particular in himself. For generative man *cares* for both the very large and the very small, i.e., what is of universal meaning but also what is of meaning only to certain individuals, certain groups, and certain cultures.

6

ERIK ERIKSON

Generative Man and
the Household of God

There is no better way to open our chapter on Erikson than with a brief meditation on a quotation from his last book, *Gandhi's Truth*. It demonstrates with characteristic Eriksonian sensitivity the common ground between the generative man and the religious reformer.

> We have seen how deeply Gandhi at times minded having to become a householder, for without his becoming committed to a normal course of life by child marriage, he might well have been a monastic saint instead of what he became: politician and reformer with an honorary sainthood. For the true saints are those who transfer the state of householdership to the house of God, becoming father and mother, brother and sister, son and daughter, to all creation, rather than to their own issue.[1]

Gandhi was not a saint; nor was he a very good father. But he was a religious reformer, and one partially because what he had learned (and failed to learn) about generating and maintaining a household of his own was later projected at a much higher level onto what he generated and attempted to maintain not only for India but for the British Empire, and, finally, for humanity itself.

To generate and maintain a world, but in such a way as to include and yet transcend one's own issue, one's own family, tribe, nation, and race—this is the essence of the generative man, the essence of his ethics and of his religious meaning. Generativity, for Erikson, is a process that stretches from man's most archaic and unconscious biological tendencies to the highest cultural products of his imagination and his reason. "Generativity" is the only word that expresses what Erikson has in mind. "No other fashionable term, such as 'creativity' or 'productivity,' seems to me to convey the necessary idea." [2] Only the word "generativity" conveys that Erikson has in mind not only the results of man's "genitality and genes" but also the results of his "works and ideas," [3] as well as the continuity between the two.

Hence, Erikson, who is often faithful to the terminology and the history of psychoanalysis, has worked more of a revolution in this tradition than is generally recognized. Generativity, not just libidinal sexuality, is the true archaic foundation of man. Certainly for Erikson, man is a creature of desire; but desire, for him, is more than sexual release or sensual enjoyment. Desire is a complex coordination of a wide range of instinctive patterns which all aim toward self-expression and self-confirmation through generativity. Erikson speaks of a "wish" for generativity. In addition, he refers to generativity as the *"instinctual power* behind various forms of selfless 'caring.'" (Italics mine.) Implicit in this shift of emphasis is a new formulation of the relationship between self and society, between the public and the private. Man's innermost private satisfaction and the outermost public relevance are found in one and the same reality—the individual confirmation that rebounds to him from the recognition and affirmation of that which he has generated.

In Erikson, there is an intimate relationship between the archaic and the teleologic in his vision of man. In fact, both are rooted in generativity. Generativity sums up that in man which is most basic and most primitive. But it also points toward that which is the end and goal of existence. If all of man's instincts propel him toward biological generativity, man's capacity for imagination, reason, and conscience make it possible and necessary for him to elevate this generativity to higher cultural, ethical, and religious levels. Generativity is not only the instinctive source behind biological procreation and care; it is also the ground for man's higher attempts to create a total environment ecologically supportive of the general health—not only of family and tribe, but of the entire human species.[4]

Erikson's great general popularity as well as the high respect often paid to him in professional psychiatric and psychological circles can be credited to the conceptual and the professional continuity that he has maintained between himself and Freud.[5] In contrast to Fromm, Erikson has been in intimate contact with the true intellectual disciples of Freud—Heinz Hartmann, Anna Freud, David Rapaport, Ernst Kris, Robert White, and others. His theory is built squarely upon the advances of psychoanalytic ego psychology, to which he has made many contributions himself.

However, most readers, even those well equipped with psycho-analytic training, fail to grasp the subtle but all-important shift from sexuality to generativity in Erikson's thought. Erikson himself has only gradually become aware of the true implications of this shift. Most of the traditional psychoanalytic concepts have been redefined in his thought in the light of this new idea. The crucial theory of the Oedipal complex receives a radically new meaning when generativity rather than sexual economics is given the seat of central theoretical impor-tance. Erikson writes that the Oedipal complex, as the concept is generally employed, "is only the infantile and often only the neurotic core of an existential dilemma which (less mythologically) may be called the *generational complex,* for it derives from the fact that man experiences life and death—and past and future—as a matter of the turnover of generations." [6]

Erikson brings the regressive and the progressive, the low and the high (the archaic and the teleologic) in man, into a closer dialectical relationship than do any of the other psychoanalytic ethicists con-sidered in this study. Erikson knows that the low, when rightly under-stood, is the true foundation of the high. But he also knows that if man is to survive, he must indeed attain the high, but a high—that is, a maturity—which is humble and modest and in intimate contact and communication with man's archaic depths. Rieff, as we have shown, trusts neither the high nor the low. Brown, we have seen, trusts only the low. Fromm trusts both the high and the low but maintains a mis-leading distance between the two. Only Erikson maintains their dis-tinctiveness, and shows the continuity between them, while yet valu-ing and trusting both.

We approach Erikson not only as a psychologist, a scientist, and a therapist. We approach him also as an ethicist and a cultural synthe-sizer. Erikson's work as a therapist and as a student of human develop-ment is really the work of an *artist*. Therapist as artist, or better, sci-entist as artist—this is the way to understand Erikson's contributions. When Erikson is observing and classifying the stages and the conflicts of human development—psychosexual, psychosocial, ethical, religious —he is also working an artistic, cultural synthesis. He gives us not only the laws of human development but also a *new cultural ritual,* a Western counterpart to the Hindu "stages of life." The careful reader of Erikson soon senses the relaxed and playful character of his mind. Erikson knows that it is in this mood of *playfulness* that the ego's best *work,* its best job of synthesizing and redressing the ambiguities of life, occurs. Erikson's stages, his contributions to the psychology of identity and to the psychology of national character, and his pioneering work in the methodology of historical biography—in short, all that is scientific, scholarly, and rational in Erikson is at the same time a grand cultural synthesis (the product of a playful mind at work) which contains both ideological and universal elements within it.

Erikson, in spite of himself, is emerging as something of a cultural guru. Yet his stature as a man of our times (as well as a leading psychoanalytic theorist) has only recently begun to be assessed. Within the last few months (after most of the research for the present study was completed) several major articles in leading periodicals (especially *The New York Times Magazine* and *The New Yorker*) and one major book by Robert Coles on Erikson's life and thought have appeared.[7] Coles's book and an autobiographical piece by Erikson himself, which recently appeared in *Daedalus,* give us important information about Erikson's life that has been largely unknown until now. In a time when most people in the West have experienced a general sense of uprootedness due to rapid social change and the erosion of inherited tradition, Erikson experienced as a youth a particularly intense form of these commonly experienced dislocations. Born of Danish parentage, he was still an infant when his parents were divorced. His mother moved to Germany and later married a Jewish pediatrician named Homberger. Erikson tells us: "All through my earlier childhood they kept secret from me the fact that my mother had been married previously and that I was the son of a Dane who had abandoned her before my birth."[8] Erikson—the man who discovered modern man's great preoccupation with his identity—has had more than a little difficulty determining his own. It was precisely his destiny to migrate one day to the United States, where indeed the problem of identity seemed to be everybody's problem. For it was the case that "in this country's history, fate had chosen to highlight identity questions."[9] But if this is the problem of America and Americans, it is also true that "problems of identity become urgent wherever Americanization spreads."[10]

Erikson left home after completing his work at the German gymnasium (his only academic degree, aside from a Montessori diploma and his accreditation from the Vienna Psychoanalytic Institute) and assumed the identity of a wandering artist. His longtime friendship with Peter Blos (later to become a famous child psychiatrist) led him to a school for the children of wealthy Americans attending Freud's institute in Vienna. There he was gradually "adopted" by the Freudian circle. (Erikson tells us that he enjoyed "a kind of favored stepson identity that made me take for granted that I should be accepted where I did not quite belong.")[11]

After marrying Joan Serson, a Canadian dancer and teacher, and completing his psychoanalytic training, Erikson came to the United States and settled in Boston. It is not surprising that Erikson as an immigrant in a nation of immigrants began to concern himself with the problems of identity. "Identity problems," he writes, "were in the mental baggage of generations of new Americans, who left their motherlands and fatherlands behind to merge their ancestral identities in the common one of self-made men." [12]

Could it be that Erikson, as one who studied so artfully both his own identity crisis and that of his age, has also given us some indices of a new ideological synthesis which could give us a method and a vision for transforming and combining our passing identities into a more inclusive new world-image ("and, in fact, a New World image")? Is it possible that his vision of "generative man" and the world which he implies and attempts to shape might constitute (or at least suggest) an outline of such a synthesis?

If this is a possibility, then Erikson emerges as a distinctively religious figure for our times. Erikson himself described the essence of *homo religiosus* in his brilliant studies of Luther and Gandhi. *Homo religiosus* is the man whose personal and existential conflicts are representative of the central conflicts of an entire age. *Homo religiosus* (the "religious actualist") makes his own patienthood and cure into a universal drama which activates and gives meaning to the people of his day. Part of the cure is likely to be a playful new ideological synthesis which combines both old and new religious, political, humanitarian, and economic patterns with present states of knowledge. Hence, the religious man is a cultural worker who creates, out of the conflicts of his time, a new identity for his age. This is what Luther and Gandhi, in different ways, did for theirs. It is intriguing to speculate whether Erikson, in a less dramatic way, is doing something of the same for his age. For in his moral vision there unfolds a subtle but arresting synthesis of a grand variety of present-day cultural and social fragments— evolutionary theory, religion (the cross, the Nativity, ahimsa), psychoanalysis, ethology, ecology, and nonviolence—all brought together to suggest a new world-image which would give controlled direction to an emerging industrial and technological world community. In searching for his own identity, has Erikson pointed to possible styles of life and cultural sources for our own? Erikson himself, with his characteristic humility, would decline such a grandiose role. It is indeed premature to suggest such a thing; only history can really tell us the answer.

Erikson would acknowledge that there are ideological and historically relative aspects to his thought and observations. He would also insist that in and through the historically conditioned aspects within his thought there also comes to light a more universal perspective on human growth and ethics. This is why his thought is so relevant for our times; he offers us a way of transcending our historical and cultural shortsightedness without making the sad mistake of forgetting who we are and where we came from.

The relationship between the historically conditioned and the universal levels of Erikson's thinking (what he often calls the distinction between "ideology" and "ethics") is a cause of much confusion for many of his interpreters. Some have said that Erikson is the psychologist of Protestantism and charge him with giving a biased psychological defense of the so-called Protestant work ethic. Others accuse Erikson of being the psychologist of the middle class, rationalizing and sanctioning middle-class preoccupations with vocation, intimacy, and parenthood. Still others have said that his concern with identity makes him the great modern-day psychologist of conformity. Is not identity, they ask, inner psychological stability through conformity with the larger group mind?

As a student of human development, Erikson knows that all men must go through a stage of ideological consolidation before they can transcend it to a more universal, ethical level. As an ethicist and a cultural synthesizer, he knows that a universal identity must both emerge from and affirm partial identities which consist of particular ways of living, working, and loving. Erikson's interpretation of the American situation and the American character culminates in an intriguing portrait of the cultural dichotomy facing the Western world. The dichotomy exists between those youth who derive their identity "from the whole ideological pack of technological expansion" and those youth whom Erikson calls the "new-humanist youth" who constitute an "intense new group of universalists." [13] The technologists are those who appear to "know what they are doing" and the universalists are those who seem to "mean what they are saying." Of course, both the technologists and the new-humanists have their respective hidden ideologies, although the new-humanists are more self-conscious in their efforts to attain a universal-ethical level. Erikson knows that these polar character types need to be defined with clarity and that their distinctiveness must not be allowed to be blurred. But it is also true that the thrust of Erikson's work is to set forth still another character type which would be a synthesis of the two: a man who would be at once a technologist and a universalist, accomplished in the dominant disciplines of our culture and yet ethically sensitive to their humanistic control and employment. Such is the nature of generative man as he will gradually unfold on these pages. As critical as Erikson is of the modern technocratic society, he sees generative man as ideological enough to be reasonably skilled in the historically dominant technics of our culture just as he will be universal enough to ruthlessly control, guide, and limit them for the true good of man.

Psychoanalysis and the Ethics of Human Ecology

Erikson is close to Fromm in his belief that psychoanalysis is a positive ethical science. He also shares Fromm's vision of having some-day a psychoanalysis that is sociologically sophisticated and a sociology that is psychoanalytically mature. In other words, Erikson calls for a superdiscipline which would synthesize psychoanalytic, sociological, and cultural perspectives. Toward this end, both Fromm and Erikson have made important contributions. But Erikson goes farther than Fromm in that he sees ecology and ethology as the new disciplines from which psychoanalysis has the most to learn. In fact, Erikson's psychology can best be characterized as a descriptive and a normative ecology and ethology of the human animal's average expectable social and psychological environment. Erikson's primary question is this: What kind of psychological, social, and cultural environment makes man strong?

Most of Erikson's observations and theories are grounded in his experience as a therapist. This is also true of his most fundamental insights into the nature of ethics for human life. For Erikson, the most important ethical implication of psychoanalytic psychotherapy centers on its unique study of "human childhood" as the "most fundamental basis for human exploitation." [14] Erikson writes: "The polarity Big—Small is the first in the inventory of existential oppositions such as Male and Female, Ruler and Ruled, Owner and Owned, Light Skin and Dark." [15] When Freud began to listen to his patients' free associations, several things happened. First, he began to give up the privileged role of the physician as "all-knowing father." This meant that psychotherapy could progress only by "engaging the fully motivated partnership of the observed individual." [16] Later, Freud's awareness of his transference with Fliess and his awareness of the habitual cycles of transference and countertransference, which invariably occur in therapy, led Freud to another principle of psychoanalysis: "You will not see in another what you have not learned to recognize in yourself." [17] Erikson probably goes beyond anything Freud had in mind when he summarizes the implications of these two discoveries with the following words:

> That shift in self-awareness, however, cannot remain confined to professional partnerships such as the observer's with the observed, or the doctor's with his patient. It implies a fundamentally new *ethical orientation of adult man's relationship to childhood:* to his own childhood, now behind and within him; to his own child before him; and to every man's children around him.[18]

In order for the therapist to relate to the adult and the child in his patient, he must learn to hear and understand the adult and the child in himself. This discovery, for Erikson, was more than an insight into the technique of the psychotherapeutic relationship. It opened, in effect, an entirely new region upon which to center ethical reflection.

The therapist, Erikson believes, is more than a neutral observer. And psychoanalysis has more to contribute to ethics than what Freud and later Heinz Hartmann suggested when they restricted the ethics of psychoanalysis to "the ethics of scientific truth only" and to "studying ethics (or morality) in a scientific way." [19] The therapist must practice a "judicious partnership" which avoids "apathetic tolerance or autocratic guidance." [20] The therapist has his commitments "to a highest good, the preservation of life and the furtherance of well-being —the 'maintenance of life.'" [21] The ethics of the psychoanalyst, both professional and therapeutic, both personal and private, must be an ethical commitment to the maintenance and the regeneration of the cycle of the generations. The question is, then, that when Erikson claims so much, does he really say anything ethically meaningful at all?

The broader significance of Erikson's ethic can be assessed if we place it side by side with other ethical positions commanding respect in present-day discussions, especially the ethics of "regard" or "recognition" found respectively in the work of Jean-Paul Sartre and Martin Buber. Erikson's psychoethical perspective in addition to being an ethic of the generational cycle is also an ethic of "recognition" or "regard," i.e., a psychology and ethic of the "face." Erikson combines his evolutionary and adaptive perspective on ethics with an existential ethic of recognition. It can be argued that the two perspectives are not in contradiction but are mutually supportive and corrective. Erikson helps us undertand the existential meaning of the adaptive and evolutionary perspective; and he also helps us to understand the adaptive significance of the existential struggle for recognition.

But Erikson's ethic of recognition is strikingly different from the Sartrean ethic of "regard" or "the look." For Sartre, human recognition or regard is always a "look," an objectifying stare which robs the other of his center of subjectivity.[22] Erikson, a clinically sophisticated psychoanalyst, would most likely classify the Sartrean regard as a pathological distortion of a deeper and more fundamentally human kind of recognition. This more fundamental kind of recognition Erikson calls "mutual recognition"; it is "mutual" because it "activates" very basic levels of human subjectivity in both parties to the encounter.

Erikson's psychology and ethic of recognition are clearly much closer to Martin Buber's famous philosophy of the "I-Thou" relationship.[23] But even here, Erikson's psychology of recognition is vastly more complex. For Erikson, the I-Thou relationship (the act of mutual recognition) is not simply a duality as it is for Buber. It is at least a quadrivium. It is not just adult meeting adult; it is the adult and the child of one person meeting the adult and the child in the other. Mutual recognition not only involves an affirmation of the adult and the child in the other; it also involves an affirmation of the adult and the child in oneself. Erikson places the I-Thou relationship (mutual recognition) within the context of everyman's internalization of the cycle of the generations in which he stands. Erikson would see the I-Thou relationship as occurring when two people with different histories, divided functions, varying gifts, and unequal powers come together and, in spite of their separateness, mutually activate and mutually affirm both the child and the adult in each other. The primordial examples are the mother-child and the husband-wife relationships. Such relationships constitute both the subject matter and the paradigms for ethical reflection. It is these relationships which have most to do with the validation and the preservation of individuals in the context of the cycle of the generations. These relationships are the most ethical of relationships, not because they are always the most pure, but because they have the most to do with the creation and the maintenance of human "strength."

Erikson's ethical psychology of recognition takes account of clinical and ethological data on the nature of recognition, the smiling response, and the importance of the face in the drama of human adaptation.[24] In one place Erikson writes:

> I would call mutuality a relationship in which partners depend on each other for the development of their respective strengths. A baby's first responses can be seen as part of an actuality consisting of many details of

mutual arousal and response. While the baby initially smiles at a mere configuration resembling the human face, the adult cannot help smiling back, filled with expectations of a "recognition" which he needs to secure from the new being as surely as it needs him.[25]

In *Young Man Luther*, Erikson applies this psychology of the face to a religious psychology of Luther's search for a confirming face, not only from his earthly father but from his heavenly Father as well. Implicit in this psychology of the confirming face is a truth well recognized in contemporary ethology and in behavioral physiology. The need for a confirming face may have its phylogenetic origin in man's secondary need for a sign of security from the person who ministers to his basic physiological needs. But secondary structures, through the course of evolution, have a way of gaining their own autonomy, their own energy, and their own independent needs for activation. As Konrad Lorenz has pointed out, certain behavioral potentials may be phylogenetically associated with more fundamental drives which they indeed stand ready to serve. However, their activation does not always depend upon the energy from the more basic drive. Just as "dogs go through the motions of smelling, seeking, chasing, biting, . . . whether they are hungry or not," [26] so may man have an independent need for a confirming face—a need not always related to his drive to fill his stomach. Man is the animal who, both as infant and as adult, has an instinctual need for mutual recognition, not simply to satisfy his hunger, but also to satisfy his humanity. Erikson's psychology of recognition grounds the I-Thou relationship in the very phylogenetic and ontogenetic archaeology of the ego.

Erikson's psychology of recognition may be at the very apex of his ethics of the generational cycle, but it is actually only one part of a larger vision. It helps bring into focus certain details of a larger picture which psychologists, ethologists, and ecologists are just now beginning to discern. Erikson assumes that man is no different from the animals in that he is born with a wide range of behavioral potentials "preadapted" to what Heinz Hartmann has called an "average expectable environment." [27] The mutual smiling response between mother and child is just one example of a grand congress of other such preadapted responses. Ethics, for Erikson, must concern itself with what is necessary for the maintenance and the enhancement of this average expectable environment in the midst of changing conditions and different historical actualities.

Erikson, like Norman Brown, believes he can learn much that is good for man by meditating upon the behavior of animals. But Erikson's mythology of animal existence is vastly different from Brown's. Brown sees in the animal an uninhibited expenditure of playful energies as it moves acceptingly toward death. Erikson, on the other hand, sees in the animal a prudent avoidance of premature death and an unconscious commitment to the preservation and continuity of its species. While Brown, in his mythology, sees a union of the life and death instincts, Erikson believes that a less anthropomorphic view of the animal reveals what he calls its *"ecological integrity;* a combination of mutual regulation and reciprocal avoidance which safeguards adaptation within the characteristic environment and with other species sharing it." [28] By ecological integrity, Erikson means to point to an "actuality" which "at all stages rests on the complement of inner and outer structure." [29] Erikson's ethics of human ecology is indeed built upon a reappropriation of the animal and the natural in man. (He wants to "nurture nature, as well as to master it.") But Erikson's naturalism is not a romanticism; nor does it overlook the thing in man which is unique to his species—his capacity for reason, imagination, and historicity. But it does, however, hold an insight shared alike by all students of human nature influenced by the psychoanalytic tradition. The problem of man does not involve so much the animal in the man as it does the man in the animal. Erikson trusts the animal in man more than does Rieff or Fromm and he trusts it in a different way than does Brown. The solution to the human predicament is for Erikson, as it was for Fromm, indeed a progressive one. The way out is up. But this means for Erikson that the way out of the human dilemma is for man to integrate his animal nature (his own deeper propensity for ecological integrity) into his higher nature (his capacity for reason, reflection, and historical actuality). This means that ethics must determine the meaning of "ecological integrity" for institutions and for culture as well as for interpersonal relationships and the physical environment.

The Ego:
Its Epigenesis, Virtues, and Necessary Rituals

Erikson believes that the ego, in contrast to the superego and the id, is the human counterpart of those regulatory capacities of animals which assure their ecological integrity. It is the ego which is the real servant of evolution, adaptation, and the cycle of the generations. The superego is the servant of the tribe; it serves neither the good of the wider species nor the good of the individual. The superego, then, is the seat of "morality"—that codified, inherited, and provincial good which serves only the continuity of the family, the tribe, or the nation.[30] The ego, on the other hand, is the seat of "ethics" and can, when it is mature and healthy, seek not only its own most enduring good but also the wider good of the human species as a whole.[31] Therefore, an ethical science of human ecology must be grounded in a study of the structures and functions of the ego—its *epigenesis,* its *virtues,* its *necessary rituals,* and its *self-interpretation,* i.e., its *identity.*

In the work of Erikson we discover a restoration of the fullness of the human ego. Moreover, in contrast to Fromm, Erikson's work on the nature of the human ego and on the so-called higher processes in man tends to be far more convincing, especially to the psychoanalytically trained audience. This is because Erikson's psychology has grown step by step with the most significant advances in psychoanalytic ego psychology. However, whereas Freud expanded the id to almost completely crowd out the ego, Erikson reverses this and expands the ego until one might wonder what legitimate room is left for the id.

The ego, for Erikson, refers to the totality of man's primary equipment which regulates and guides his relationship with the wider physical and social environment. Most of the ego is unconscious, but at the very top of its hierarchy of functions is that center of consciousness which Erikson calls the "I." [32] The "I," which is the very seat of our personhood and the center of our capacity to consciously direct our will and our actions, must be distinguished from the larger ego which is the center of Erikson's interest. The ego is that silent inner agency which seeks a sense of *wholeness,* an *active mastery* over the vicissitudes of outer experience and inner impulses, and an abiding sense of inner *centeredness.* The mastery which the ego seeks is, as Erikson sees it, very similar to what Robert White has called the need for "effectance" and "competence." [33] But mastery and competence have more organic, ecological meanings for Erikson than they do for White. Not so much the wish to be a "cause" (White) but the desire to regulate and be regulated by a supporting and activating environment—this is the meaning of mastery and competence for Erikson. Nor is the mastery and competence about which Erikson speaks the mastery of technological domination or the controlling maneuvers attributed to the classic Western prototype of the self-made man. Readers of Erikson who associate his understanding of the functions of the ego with these cultural distortions are fighting ideological word battles. The mastery which the ego seeks is an ecological coordination and regulation between inner structures and outer realities.

The ego can best be understood as an active agency of synthesis.

It forever seeks to coordinate the various fragments of one's experience into a meaningful *whole*. In contrast to Rieff, who believes that man has no fundamental need to discern his place amid the whole of things, Erikson believes that this is the quite spontaneous, central function of the silent workings of the ego. In his dreams, his play, his poetry, and his rituals, man is always trying to weave together—through analogies, subtle omissions, and selective observations—a meaningful and manageable whole out of the frightening welter of life's experiences. Only when experience becomes too unpredictable, too threatening, or too mysterious does the ego convert its quest for wholeness into an overdetermined drive for totalistic control, domination, and tightfisted mastery.[34]

In the process of synthesizing experience, the ego is always converting inner and outer influences into experiences either actively chosen, actively accepted, or actively rejected. The ego seems to have the inner need to turn the passivities of life into experiences which, if not actively chosen, are at least actively affirmed. As we will see later, the ego actually gains its most fundamental sense of activeness when it accepts and affirms those most primordial passivities which undergird the beginning of every human life and which continue to touch it throughout its pilgrimage.[35] For Erikson, genuine passivity is in reality a very basic kind of activeness. Therefore, in contrast to Fromm, who is forever contrasting the evils of passiveness with the virtues of activeness, Erikson places the dichotomy between *activeness* (along with its passive forms) and various forms of debilitating and maladaptive *inactivation*.[36]

To say that the ego is the seat of ethics becomes more convincing when we are reminded that the ego has an epigenesis—a developmental history—and that its capacity for ethics is an emergent phenomenon. The truly ethical stage of development does not begin to be visible until adolescence and does not mature until the stages of "generativity" and "wisdom" which occur during the middle and later stages of adulthood. But all the preceding stages are important for later ethical capacities. The capacity for higher generativity (which is of the very essence of ethical living) has its foundations in the very beginning of life.

In his introduction to *Identity and the Life Cycle*, David Rapaport points out that Erikson has complemented Freud's theory of psychosexual development with a theory of ego epigenesis.[37] The theory of epigenesis, which Erikson borrows from biology, when applied to ego development simply means that the various aspects of the ego grow from "a *ground plan*, and that out of this ground plan the *parts* arise, each part having its *time* of special ascendancy, until all parts have arisen to form a *functioning whole*." [38] To illustrate the principle of epigenesis, Erikson discusses various preadapted modes of bodily response which center around certain bodily zones, or schemas. For instance, there are the various modes of receptive and aggressive *incorporation* which center around oral-sensory-respiratory zones. During the second year, the modes of *retention* and *elimination*, which center around the anal-urethral-musculature systems, gain prominence. Finally, during the so-called Oedipal age, the modes of *intrusion* (for boys) and *inclusion* (for girls), centering around phallic-locomotor systems, become of crucial importance. The bodily modes are the basis of certain psychosocial "modalities" which constitute a basic fund of preadapted ego patterns for relating to significant persons in the social environment. Erikson traces the modalities through all the stages of life, but for the purpose of illustration, we mention only the earlier ones: "to receive" and "to get" (related to incorporative modes), "to hold" and "to let go" (related to the retentive-eliminative modes), and "to make" and "to be on the make" (related to the intrusive-inclusive modes).[39] These modalities, built as they are around specific modes of the body, constitute the basic patterns of action for the ego.

This part of Erikson's thought is well known and quite popular. Therefore there is no need to labor the details here. However, at least one observation should be made. It is clear that from the beginning, Erikson's theory of ego epigenesis was built on an implicit revision of the traditional Freudian theory of psychic energies. This revision became clearer as Erikson's career progressed. *Instinctive structures* and patterns, rather than specifically *libidinal energies,* have always occupied the prominent position in Erikson's theory of motivation. In one place he refers to that which is instinctive in man as "pre-formed action patterns which under certain conditions can call on some ready drive energy for instantaneous, vigorous, and skillful release." This, of course, is very similar to the relationship between energy and structure which we met in the work of Robert White. It seems that Erikson posits a general psychic energy (instinctual force) which can be put to use by a variety of preformed and relatively autonomous instinctive patterns. But finally, for Erikson, it is the "configuration" of the action pattern, rather than the source of its energy, that is important for understanding behavior.[40] Therefore, when Erikson speaks of modes and modalities rooted in the oral-sensory-respiratory, the anal-urethral, musculature, or phallic-locomotor "zones," he does not mean to use "zone" in the specifically erogenous sense of traditional Freudian psychology. These zones, as Peter Wolff has pointed out, are really systems of the body which share certain common "schemas," or patterns of bodily action.[41] It might be better to speak of certain erogenous modes (oral-anal-phallic) and certain nonerogenous modes (sensory-musculature-motor) which share *common* and *analogous* action potentials.

Since modes and modalities (rather than instinctual energies as such) are what is emphasized in Erikson, it is fair to say that from the beginning Erikson saw man in the same way as do many existential phenomenologists such as the later Husserl, Heidegger, Sartre, Merleau-Ponty, and Binswanger. All these thinkers study man from the perspective of his "being-in-the-world." A mode or a modality of action is really a pattern or style of being-in-the-world.[42] Erikson's contribution is that of demonstrating a developmental order to man's being-in-the-world as well as suggesting how the basic patterns of the ego's hierarchy of states and action possibilities make up the ground plan.

It is also clear that although Erikson makes only a passing acknowledgment of the affinity of his thought with that of Robert White, he all but explicitly buys the latter's concept of independent ego energies. For example, a body mode such as intrusion may be characteristic of both erogenous (phallic) and nonerogenous (motor system) parts of the body. The ego, for Erikson, is very much a body ego. But to say this is not to say that the source of its energy is libidinal in all respects.

The action patterns—the modes and modalities—are all present in the ground plan from the beginning, yet they have their special time of ascendancy. But they are also dependent upon a favorable average expectable environment for their activation and support. Those aspects of a person's environmental, interpersonal, and institutional relations which are most relevant to the activation and support of these pre-formed potentialities constitute "reality" for that person. But Erikson chooses to refer to "reality" in this sense of the word (as distinguished from phenomenal reality or the "reality principle" of Freud and Heinz Hartmann) with the word "actuality." Actuality for a person is that part of his total relationship with his social and institutional matrix which "actuates" him as he activates it. Erikson says it well when he writes:

> *Mutual activation* is the crux of the matter; for human ego strength, while employing all means of testing reality, depends from stage to stage upon a network of mutual influences within which the person actuates others even as he is actuated, and within which the person is "inspired with active properties," even as he so inspires others. This is *ego actuality;*

largely preconscious and unconscious, it must be studied in the individual by psychoanalytic means. Yet actualities are shared, as are realities. Members of the same age group share analogous combinations of capacities and opportunities, and members of different age groups depend on each other for the mutual activation of their complementary ego strengths. Here, then, studies of "outer" conditions and of "inner" states meet in one focus. One can speak of actualities as co-determined by an individual's *stage of development,* by his *personal circumstances,* and by *historical and political processes*—and I will, in fact, speak of all of these.[43]

And indeed Erikson does. In his historical biographies, his case studies, his social analysis, he is using psychoanalytic means to discern in man's personal circumstances and political and historical processes that coincidence of inner and outer conditions which makes for his strength and his inner sense of reality. The capacity to be faithful to these conditions oneself and the ability to provide them for others constitutes the essence of the generative personality.

The concept of actuality is a clarifying perspective from which to view Erikson's important discussion of the meaning of "virtue" in human life. It is the integrity of the actuality and mutual activation in the sequence of the generations which determines the quality of each man's inner strength and his virtue. Virtue is the very end of ethical action—to create virtue in others and to enhance virtue in oneself. Human society, its institutions, its technology, and its world view should all be aimed toward this end. Erikson's list of virtues serves as an index of moral action on the part of people and institutions. The good man (and the good institution) is the man whose action creates strength (virtue) in others while at the same time creating strength (virtue) in himself.

Erikson uses the word "virtue" to refer to that "active" and "spirited" quality which is the very essence of what psychologists often call "ego strength." [44] A virtue is always a matter of synthesis. It refers to the ego's capacity to gain a favorable synthesis out of the positive and negative dimensions of life's developmental crises and nuclear conflicts. Recall, for a moment, Erikson's famous list of developmental crises: the childhood crises of *trust* versus *mistrust, autonomy* versus *shame and doubt, initiative* versus *guilt;* the latency and adolescent crises of *industry* versus *inferiority,* and *identity* versus *identity confusion;* and finally the adult crises of *intimacy* versus *isolation, generativity* versus *self-absorption,* and *integrity* versus *despair.* Virtue is that active capacity for synthesis which enables one to take due account of the negative aspects of each of these nuclear conflicts while still tilting the crisis in favor of the positive. The active syntheses, when successful, leave certain deposits for the future which constitute adaptive strengths not only for the individual but for the larger evolutionary cycle of which he is a part. Although our focus of concern in this study is the adult virtues of *love, care,* and *wisdom,* we will have occasion to note later how these so-called adult virtues build upon, respond to, and in turn help to develop in the young those virtues of childhood (*hope, will, purpose, competence*) and youth (*fidelity, love*) which precede them.

Erikson's understanding of the meaning of virtue brings important new perspectives to the field of ethical reflection. Fromm can say that the good is that which fulfills man and that the bad is that which frustrates this fulfillment. Erikson brings a slightly different tone to his definition of good and evil, but the meaning is very much the same. For Erikson, the good is that which makes man "strong" both in his individual ontogenetic development and in the phylogenetic evolution of the larger cycle of the generations. The opposite of goodness as strength is not so much evil as it is "weakness." Evil is that which renders man ontogenetically and phylogenetically weak.

The concept of virtue, however, is not simply an overextension of a biological principle, thereby committing the "naturalistic fallacy" of reducing man to the impersonal laws of evolution. Every virtue involves a synthesis of psychosexual, psychosocial, and cognitive stages of development, as these epigenetic elements not only shape but are shaped by external, familial, institutional, cultural, and historical factors.[45] Man's epigenetic potentials shape and form this external, institutional, cultural, and historical environment just as much as these external factors shape, support, or frustrate (as the case may be) these epigenetic potentials. In fact, Erikson gives us a "dialectical" relationship between internal and external, child and adult, nature and culture.

Therefore, the picture of evolution presented by Erikson is vastly different from that preferred by either the Darwinian or the Freudian view, especially in their degenerate popular versions. Erikson's use of the word "strength" should not conjure up images of a "tooth and claw" struggle for survival or of an Oedipal battle between father and son over scarce pleasures. Human evolution, for Erikson, is the history of the emergence of man's epigenetic biological potential as it shapes and is influenced by society, culture, and history. It has always the goal of finding ever-better patterns (or rituals) of mutual activation and regulation. These patterns, or rituals, are the essence of culture. Culture is not simply a system of *prohibitions* and *permissions,* as Philip Rieff would have us believe. It is instead a complicated *pattern of mutual activation and regulation.*[46] Erikson's formula tells us much more. The Rieffian definition, as did the Freudian upon which it is so faithfully built, ends with the vision of each man's boundless desires pitted against those of all his neighbors and of society as a whole. The Eriksonian vision, which is more ecologically and ethologically valid, sees self and society more as a system of complementary needs which are mutually activated and mutually regulatory of each other. Society's prohibitions and penalties are its protection against man's miscalculated inventiveness and his inevitable impatience. But by themselves, prohibitions never constitute the true essence of even the most oppressive civilization.

Care and the Anthropology of Generative Man

The first thing to be said about generativity is this: generativity is a work, a product of a delicate synthesis. Erikson can speak about the instinctive patterns behind the various developmental tasks and the various virtues that may accrue from their successful resolution. But the successful resolution of a developmental conflict and the achievement of virtue is never simply a matter of instinctual unfolding; rather, it is always the result of an act, a synthesis, a work. Erikson would probably not object to the use of Frommian language if we were to assert flatly: generativity is an "art."

Generativity is an artistic achievement—a synthesis—which depends upon the successful achievement of several earlier although no less complicated syntheses. When a man and a woman have more or less achieved a successful resolution to the nuclear conflicts of childhood and youth and have established a workable identity and learned to share this identity with each other in the context of a genital relation, then, Erikson tells us, these mates will "soon *wish* . . . to combine their personalities and energies in the production and care of common offspring." [47] In later revisions of the article from which this quotation was taken, Erikson deletes this sentence, probably to guard against an overly concrete association of generativity with biological parenthood. In his later thought, Erikson is satisfied to say, "Generativity, then, is primarily the concern in establishing and guiding the next generation." [48] Then Erikson hastens to add that certainly there "are individuals who, through misfortune or because of special and genuine gifts in other directions, do not apply this drive to their own off-spring." [49]

But even though generativity is very much a work and a synthesis and does not even necessarily refer to the biological act of procreation, Erikson reminds us that it does indeed have its evolutionary and instinctive foundations. In one place he writes: "Evolution has made man a teaching as well as a learning animal, for dependency and maturity are reciprocal: mature man *needs to be needed,* and maturity is guided by the nature of that which must be cared for." [50] Something very fundamental happens to man when his needs for generativity are not met, something quite central to the direction of his energies and to his relationship to himself. Individuals who fail to achieve this delicate synthesis which generativity demands often become "stagnated" and "begin to indulge themselves as if they were their own—or one another's—one and only child; and where conditions favor it, early invalidism, physical or psychological, becomes the vehicle of self-concern." [51] The reasons why some people cannot achieve true generativity are varied and "are often to be found in early childhood impressions; in faulty identifications with parents; in excessive self-love based on a too strenuously self-made personality; and . . . in the lack of some faith, some 'belief in the species.' " [52] Whatever the reasons, an inadequate capacity for generativity not only brings subtle diminishment to those who suffer from it, but it passes itself on to succeeding generations. The sins of the fathers are indeed visited upon their children and upon their children's children.

The virtue that emerges when generativity is dominant over stagnation is "care." "Care is the widening concern for what has been generated by love, necessity, or accident; it overcomes the ambivalence adhering to irreversible obligation." If such definitions make Erikson sound like an idealistic moralist, a closer reading will demonstrate that it is *ethology* rather than either philosophical or religious traditions which guides his vision. He writes:

> *Care* is a quality essential for psychosocial evolution, for we are the teaching species. Animals, too, instinctively encourage in their young what is ready for release. . . . Only man, however, can and must extend his solicitude over the long, parallel and overlapping childhoods of numerous offspring united in households and communities. As he transmits the rudiments of hope, will, purpose and competence, he imparts meaning to the child's bodily experiences, he conveys a logic much beyond the literal meaning of the words he teaches, and he gradually outlines a particular world image and style of fellowship. All of this is

necessary to complete in man the analogy to the basic, ethological situation between parent animal and young animal. All this, and no less,
makes us comparable to the ethologist's goose and gosling. Once we have
grasped this interlocking of the human life stages, we understand that
adult man is so constituted as to *need to be needed*.[53]

Therefore, Erikson can say such things as "man *needs* to teach" and that
he has a "teaching passion." But this generative, teaching, caring passion must, to some extent for all and to a considerable extent for the
most sensitive and talented among us, extend to whatever "man
generates and leaves behind, creates and produces (or helps to produce)."[54] In addition to that, the generative man must learn how to
"restrain his capacity for unlimited propagation, invention and expansion" to at least that for which he can be responsible in a way which
surpasses his most reckless recent history. *For it is irresponsible
creativity devoid of a quality of enduring care that is man's grandest
temptation and greatest fault*, not only throughout all of his history but
most specifically during modern times. The real problem with man's
Promethean will (the high in man) is not that he aspires to do too
much, but aspires to do more than he is able or willing to care for.

This is the essence of Erikson's startling interpretation of modernity.
The problem of modern man is his *nongenerative mentality*—his inability to care for what he creates, what he generates. We see it in the
way he treats his children, builds his buildings, conducts his science,
experiments with his technology, and ravishes his environment. It is
not that modern man's creativity—as seen in his science, technology,
industry, and urban mobility—is itself a product of repression, as
Norman Brown insists. The capacities for such enterprises are given in
man's basic potentials; they are a natural expression of both his never-
ending desire for mastery (which for Erikson means mutual activation
and regulation) and the sheer enjoyment (function pleasure) that
comes from the exercise of all of man's functions, even his higher
capacities for creativity. But for modern man, his generativity has
degenerated into mere creativeness, experimentation, and inventiveness; it has become torn apart from that deeper capacity for care which
completes and limits the truly generative impulse. Modern man appears
to be generative because he creates so much; in reality his problem is
his nongenerative mentality which is seen in the fact that he cares so
poorly for that which he creates. Buildings which are made to last no
more than thirty years; the acres of urban rubble which witness to his
unsteady creativity and impatient destructiveness; his reckless tendency
to produce more children than he can either educate or provide for;

his unwitting habit of building cities that are uninhabitable for families and children; his penchant for pursuing careers at breakneck speed without regard to their effect upon his offspring; his knack for constructing societies so specialized and differentiated as virtually to segregate all children and young people from adult life; and finally, his heartless capacity to conduct wars that call for no sacrifice to himself but that end in the sacrifice of his sons and daughters—all these things and many more testify to the nongenerative character of the modern mind and its strange proclivity for creating more than it can either care for or maintain. Perhaps Norman Brown is partially correct. Maybe all of this unrestrained expansionism and creativity is a result of modern man's fear of death. I doubt if Erikson would object to this as a possible explanation. But it is one thing to say that modern man is fleeing death, and quite another thing to say that thought itself, science itself, philosophy itself, and rationality itself are in their entirety a result of repression and the fear of death. In the modern situation we are witnessing a distortion of activities and potentials that are in themselves human and natural. But this distortion is in itself enough to corrupt the integrity of the evolutionary pilgrimage, the cycle of the generations, the strength of the young, and the very life of us all.

But from where does this nongenerative mentality which has grasped American life come? The answer is complex, and to force a systematic answer from Erikson would certainly be unfair. Erikson is a clinician and not a systematic social and cultural analyst. Yet in and through his case studies and psychohistorical biographies, Erikson gives us a rich discussion of the sources of modern man's proclivity for generating more than he either wants or is able to care for. A close reading of Erikson's thought suggests that our profligacy comes from the unfortunate coalescence of streams which flowed into the major currents of American life: (1) the Protestant ethic, (2) the uniquely American experience of an inexhaustible and ever-expanding frontier, and (3) the highly differentiated character of advanced industrial societies. All these factors mean that modern Americans travel too fast to take the time to care for or know that which they generate. It is only when one keeps in mind all these trends in American life that one can comprehend how Americans learned to take their place on a veritable roller coaster of history, believing all the time that they were doing their God-ordained duty just by managing to keep up with the breakneck speed. In the following section we will look at these three trends, starting with the last first.

Identity and Modernity

Before we can understand the effect of highly differentiated, rapidly changing advanced technological societies on people, we must add a word or two about the concepts of "identity" and "ideology."

Certainly the concept of identity has been at the heart of Erikson's interest during the three decades that span the peak of his professional career. Yet no concept of Erikson's and possibly no other concept in the recent history of psychology has suffered from as much misinterpretation. It has fallen prey to both conservative and radical ideologies, but certainly the conservative ideologies are more obvious and more widely prevalent. In the name of the need for identity, evangelists for a variety of causes, both religious and political, go forth to reindoctrinate the young in the wooden truths of another age, often with a copy of Erikson under their arm. But man's need for a viable identity means something more than a simple and all-too-exploitable need to have "something to hold on to."

The process of identity formation and the functions that identity serves are a part of the larger process of maintaining and regenerating the cycle of the generations. Ideally, then, identity (as is the rest of the generational sequence) is a product of mutual activation and mutual regulation. This means that identity is never something simply given by the old to the young, by history to the generations "to come," or by established institutions to those who need socialization to "our way of life." This is what is meant when Erikson defines identity as the "accrued confidence that one's ability to maintain inner sameness and continuity . . . is *matched* by the sameness and continuity of one's meaning for others." [55] This means that identity must somehow be a *match* between a child's individual (and albeit somewhat idiosyncratic) ways of maintaining continuity and sameness and those outer definitions suggested by the perceptions and recognitions of his community. Erikson states it differently when he writes in another place: "The growing child must derive a vitalizing sense of reality from the awareness that his individual way of mastering experience (his ego synthesis) is a *successful variant* of a group identity and is *in accord* with its space-time and life plan." [56] For individual identity to be "a successful variant" and yet "in accord" with the identity of the larger group of which it is a part it need not reproduce with slavish detail the exact content of that larger identity. But the objective pole of individual identity does indeed compose itself out of the material of the wider group identity, although invariably giving it a certain unique organization. And in the case of men of genius, such as Martin Luther, Freud, or Gandhi, their unique synthesis of the larger group identity may be nothing short of revolutionary. Therefore, for Erikson, as it was for Rieff, culture seems to be very much the product of the unique syntheses of old identities which men of genius perform for an age and out of which succeeding generations live (although never simply reproduce) sometimes for centuries. Erikson's concept of identity is very similar to Fromm's idea of the need for a frame of orientation and devotion. The primary difference is that Erikson, because of his more detailed interest in the restorative, regulating, and synthesizing capacities of the individual ego, can explain with more concreteness the various ways men go about reshaping as well as internalizing the specifics of their larger group identities.

All people, but most especially young people, need an ideology that will support and give content to their identity. An ideology "at the least . . . is a 'way of life,' or what the Germans call a *Weltanschauung*, a world-view which is consonant with existing theory, available knowledge, and common sense, and yet is significantly more: an utopian outlook, a cosmic mood, or a doctrinal logic, all shared as self-evident beyond any need for demonstration." [57] *Ideology*, for Erikson, stands somewhere between *morality* and *ethics*. Morality is the blind acceptance of tribal tradition and values. Ethics is a more universal perspective which transcends tribal loyalties in its efforts to determine the good. The emergence in adolescence of a "historical perspective" leads many young people to experience the pluralism of modern societies as threatening and confusing.[58] This leads many young people to search for an ideology which will rise above yet include old moralities within an expanded yet firmly delineated world vision. An ideology must always synthesize the "past" with an anticipated future; it must "include but transcend the past, even as identity does."

Ideology, as Erikson uses it, is the transference to the level of historical existence of that general ecologically grounded need for what Heinz Hartmann called "an average expectable environment." At the level of ideology, it means that man has a need to know and to trust history. Man, and especially the adolescent, has a need for what Erikson calls "fidelity" in historical actuality. He has the need to know and to synthesize into manageable symbols and condensed prototypes what is trustworthy and untrustworthy, good and bad, about his past, and about the present state of affairs, and what their influence is on the probable future which stretches before him.

Hence, ideology contains within it an incipient ethical view. Its quest for the trustworthy and the faithful leads it to search for the truly universal in its own partial history. But because of the fragileness of their identity and their ideological synthesis, many adolescents need closure and certainty more than universality. Therefore, the emergence of the truly ethical and universal perspective must often wait until adulthood and the age of generativity, although it may not come even then. But even here, man's need for wholeness persists. This means that all universal perspectives must still be perspectives which can be stated and made meaningful in the light of the given past, present states of knowledge, existing theory, the going political situation, and preferred techniques for living and making a living. Even the revolutionary religious and ethical genius is very much a product of his times.

Man's need for wholeness is certainly ambiguous. In response to the anxieties of attack, rootlessness, and change, it so easily expresses itself in *totalism*. Totalism treats partial identities and relative ideologies as if they were indeed universal. The group identity of some fraction of the human species—a *pseudospecies*—becomes a totalism and is assumed by its adherents to be normative, of universal validity, and exclusive of the identities of all other peoples and tribes. If one assumes that one's own pseudospecies is the center of the universe, other tribes often appear dangerous and are useful only as objects upon which to project those "negative identities" which are the necessary if uncomfortable counterparts of our positive identities. Finally, this projection, in conjunction with a sense of territoriality, gives "men a reason to slaughter one another in *majorem gloriam*." [59]

Clearly, when Erikson roots the core of man's fallibility in the ambiguity of man's need for identity and ideology, he is following closely in the tracks of both ancient and modern theological traditions. Man's sin is primarily spiritual. It is grounded in his twofold need for *transcendence* and for *rootedness*. His capacity for transcendence gives him the ability to imagine the infinite, the center, the absolute, and the invariant. Yet, his finitude and the particularity of his style of life lead him to posit the transcendent and the infinite in the finite and in his own partial experiences. As we saw in an earlier chapter, this analysis of the human condition has had great prominence in theological existentialism through the work of Søren Kierkegaard, Paul Tillich, Rudolf Bultmann, and Reinhold Niebuhr. It has also found prominent exposition in the philosophical existentialism of various writers and is presently being forcefully stated by Paul Ricoeur and Erich Fromm.

However, Erikson states this same insight in the context of man's evolutionary struggle for the continuation and advance of the species. It is true that Erikson does not speak of man's general tendency to absolutize the relative, as do many of the theological and philosophical existentialists mentioned above. He speaks more of man's specific tendency to absolutize the relative ideology of his own pseudospecies. It is this particular tendency, which is both so necessary and so dangerous for man's ecological integrity, which seems to Erikson to be the crucial problem facing man as he stands on the brink of mutual extermination on an international scale. And the crucial solution, for Erikson, is for man to raise the level of ideological thinking from pseudospecies to the human species as a whole. When this happens, of course, ideology must give way to ethics. Ethics is that specific kind of thinking and acting which keeps in mind the generational integrity of man as a whole—the total species. But even here, ethical thinking and acting (the style of the generative man) must be sensitive to and appreciative of the provincial ideologies which the various human pseudospecies bring to the quest for a universal identity.

Man's general human proclivity to transform his need for wholeness into totalism has some notable modern expressions. At first glance, Erikson appears to have no systematic and specifically psychoanalytic interpretation of modernity. In this respect, he appears somewhat eclectic, very much in the fashion of Philip Rieff. The forces that create modernity are, for Erikson, very much the standard ones related to the principle of structural differentiation discussed by a large number of sociological and cultural analysts—i.e., pluralism, rapid social change, individual mobility and uprootedness, and increased rationalization of life in the form of bureaucracy and corporate capitalism. These are strictly sociological and structural phenomena. However, Erikson brings to these factors of modern life a specifically psychoanalytic concern. At all times Erikson's interpretation or evaluation of these sociological forces of modernity is guided by a single question: *How do these various forces affect the ego's task of synthesizing and gaining active mastery over its experience?* Erikson's verdict is sobering. In general, he sees modernity as an unfavorable ecological environment for the synthesizing functions of the ego. But his solution is neither one of escape nor one of accommodation. In spirit and in content, Erikson is nearer to Fromm; man must confront the forces of modernity with an *advance*—an advance in humanness and an advance in responsibility. But Erikson couches this solution in a rhetoric and a terminology which is less likely than is Fromm's to be absorbed into the standard American success ideology of "better and better and higher and higher."

Erikson's concentration on the ego and its identity in the modern environment is notable in contrast to Rieff's concentration on the superego. For Rieff, modernity means the collapse of a cultural superego built around a pattern of restraints and prohibitions. Erikson is less concerned with modernity as working a collapse in cultural restraints as he is with modernity as fragmenting and eroding those integrating cultural and social rituals of mutual activation and regulation.

What are some of these modern forces which upset the integrity of social ritualization? There are several and their interrelations are subtle.

First, Erikson is aware that modern societies differentiate their role possibilities, opening up many new professions and professional subgroups with their own relatively autonomous rules of conduct and perspectives on society. This heightened pluralism of viable occupational prototypes gives every adolescent more to choose from yet more to synthesize and more to eliminate and repudiate.[60] Erikson also knows that along with structural differentiation and professional specialization, children become more isolated from society as a whole, less a part of the meaningful occupational pursuits of their fathers, more a separate subculture unto themselves. This means that the bridging rituals—the rituals between adults and children designed to recognize and to educate the child as well as to confirm and to renew the adult—are weakened, if not altogether destroyed. With these rituals of transmission and inclusion weakened, the child and the adolescent have a greater task of synthesis to accomplish, often under greater pressure and with fewer supports.[61] This pluralism and generational distance is further aggravated by a frantic rate of technologically induced social change and general social and financial mobility. This means that aspired-for futures are always undermining the identity consolidations of lost, forgotten, or actively repudiated pasts; this further strains identity formation and ego synthesis by demanding that people become something new while either forgetting or repudiating what they once were.

Erikson is also aware of the effects of mass communication on the ego's synthesizing functions. Although mass communication offers the ego a more universal and a more immediate participation in the total global village, as Marshall McLuhan has suggested, it also threatens the ego with a kaleidoscope of undigested images which threaten fragile past consolidations with attractive yet unsubstantial possibilities for the future.

Hence, modernity tends to produce a general sense of "uprootedness"

(Fromm called it "loneliness"). Uprootedness tends to deprive modern man, and especially the children of modern man, of that one essential nutriment for ecological virtue and strength—that sense of activating "recognition" which confirms one's uniqueness while it gives definition and support to one's possibilities. Erikson writes that a "deeply upsetting or uprooting experience brings about a partial regression . . . to the basic hope for recognition. . . . It is for this reason that uprooted people often seem hardly to hear what you say, but 'hang on' to your eyes and your tone of voice." [62]

Is it possible to survive in such an environment? The answer, of course, is yes. But the man who can successfully endure this uprootedness is the man whose identity contains the "resiliency of maintaining essential patterns in the processes of change." The man with the well-established identity is the one who has organized it "around basic values which cultures have in common." [63] In other words, the man with the truly resilient identity is the man whose identity is built around universal principles, which are so clearly perceived and so firmly held that few experiences can seriously threaten them. His own self-consistency with these principles gives him an inner sense of abiding recognition by a face of universal proportions, be it the face of God or the generalized face of man idealized and projected into a more perfect future. But such a man, who is in fact the "generative character" himself, is the man of maturity—the product of a reasonably favorable environment, many years of struggle, and perhaps a bit of genius. It is Erikson's conviction that it is precisely this kind of man who may be more and more difficult to come by in our contemporary civilization, so devoid as it is of ecologically viable rituals of recognition. Therefore, although it may be theoretically possible to thrive in the environment of modernity, this society may, in fact, be devoid of the very resources necessary to produce the kind of man who can do it.

The forces of pluralism, structural differentiation, technologically induced social change, and generational isolation are characteristics of modernity which America shares with the rest of the West and to a lesser degree with the entire world. In addition to these sociological trends, Erikson is very interested in the ideological and cultural influences distinctive to American life. In fact, in order to understand how it happened that America climbed with such relish onto its present bandwagon of urban, industrial, and technological expansion, one must know something about the cultural forces that dominated our early history. Erikson speaks primarily of two ideological influences—Protestantism, and the frontier motif. Of the four authors reviewed in this study he is the only one who attempts to make more than the most cursory statements about what is distinctive about American life in the context of modernity.

Of course, Erikson would agree with Rieff, Fromm, and Brown in their assessment of the importance of the Protestant experience for the formation of the American approach to economic life. Yet Erikson's handling of Protestantism is in a style vastly different from that of any of these other authors. As we have seen, Rieff discusses the Protestant experience very little but merely assumes the Weberian analysis of the importance of both Luther and Calvin, and, of course, primarily Calvin. Brown limits his analysis primarily to Luther and absorbs Luther's doctrine of *theologia crucis* into his reductionistic dialectics of the life and death instincts. Erikson's handling of Protestantism is closer to that of Fromm, but even here there are important differences. Erikson has very little to say about Calvin and Calvinism and even his book *Young Man Luther* makes no particular effort to trace the relationship between Lutheran theology and various developments in modern characterology, which, of course, is the primary interest of Fromm. Rather, *Young Man Luther* is a biographical study of Luther himself. It attempts to show the interrelationship between psychological infrastructures and theological ideas. It seeks to demonstrate the way in which Luther's relationships with his father, his father's class and ambitions, the cultural and social currents of the Renaissance, and German economic and social life all helped to shape Luther's struggles with the pope, with Christ, and, finally, with God. But even more, Erikson attempts to demonstrate how Luther's own confrontation with Scripture, especially the doctrine of justification by faith alone, helped to liberate Luther and the people of his age from their bad consciences and enabled them to regain that deeper activity which is first granted by a mother's recognition of her child but which needs always to be reborn at successively later stages of life.[64] Of course, Erikson is well aware of how in Lutheranism this deeper activity (a recapitulation at a higher level of those first passivities associated with a mother's recognition) so quickly became domesticated, and how, through the Lutheran doctrine of "calling" (*Beruf*), it was so rapidly directed toward an activistic, dutiful, and quite unwitting conformity to the demands of the new authorities—the authorities of state, nation, and the emerging capitalist economy. So Erikson can write:

> The Protestant Revolution thus led to a way of life in which a man's daily works, including his occupation, became the center of his behavioral

orientation, and were rigorously regimented by the church-state. Such a condition Luther had once decried as "Mosaic law." Now he rationalized it: since a Christian man has not only a soul, but also a body living among other bodies, he must "resign himself to Moses" (*sich in Mosen schicken*). Even praying man should take council not only with himself, but with the rulers, in order to be sure of perceiving all the signs of God's plan. This new face of a God, recognizable in prayer, in the Scriptures, *and* in the decisions of the *Landesvater*, became the orientation of a new class, and of a religiosity compliant to the needs of progress in the new, the mercantile, line of endeavor. In spite of having reacted more violently than anyone else against indulgences and against usury, Luther helped prepare the metaphysical misalliance between economic self-interest and church affiliation so prominent in the Western world. Martin had become the metaphysical jurist of his father's class.[65]

Erikson seems to be aware that the birthright of Protestantism is more than that subtle combination of activistic and dutiful conformity bequeathed to the modern world by the sociological consequences of Luther's theology. He seems also to assume that additional *ascetic* element generally associated with Calvinism as well as the peculiar logic of the doctrine of predestination so prominent in American Puritanism. However, he says little about this. The growing edge of Erikson's contribution to an understanding of American ideology rests in how he portrays the specific way in which these Protestant motifs interact with another source of the American identity—the overwhelming presence of a geographical fact, a seemingly limitless American *frontier* which grasped and organized the imagination of the adventurous in spirit throughout the early history of this new nation. It is only by understanding how the presence of the frontier shaped the perception of space and time in the American consciousness that we begin to gain a full picture of the specific way our Protestant heritage expressed itself in the American character.

The American character—or "identity," as Erikson prefers to call it —is composed, as are all national identities, of a series of *dichotomies*. National identity is always a synthesis of disparate elements into a relatively stable whole. It is this insight, recognized by many investigators but stated most forcefully by Erikson, which saves him from the error of postulating momentous discontinuities in the American character such as Riesman's theory of the shift from the inner-directed to outer-directed character. Early in our history the "functioning American" learned to base his "final ego identity on some tentative combination of dynamic polarities such as migratory and sedentary, individualistic and standardized, competitive and co-operative, pious and freethinking, responsible and cynical, etc." [66] This kind of thinking about American identity is more consistent with the thought of Seymour Lipset as expressed in his book *The First New Nation*[67] than it is with the thought of either Riesman or his mentor, Erich Fromm. Lipset, speaking specifically of the polarity of equality and achievement, believes that these somewhat contradictory values have "been a constant element in determining American institutions and behavior." Riesman and Fromm, on the other hand, tend to see the American character developing in relatively discontinuous stages.[68] Erikson, however, tends to see the varieties of American identity as playing out one or more extremes of a polarity of characteristics, every particular expression of which assumes and to some degree defends itself against its opposite.

For Erikson, these polar opposites tend to contain a common element, an element that grants some synthesis to the dichotomies latent in the American identity. The individual American is likely to feel relatively secure in his identity "as long as he can preserve a certain element of deliberate *tentativeness* of autonomous choice." [69] The individual must be able to feel that "the next step is up to him" and that whether he is "staying or going," settling down or moving on, he is not being told to do either and that the options are basically up to him. Erikson believes that one of the central components of the American ideology supporting this element of openness and tentativeness in the American character has to do with the crystallization of images of movement, open space, free mobility, and rapid change centering around the physical presence of America's grand frontier. The American identity seems to be grounded on a vision of "unlimited space" and a "limitless future" in which to develop and to test its social experiments. Erikson believes that the space-time perceptions of a people are always important factors in shaping their identity. Just as the open prairie and the tasks of buffalo-hunting gave the Sioux a *centrifugal* space-time identity,[70] and just as the presence of the Klamath River and the vocation of salmon-fishing gave the Yurok a *centripetal* space-time identity,[71] so the frontier helped to shape the Protestant identities of Americans into a complex set of dichotomies of which "tentativeness" may indeed be the central element.

The importance of "limitless space" for American identity has been investigated in depth by such historians as Sidney Mead and R. W. B. Lewis. Sidney Mead states it beautifully when he suggests that from "time immemorial the peoples of the Orient, of the Near East, and of

Europe have been a people hemmed in, confined within the spatial boundaries set by geography and by the closely related boundaries set by tradition and custom." [72] On the other hand the first emigrants to America "experienced a new birth of freedom—the possibility of unconfined movement in space." [73] R. W. B. Lewis takes up much the same theme in his classic *The American Adam*. He conceives of early American history as a great dialogue between what he calls the Party of Hope, the Party of Memory, and the Party of Irony. The Party of Hope reflected the dominant mood of the country. This party repudiated the past and celebrated the limitless possibilities of this new country and its inexhaustible frontier. Oliver Wendell Holmes exemplifies the spirit of this group with the statement, "The expansive future is our arena." [74] The New Adam, the new man in America, Lewis tells us, finds his habitat in "space as spaciousness, as unbounded, the area of total possibility." [75]

Erikson's work on the American identity, published prior to either of these studies, was the first introduction of space-time factors into psychiatric studies and possesses the additional merit of demonstrating the importance of space-time considerations for more traditional psychiatric concerns such as child-training, identification, repression, etc. Most specifically this contribution helps to explain the peculiar role of the mother in the American family (the institution of "momism") and her contribution to the formation of the strengths and the weaknesses of the American character. The mother has gradually become the center of power in the American family, largely out of necessity. In a space without limit, which offered an endless horizon of hidden attractions to the more mobile and ambulatory male to which she was married, the American mother was frequently the only source of stability and order in the home, checking and restraining the more exploratory instincts of her husband and her sons. Generally preferring to remain "settled" herself, she still, with a mother's instincts, raised her sons to survive and to flourish, if possible, in an open and mobile space of limitless possibilities. To train a son for mobility, initiative, and opportunity meant, for her, to capitalize on certain resources in the Protestant heritage—its doctrine of asceticism, hard work, and success as a sign of right relationship with God. Hence, when it was time for the son to leave home, the mother could "trust" him; she had literally starved the more "sensual" and "rebellious" elements out of him, leaving him only with a desire to *move*, but to do so safely. As the frontier began to close, the son, if he could not move in space, could at least move up in business or in the organization. From the mother's standpoint, this would be better, since it would permit the son to be settled, and this is what the mother always preferred to begin with. Hence, the polar opposites of "migratory" and "sedentary" not only were differences that distinguished those who "moved on" and those who "stayed behind" and settled; they were characterological ambiguities bred into the identity of many Americans, setting the stage for a more familiar and later development—a polarity between "individualism" and "conformity."

If industrialization, the factory, and the rapidly expanding corporation were to become the new substitute for the American frontier, then the mother's Puritan asceticism in raising her children would soon resonate with an emerging ideology of the machine and she would soon attempt to raise her child with factorylike precision, punctuality, and order—all in the name, once again, of endless expansion, mobility, progress, and success. This deep identification with the machine is something like the Sioux's identification with the buffalo or the Yurok's with the salmon. It is a modern instance of magical thinking which tries to master external realities through unconscious identification with them. This magical identification with the machine was an identification, however, for which Americans were well prepared by the combination of asceticism and dutiful activism inherited from their Protestant legacies.

Whatever its origin, such a system of child-raising, during the last part of the nineteenth century and the first third of the twentieth, was efficient in producing a type of man who had at the same time both high initiative and a high capacity to conform to the demands of America's corporate capitalism. Erikson does not minimize the virtues of this kind of man. His problem, however, is primarily a lack of a more universal ethic, a lack of a true sense of generativity. His initiative and conformity permit him to be an excellent "little boss"; the trouble is, he leaves far too many decisions to the "big bosses," the government, the higher powers. Consequently, he has little interest in and little desire to question very deeply the ethical meaning of the *context* within which he works. Hence, the boss, the corporation, and the machine constitute, for Erikson, a threat to America because they present to all the "little managers" of our nation the possibility of an "autocracy of irresponsibility." And, of course, an autocracy of irresponsibility would be, for Erikson, an autocracy of the nongenerative mind.

Hence Erikson, I believe, would not be entirely satisfied with Riesman's concept of the "other-directed" person or Fromm's concept of the "marketing" character. The emerging technological man still has much of the capacity for initiative, self-starting, and ascetic discipline of the "inner-directed" man, just as he, at the same time, has a great need for and tendencies toward conformity, settledness, and safety. He still, most probably, needs to feel that he is a part of an ever-expanding and a freely chosen environment, if not the frontier, then possibly some new colossal technological or machine-created universe. Erikson invokes neither the death instinct of Brown nor the concept of necrophilia of Fromm to explain this strange coalescence between the image of the frontier, our Protestant asceticism and vocationalism, and our fascination with the machine.

In a strange way, Erikson agrees most with Rieff. Most Americans have in common a pervasive and nearly unrestrainable need to "keep moving" (Rieff) or to stay "tentative" (Erikson). It is the characteristic that is shared in common by the settlers and the migrators, the conformers and the individualists, as well as all those (and this includes most of us) who are strange mixtures of all these tendencies. As we saw earlier, Erikson sees the major dichotomy developing in America today to be that between the so-called "technologists" and those whom he calls the "new-humanists." Certainly the technologists, at their various levels of competence and incompetence, contain more of that standard Protestant synthesis of initiative and conformity than do the emerging humanist youth. But as most researchers into humanist youth (especially Kenneth Keniston) have shown, many of these young people, in addition to their seriousness, honesty, and idealism, are very much committed to a life of constant change, fluidity, openness to the future, and a deep fear of being trapped in the "System." [76] It may be that it is the characterological weakness of both the technologist and the new-humanist that they do not really know how to live with "containment" and "limitation." What does it mean to live in a world where there is no more space (except outer space), where adulthood may entail entangling commitments, where new nations will emerge to limit the autonomy of old and larger ones, where every new scientific advance seems to be more ominous of destruction than of beneficence, and where advanced technology requires more rationalization of both job and leisure than most Americans prefer? This is the question which we will pose now and attempt to address more completely at a later time. Then we will ask the question, Does generative man, as sketched by Erikson, provide us with a characterological type that truly possesses resources to live in a technological world with a new style of active mastery, communal responsibility, relaxed enjoyment, and ethical control over the cancerous expansiveness of our scientific and economic enterprises? In other words, will generative man have new capacities to live with containment, limitation, and that kind of communal responsibility which knows how to generate and to care?

7

THE EMPIRICS
OF GENERATIVE MAN

In this chapter, I will extend the vision of generative man. I will investigate his essential nature and clarify the specific ways he must live his life in the face of modernity. What is said about generative man here will seek to remain faithful to Erikson's own writings about the adult stages of life, but there will be moments when I will expand what he says in ways which may seem somewhat foreign to Erikson himself.

In organizing this wider discussion of generative man, I will follow the usual order of discussing his relationship to himself, to time, to his social world, and to the "other."

The Dialectics of Receiving and Acting

The relationship of generative man to himself should be understood as an extended dialogue between that part of himself which is involuntary and that part of himself which transcends the involuntary. Erikson believes, as Fromm does, that both of these facets of man are natural and given. By nature, man is a thinking, imagining creature who can gain a historical perspective on his life and on the lives of others. By nature, also, man is an animal, and for a portion of his life, he is also a child. Erikson believes that man regulates his life through a constant dialogue between the "I" (the highest level of personal and historical consciousness) and the deeper processes of ordering which come forth from man's child and animal nature. Hence, Erikson is neither an existentialist trusting only the lucidity of man's historical consciousness nor a determinist trusting only the rigid laws of behavior which are often erroneously attributed to the animal and to the child. In terms of the now-famous French intellectual scene, Erikson has little affinity with either the existentialism of Sartre or with that brand of determinism represented by his arch-opponent, Claude Lévi-Strauss. He has a greater affinity with those moderating figures such as Paul Ricoeur or Maurice Merleau-Ponty who tend to see life as a subtle interplay between man's involuntary bodily tendencies and his higher capacities for self-awareness, reflection, and freedom.[1] Of course, the source of Erikson's position on this issue is Heinz Hartmann and his vision of the relationship between the rational and the irrational in man which we have already reviewed in Chapter 4. For Erikson, the child and the animal in man make a positive contribution to the order- ing and the renewal of life at the level of the adult historical ego. The adult "I" simultaneously opens itself to and yet directs the deeper activities of the more involuntary dimensions of life. Erikson sees an underlying compatibility between the transcendent and the involuntary dimensions of man, but this deeper harmony must sustain a variety of conflicts and contradictions which may indeed possess less ontological foundation but which are no less an inevitable dimension of the human career.

We will view generative man's relationship with himself from the perspective of his developmental stages. When the human situation is viewed from this perspective, we must admit that Erikson gives us a somewhat tragic or ironic view of life. Man's odyssey toward maturity and generativity is punctuated by a series of confrontations with the darker, more destructive dimensions of life. Maturity, or full genera- tivity, is born out of a series of confrontations with *mistrust, doubt, limitation, powerlessness,* and *confusion.* Human strength and maturity, or generativity, come not so much from victory as from *synthesis.* These negativities are not vanquished; instead, they are synthesized into a delicate balance with man's strengths. Generative man is one who recognizes and includes within his higher affirmations the deeper untrustworthy, humiliating, limiting, inferiority-producing, and frag- menting dimensions of life.

Generative man's relationship to himself will be examined from the perspective of the psychosocial stages and virtues that contribute to the grand final synthesis which we call generativity. Our goal is to restate these stages and virtues, not so much from the perspective of their ontogenetic development, but from the perspective of their final culmination in maturity and generativity. Generativity is the normative center of Erikson's thought; however, in some ways, he has less to say about this stage than about any other stage of development which he discusses. Yet the center of life and the essence of the good man are to be found here. To understand generativity in all its richness, we must restate all the stages and virtues in terms of what they mean for the true goal of life. This procedure is both justified by and implicit in Erikson's idea of the epigenetic principle. If all parts of the ground plan of human development are present at the beginning of life (in the original ground plan, or pattern), then all the developmental stages have as their aim those later stages of maturity—specifically generativity. And their final deposit to human strength is to be seen in what they contribute to that grand central synthesis of life which Erikson calls generativity. This point of view, implicit in the logic of all that Erikson has to say, is truly a revolutionary idea to introduce into psychoanalytic theory. The meaning or end of life is not to be found by studying the origins or beginnings of life. The meaning of life is to be found in the end of life, in the purpose of life as it expresses itself in maturity and generativity. Hence, we study the beginning of life to understand what it contributes to the end. *Erikson's epigenetic principle calls for a reverse of the logic of psychoanalytic thinking. The end of life must not be understood in terms of the beginning; rather, the beginning must be understood in terms of what it contributes to and how it is directed by those emerging potentials which arise late in development but which are just as fundamental to life as that which appears much earlier.* This rather Aristotelian-sounding idea is implicit in the meaning of the epigenetic principle and justifies the procedure we are about to follow in our effort to state the fuller meaning of generative man's relationship to himself.

I will be looking at Erikson's developmental stages and virtues from the perspective of the normative center of his thought—the stage of generativity. It will be helpful, I think, to be reminded, once again, of their age and sequence of emergence.

Age	Nuclear Conflict	Virtue
1. Infancy	Trust vs. Mistrust	Hope
2. Early Childhood	Autonomy vs. Shame	Will
3. Play Age	Initiative vs. Guilt	Purpose
4. School Age	Industry vs. Inferiority	Competence
5. Adolescence	Identity vs. Identity Confusion	Fidelity
6. Young Adult	Intimacy vs. Isolation	Love
7. Adulthood	Generativity vs. Self-absorption	Care
8. Old Age	Integrity vs. Despair	Wisdom

To represent the structure of the coming discussion, Figure 2 may be helpful. It represents the relationship of each stage (trust, autonomy, etc.) and each virtue (hope, will, etc.) both to the negative dimension of its developmental conflict (bottom) and to the stage of generativity (stage 7, shown at top).

DEVELOPMENTAL INTERRELATIONSHIPS IN ERIKSON

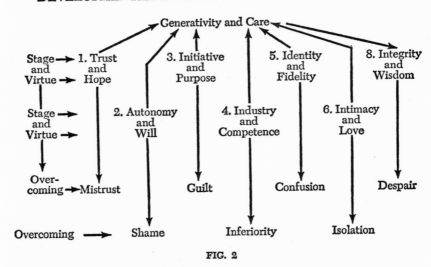

FIG. 2

Generative man contains within himself a fund of *basic trust* in the world and *hope* for the future. This unconscious reservoir of emotional and cognitive assumptions about the basic responsiveness of the world was first bestowed by the mutual regulation and mutual satisfaction of the infant-mother relationship. If it is supported by later analogous experience, this basic trust and hope can be progressively restated and generalized to successively higher and more inclusive levels of experience. It often finds its highest articulation in mature religious and philosophical world images and ideologies. This basic trust applies to the self and to the world; it grants one both a fund of positive feeling toward one's own inner needs and a faith in the capacity of the outer world to meet these needs. It gives generative man hope and faith that the dark denials, deprivations, and frustrations of life, as real as they are, will not in the end outweigh its satisfactions. This basic trust and hope of generative man makes a certain kind of receptivity, openness, and passivity the fundamental modality of his life. In contrast to Fromm, who has a disparaging view of passivity, Erikson sees authentic receptive-passivity and authentic activity, at their deepest levels, as identical.[2] Generative man has access to this deepest level of receptivity which is the foundation of all later activities, i.e., autonomy, initiative, and competence.[3] It is most important to remember, however, that the basic trust and hope of the generative man has a specifically phylogenetic meaning; it gives him the trust not only to continue his own existence but to share in the generation of succeeding generations and to help care for and sustain their lives with hope. This basic trust and hope gives generative man faith in the future of the species. The basic trust and hope that has accrued to him through a favorable coincidence of internal equipment and external environment is now something he is concerned both to pass on to and elicit from others.

Generative man also has a capacity for *autonomy* and the virtue of *will*.[4] This is to say, he trusts those deeper forces within himself which propel him toward growth and individuation. In addition, he has trusted those external pressures and affirmations which are designed to guide and support this process. The autonomy of generative man is an autonomy that is grounded in a prior receptivity. This means that he has learned to trust his own powers partially because he has first learned to experience the basic reciprocity between his powers and the powers of the external world. He has learned that to exercise his own powers—his own autonomy—is neither to destroy the external world nor to cut himself off from its support and confirmation. In addition, he has learned that when he exercises his own powers, the world will not respond in such a way as to humiliate and *shame* him, rendering him *doubtful* about his capacity to successfully order crucial aspects of his own life. For a man to have autonomy and will, he knows that there are some things he must *hold to* and other things that he must *expel* or *repudiate*. Generative man has learned to exercise his will and autonomy in such a way that his *holding* is not defiance or stubbornness and his *repudiations* are not violent destructiveness. All this means that generative man can accept the limitations of his will without losing his basic confidence in his right to exercise it. He also can assert limitations on the will of others without undue fear of destroying the other. His capacity to endure reasonable limitations without unmanageable shame or doubt makes it possible for him to submit both himself and his progeny to the prudent restraints of an institutionalized legal order.[5]

The relationship in generative man between receptivity on the one hand and autonomy and will on the other sets him off clearly from all three of the previous character types we have studied. Generative man's autonomy and will are *embedded* in a deeper receptivity of trust and hope. Autonomy is finally, for Erikson, of equal ontological status with receptivity. This is where he differs so profoundly with Brown. Regardless of Brown's explicit intention to maintain the onto-logical grounds of individuation (autonomy), the very fact that he grounds individuation and autonomy in the death instinct deprives him of this accomplishment. In Erikson, man's drive for autonomy builds on a foundation of receptiveness but yet has its own ontogenetic basis and schedule for emergence. Autonomy can function to bring the need for union and receptivity to a higher level of expression. Erikson shares the insights of Robert White and of Jean Piaget in seeing man's drive toward autonomy (individuation) as a part of a general aim to know and experience a *wider* environment. Leaving the womb is not anti-thetical to union; instead, it is the first step in a long journey toward a higher and more inclusive union.

In addition, the receptivity and union about which Erikson speaks is not the union by fusion preached by Brown. Generative man seeks a union of mutual recognition and not a union of self-obliteration and self-absorption. Generative man seeks a union of reciprocal patterns of regulation and mutual activation. It is a union that protects his individ-uality as much as it overcomes his loneliness. It is a union that seeks to "know even as we are known." Generative man seeks a wider and more inclusive union which can give recognition, regulation, and com-munion to his own inevitable uniqueness.

If the meaning of receptivity and union in Erikson differs from that of Brown, so does the meaning of autonomy and individuality differ from that of both Rieff and Brown. Rieff's psychological man, in some respects, is sheer activity. Technical reason in psychological man makes him hyperconscious, forever surveying and controlling the lower pas-sions with the vigilant guidance of psychoanalytic insight. For Rieff, the passions of life have little if any adaptive or regulative significance. It is true that release is the major modality of psychological man, but not because man's passions or instincts have any adaptive significance; rather, it is because they mediate to consciousness certain pleasurable states, especially when wisely guided by the prudence of psychoana-lytic insight. On the other hand, generative man is not all activity and not all consciousness. He is open to his deeper passions not only be-cause they bring pleasure, comfort, or balance but also because they bring patterns of regulation deeper and wiser than consciousness by itself can either know or devise. In a strange way, Rieff's psychological man is akin to the Western prototype of the self-made man; both are overdifferentiated toward consciousness and control. Both are indeed Apollonian in ways that generative man is not.

Productive man is also Apollonian in ways that generative man is not. However, Fromm's productive man has been rendered Apollonian in style and vocabulary more than in the actual details of his formal conception. Yet Fromm's habitual tendency to associate "passiveness" with evil and immaturity and to associate "activeness" with virtue and maturity perpetuates the existential fallacy, generally associated with the thought of Jean-Paul Sartre, that man makes himself in all respects. It also promulgates the assumption, widely held in the Western world, that man's higher rational and conscious powers, mobilized and kept in a constant state of hyperalertness, are the key to maturity. Generative man knows better; for him, higher-order rationality and consciousness are gentle guides and complements to basically adaptive, although never completely automatic and infallible, lower-order passions.

Generative man has the capacity to sharpen his autonomy and will into the capacity for *initiative* and the virtue of *purpose*.[6] Whereas autonomy and will have to do with that more diffuse desire "to do it for oneself" and to enjoy a kind of "freedom from," initiative and purpose entail more specifically goal-directed activity and involve more directly another kind of freedom—a "freedom to." Just as autonomy and will include and surpass inevitable feelings of *shame* and *doubt*, so initiative and purpose include and surpass inevitable experiences of *guilt*. The point is that generative man is not without those residues of guilt which come from an internalization of familial and tribal limitations and moralities. Generative man knows that there is a place in life for those elemental limitations which come from one's own family and one's own province. Here Erikson would distinguish between guilt at the level of morality and that higher kind of existential guilt which comes from one's sense of failure or inadequacy in contributing to the general maintenance and strengthening of the cycle of the generations. The basic helplessness of the human infant and its long period of dependence upon parental figures necessitates the development in the human child of a superego. This mental institution assists in the guidance of the child until physical and mental maturation become stabilized. The superego is, for Erikson and the generative man that he envisions, a phylogenetic and ontogenetic necessity.

Erikson does not see in man's initiatives any basically overdetermined tendency to dominate and control the other. Essentially, man's initiatives aim toward complementarity and not toward domination. However, in the context of the child's limited vision or at other times in situations of scarce resources, initiatives to "become equal" or "to be like" someone else often express themselves in fantasies and in behavior to "usurp" the other person and to "take his place." Of course, this is the essence of the Oedipal conflict between father and son and between mother and daughter. Here differences in competence and developmental schedule necessitate placing limitations on the child's premature efforts to be like mother or father and to fulfill the specifics of these parental roles.

In generative man, these limitations have been administered in such a way as not to suppress completely those fantasies and initiatives which are aimed at becoming "equal to" or "like" admired persons of power and competence. Generative man will possess and respect those vestiges of inherited morality which inculcate the specific patterns of permissions and restraints characteristic of his native culture. But his morality will stop short of moralism—those blind and totalistic rejections of all people and experience which cannot conform to his own customary ways. In addition, his own superego and the specific morality that it transports will have undergone a higher negotiation with his own maturing ego. Hence, certain aspects of his inherited prohibitions and of his inherited ideals will undergo revision, sometimes born out of considerable agony, with a new synthesis being the result. Some prohibitions and ideals are affirmed not only as inevitable but as wise, whereas others are respectfully set aside. In the end, generative man can affirm, both in principle and to some extent in specific detail, his own inherited morality and superego, while at the same time trusting and giving expression to the initiatives and specific purposes they were designed to limit and guide judiciously.

Because generative man can appreciate the usefulness of his own inherited morality (regardless of its acknowledged imperfections and the later qualifications he will inevitably place upon it), he will not hesitate to pass on to succeeding generations a morality suitable for their time, place, and major enterprises. The superego and morality (and the guilt which always accompanies them) that generative man passes on to others will not be identical to the ones that he received, nor will they be totally discontinuous with them. His qualified acceptance of his own inherited moralities makes it possible for him to convey to the issue of his own generativity a *flexible* link with the past. The progeny of generative man will be liberated for the future and for a wider universalism. But their journey toward the future and toward a wider universalism is never without the support of more provincial moralities which give them a sense of rootedness in their own time and place and a sense of connectedness with their own past.

All the psychoanalytic ethicists reviewed in this study share a common concern about the destructive potentials of the superego. Rieff, Brown, Fromm, and Erikson alike share the hope of mitigating the influence in human affairs of man's more rigid moralism, his masochistic or sadistic preoccupations, and his projections of his own most deeply feared sins onto foreign groups and tribes. All four men are typically "psychoanalytic" in seeing the "high" in man—primarily his moralisms—as being the major seat of his difficulties. In this, strangely enough, they agree with the central witness of the great tradition of the Christian churches in the Western world; the churches too have tended, in their best moments, to center man's fallibility in his spirit —more precisely, in an orientation of his spirit—rather than in his flesh or in his drives, as did the Manichaean tradition. *But Erikson is the only one of the four who retains both a phylogenetic and an ontogenetic significance for morality and the superego.* Of course, for Brown, the superego is considered a phylogenetic catastrophe from the beginning. Rieff and Fromm are more charitable. Both men admit that from the perspective of the history of the race, the superego was a necessity. For Rieff, it was, in all former ages, the essence of culture forcing upon man the renunciations essential for civilized community. For Fromm, morality and the superego are phylogenetically mandatory to help man rise above primitive embeddedness with nature. However, both of these men envision a time when morality and the superego will be extinct—when they will be ancient curiosities no longer relevant to the socializing process of advanced societies. Rieff would replace the superego with the conscious controls of psychoanalytic insight. Fromm believes that the superego can be replaced by a rational positive ethic built on psychology as the science of man. Neither Fromm nor Rieff says anything about the continuing importance of the superego in the ontogenetic development of the child, even the children of modernity.

Of course, Erikson too envisions a time, in the history of the race as a whole and in the development of every individual in particular, when the restrictions and the ideals of the superego would finally submit to the more realistic and autonomous ethics of the ego. But in the transition from a morality of the superego to an ethics of the ego, Erikson sees the ego (each man's ego as well as the collective ego of the race) selectively *affirming* certain traditions and values of the superego. Hence, generative man will see the superego as an ontogenetic necessity. The children of generative man will have their superegos—their cluster of only dimly perceived and understood prohibitions and ideals. But generative man, in contrast to some of his predecessors, will enter into an extended, intense, and often agonizing dialogue with succeeding generations, helping each to decide which old values in their inherited morality and superego must be retained and which new ones must be added and passed on to the young of future ages.

Because his accumulated sense of limitation does not completely cripple his deeper initiatives and spontaneities, generative man has considerable capacity for "play." The capacity for *meaningful* play, which first emerges in late childhood, is never lost for generative man. In Erikson's thought, play is man's major means of restoration—his preferred therapy.[7] Play is the way the ego repairs itself in the face of the threats and challenges of life which tend to rob the ego of its sense of active mastery. Erikson writes: "To hallucinate ego mastery and yet also to practice it in an intermediate reality between phantasy and actuality is the purpose of play—but play . . . is the undisputed master of only a slim margin of existence."[8] Erikson realizes that there are forms of play, to be found in infancy and early childhood, which do not have the recuperation of a sense of ego activity or mastery as their primary purpose. However, about the fourth or fifth year, a kind of play emerges that rehearses interpersonal situations which constitute a potential threat to the child's social competence. Erikson calls it *macrospheric play* in contrast to *microspheric play* (play in the world of manageable toys) or *autocosmic play* (play that begins with and centers in the child's own body).[9] For Erikson, there is no great difference between the play of children and the play of adults. Both use play to regain a sense of ego integration, wholeness, and mastery; through play, both the child and the adult attempt to convert the more capricious and obstinate aspects of life into something at least acceptable and manageable if not actively willed. The play of the child, however, is in many ways closer to work than is the play of the adult. When the child plays, he is preparing through rehearsal for mastery of an eventual reality. The adult plays by withdrawing from a rigid and all too confining reality to a more limited sphere (the bowling alley, the card game) where he can achieve a sense of mastery in an area of experience that is relatively discontinuous with the rigors of everyday work. Hence, the adult's play is recreation, whereas the child's is preparation. And yet, all through Erikson's work is the implication that the creative adult (the generative adult) is precisely the person who can infuse his work with play; he is the person who can stand back from the reality situation of his work long enough to fantasy a more human way of coping with its confinements, tensions, and dichotomies. Moreover, generative man can take the further step of infusing, once again, the reality of work with the more humane modalities of his play. Even the great cultural synthesizers—the religious, political, and cultural geniuses such as Luther, Freud, and Gandhi—were supreme in their playfulness, especially in their work. Their great works of synthesis were personal attempts to restore the active mastery of their egos in the context of the tensions and dichotomies of their personal and public historical situations. All great historical syntheses are as much play as they are work. They are work because they are indeed attentive to the real contradictions and tensions that most people of a given historical period both sense and suffer. They are a result of play because the creative genius does not simply conform to, adjust to, and accommodate to these tensions. Instead, he bends and reshapes these tensions until they submit to a new synthesis which not only enlivens and activates him but which also enlivens and activates a whole people and an entire era.

In his understanding of the meaning of play, Erikson is close to the concept of play to be found in the writings of Jean Piaget. As we have already seen, play, for Piaget, occurs when assimilation is dominant over accommodation in a person's efforts to adapt to reality.[10] Play is never without its features of accommodation, just as work is never without its elements of assimilation. Play and work, for Piaget and Erikson, are placed on a continuum and become differentiated through accentuating elements in one or the other that are common to both. More important, both Piaget and Erikson see play as part of the total adaptive process. They do not make the error, committed by Johan Huizinga and Adolf Jensen, of seeing play as independent of man's struggle for adaptation. Huizinga and Jensen have made contributions to our understanding of man by pointing to the play motif in man's cultural and religious creations.[11] However, both have tended to distinguish play from man's broader adaptive processes. Neither Erikson nor Piaget makes the mistake of restricting the meaning of adaptation to mere adjustment or simple pragmatic usefulness. Since Huizinga and Jensen make this error, their writings continually put play and adaptation in opposition to each other. Consequently, their understanding of the role of play in the development of culture and of religion obscures how man's drive to playfully express himself *and* his struggle for adaptation *come together* in his great religious and cultural creations. Piaget and especially Erikson—because he takes these insights farther into the area of cultural and historical analysis—make the more profound contributions. They demonstrate in a way more consistent with the realities of life how man, in his everyday activities as well as in his grander cultural accomplishments, seeks to express playfully his humanity in his work while at the same time striving through his work to shape a world more favorable to the innermost needs of his humanity.

Generative man, then, is what one might call, rather clumsily, a "romantic adaptationalist." His belief that his play—as well as his dreams and his art—contains wisdom as well as pleasure, adaptive strength as well as satisfying expressiveness, gives his romanticism a certain kind of hardheadedness. Generative man knows that there are important adaptive potentials in man's more relaxed and sometimes unconscious processes of play, dreams, and art. The result of this brand of romanticism is to broaden the concept of rationality to include the low—the playful, the instinctive, and the so-called irrational. Rationality, for generative man, is associated with the total wisdom of the organism—the total adaptive task of conforming to the specifics of reality while at the same time forcing reality to conform obediently to man's needs and propensities.

Of course, this is vastly different from the thought of Freud, Rieff, or Brown. Freud saw in man's play only an effort to restore the organism, through repetition, to a state of equilibrium. Rieff, critical of this reductionism, commits an excess in the other direction and understands play as spontaneity and abundance, but a spontaneity and an abundance which contribute little to man's larger adaptive struggle. As we recall, adaptation was, for Rieff, primarily the task of the sly and crafty ego and the wily ways of technical reason. Of course, for Brown, play is all release and all spontaneity; it contributes nothing directly to adaptation. For Dionysian man, adaptation is man's method of avoiding death by repressing life—by repressing play. For Dionysian man, work and play are antithetical; work and adaptation constitute the repression of play and cause its eventual sublimation into cultural and religious projections. For generative man, adaptation (and finally rationality itself) is a *synthesis* of play and work. It is under the rubric of synthesis (rather than repression or sublimation) that generative man understands the relationship of play and work in all his adaptive activities as well as in his cultural and religious creations.

Generative man is also a man of *industry* and *competence*. By this, we do not mean that he is necessarily an industrialist, an expert, or a highly trained specialist. It does mean, however, that generative man has managed to focus his natural spontaneities—his autonomy and his initiative—into the learning of culturally valued skills at both a general and a more specialized level. This is to say, then, that generative man has had a successful latency period—that long period from late childhood to puberty when a child's primary interests center around school, hobbies, and interest group. Erikson acknowledges the possibility of a generalized need for "competence," as Robert White calls it. He also believes that this need may have its own specific period of epigenetic ascendancy.

But whatever truth there is (and as I have indicated, I believe that there is considerable) in the idea of a need for competence—or a sense of industry, as Erikson describes it—comes about when skillful parents, teachers, and friends lead a child's natural spontaneous play toward the mastery and completion of new skills which the child, by himself, might never discover. Hence, the capacity for industry and competence, as Erikson uses these terms, is a capacity for culturally meaningful *work* and *discipline* which builds on but also extends and possibly exceeds the natural inclinations of play.

Every culture, Erikson believes, teaches its children the basic rudiments of the particular techniques upon which that culture is built. This is true whether the culture is primarily a buffalo-hunting culture such as that of the Sioux, a salmon-fishing culture such as that of the Yurok, or a literate industrial and scientific culture such as that of Western society. Erikson is fully aware that the basic technology of any culture—be it hunting, fishing, or industry and science—grants its own particular ratio of blessings and dangers. It is clear that Erikson believes that the generative man of today and of the future will share the skills of the literate, industrial, scientific culture toward which Western society has been evolving for the last three hundred years. For Erikson, the generative man of every culture knows the selected technology of the culture of which he is a part; this means that generative man in the modern world must know and participate to some extent in the dominant technologies of his culture.

This does not mean, of course, that generative man is completely subservient to the preferred technologies of his culture, that he will not fight its rigidities, or that he will not control its excesses. We will discuss, at a later time, the moral response of generative man to the terrifying difficulties of advanced technological and corporate society. What interests us here is the importance—the necessity—for generative man to have as part of his ego structure, his identity, and his overall synthesis a repertory of basic skills which give him a ground for independence as well as the ability to make a meaningful contribution to the larger corporate good. It is a part of his general pattern of generativity. His skills give focus to his random initiatives, enjoyment in their exercise, and recognition from the contribution they make, not only to his own well-being but to that of the wider community and to that of succeeding generations. In other words, industry and competence help to overcome that sense of *inferiority* which may come with the growing awareness that one is not making a significant contribution to the community to which one owes one's very existence. A more definitive analysis of generative man's attitudes toward the specific technologies of modernity must wait for our later discussion of generative man and his relation to his social world.

We must proceed toward our goal of delineating the structure of generative man's relationship to himself. Generative man possesses a viable *identity* and a well-consolidated style of *fidelity*.[12] We have already discussed these qualities in our earlier section on "Identity and Modernity." Here we pointed out that identity must be a result of mutual activation—a match between individual styles of ego synthesis and the recognition and confirmation of one's community. We also pointed out that fidelity is the transposition to the level of historical actuality of the general ecological need for an average expectable environment.[13] Another way to say it is this: identity deals with the question of "who one is," whereas fidelity deals with the complementary question of "whom one can trust." Generative man has personally satisfying and publicly convincing answers to both of these questions.

But to talk about identity and fidelity under the rubric of generative man's relationship to himself is to bracket, as much as possible, the more objective, societal dimension of these characteristics. From this inner point of view, it is important to note the great internal richness out of which a sense of identity is forged. Also, it must be acknowledged that one learns to trust precisely those people, ideologies, and historical situations which "feel true," which "enliven," "actuate," and help to unify the various needs and potentials that make up the raw material of ego identity.[14] Identity formation is the great task of youth; it is during youth that most of the physiological and social givens which must find a place in the grand synthesis of identity finally make their appearance. What are some of these givens which make up the components of identity? In one place Erikson gives a list. He writes: "The process of identity formation emerges as an *evolving configuration*—a configuration which is gradually established by successive ego syntheses and resyntheses throughout childhood; it is a configuration gradually integrating *constitutional givens, idiosyncratic libidinal needs, favored capacities, significant identifications, effective defenses, successful sublimations, and consistent roles."* [15] Another way to think about the components entering into an ego synthesis is to understand it as a realignment of the *natural hierarchy* of one's developmental stages with the emergence of sexual awakening and the anticipation of vocational choice and marital commitment specific to youth and young adulthood.

Generative man has achieved a viable identity and a discernible style of fidelity. Identity and fidelity are not static formations. Instead, as Erikson says, they are configurations, they have certain contours and boundaries, but their inner structure and outer limits are constantly undergoing a change within a larger sense of continuity. The identity of generative man has its various parts, its various components. The unity that marks his identity is not a rigid tyranny exerting an absolute rule over the various parts. The parts have a kind of individuality of their own; they enjoy a relatively individuated status. For instance, one can perceive one's sexuality as relatively differentiated from one's role as parent, just as one can differentiate one's personal style of parenthood from those earlier identifications with one's own parents. Yet the various parts possess an overall unity, hierarchical ordering, and larger aim. Because this synthesis has occurred, generative man has confronted and overcome the possibility of *confusion* with regard to his identity and *cynicism* with regard to his commitments and fidelities. Out of a variety of alternative self-definitions and a range of possible commitments, he has forged a workable unity. And because he has within himself a workable identity and a sense of what is trustworthy in himself and in life, generative man can present himself to succeeding generations as a tangible identity from whom they can learn and against whom they can test their own emerging self-definitions. He can also present himself as one who can be trusted, just as he can help guide others to their own discovery of that which is worthy of their commitment and loyalty.

Generative man has the capacity for *intimacy* and the virtue of *love.*[16] To say this is to assert something which is at once very concrete and very symbolic. Intimacy and love are general qualities of life; yet they are also attributes that emerge and crystallize during specific periods. They often refer to the strengths found in the arrangements between a man and a woman expressed through the institution of marriage. What we say here about intimacy and love is focused in marriage, but extends far beyond it. The unmarried must be, in principle, capable of their own kind of intimacy and their own very specific, even bodily, forms of love, although neither quality may ever express itself in actual sexual union with commitment to a selected mate.

Of course, love, in the broadest sense of the word, is best expressed for Erikson by what he generally calls "care," the virtue specific to the "generative stage" of life. In one place he writes that "love in the evolutionary and generational sense is, I believe, the transformation of the love received throughout the preadolescent stage of life into the care given to others during adult life." [17] But Erikson is struck by an additional fact which must have had important evolutionary meaning —the "fact that man, over and above sexuality, develops a selectivity of love." [18] Man appears to have had the dreary habit of selecting specific mates to whom he commits himself and with whom he develops a shared identity and a shared style of life. In the context of this shared identity the partners perform complementary acts, both sexual and otherwise. The phylogenetic purpose of such selectivity, widely visible throughout the animal kingdom, is to provide a stable, stylized, and ritually effective context for the birth and nurture of children.

At the human level, intimacy and love are important complements to this stabilizing process. But in addition, they are designed to guarantee the human partners a range of individuality and uniqueness not readily discernible in the animal kingdom. By intimacy, then, Erikson means the capacity for two people to develop a shared commitment without the loss of a sense of individual identity. Hence, intimacy requires a prior sense of identity strong enough to risk the development of a shared commitment without fear of complete self-loss in the process. Such a capacity for intimacy has great implications for adult genitality. Giving to another and being lost in orgasm occur most readily when identity is firm enough to be relaxed and momentarily suspended without fear of irretrievable self-loss. Love seems to be predicated on the capacity for intimacy. It is the capacity to enter into "the mutual regulation of complicated patterns" both in genital sexuality and in wider daily activities. It is the capacity to give and to receive that most profound of all affirmations which comes when relaxed and ready bodies are offered for mutual enjoyment. Finally, love is the capacity to tolerate and to affirm the polarity of the sexes, the differences which make for a natural division of labor, both in the celebrations of genital love and in the larger generative enterprises of caring for one's own and others' offspring. As Erikson writes: "Love, then, is mutuality of devotion forever subduing the antagonisms inherent in divided function." [19] Love is precisely that behavior, in genital sexuality and beyond it, which weaves individual personalities and divided functions into larger commitments while granting a portion of respect and uniqueness to the specific personalities involved.

Generative man is, in principle, capable of such a love and such an intimacy. He may not, because of circumstances or the specific shape of larger commitments, choose to exercise it in genital and marital expressions. But he has the capacity for the kind of intimacy and love specifically required by these institutions. Consequently, he has confronted and to a degree overcome that *self-absorption* which develops when one's identity is so fragile that one cannot risk sharing either one's body or one's hopes with other people. Because generative man can share his identity with others in mutual positive commitments, he can also mobilize his identity against that which he *repudiates,* i.e., that which he cannot affirm or accept and which he must finally isolate and possibly destroy.

Intimacy and love, as we have discussed them here, are phase-specific developmental tasks which generative man has integrated into his maturity. It is now possible to give a more schematic statement of their meaning for mature generative man. *Intimacy and love are analogous to each other. They are parallel yet interacting modalities of giving and receiving—that is, of sharing. Intimacy refers to the forgiving and receiving identities. Love (at this level) refers to the capacity of giving and receiving complex patterns of bodily pleasure. Both intimacy and love take place within the context of "divided functions" and "larger commitments."* Obviously, this kind of love is very close to "productive love" as Fromm defines it. At the same time, it is very far from the concept of love as fusion and incest, as Brown defines it, or love as submission, which seems to be the only kind of love that Rieff believes to actually exist.

But, of course, intimacy and love, at this level, are never completed until set within the context of that "larger commitment" mentioned above. This larger commitment is summarized by the capacity for *generativity* and by the virtue of *care* which are, finally, the central characteristics of generative man and the final culmination of the meaning of *love* in the wider and grander sense of the word. We have already discussed the specific meaning of generativity and care. We need not repeat this discussion now. What is important to mention here, however, is that generativity and care rest upon and synthesize all the preceding modalities, capacities, and virtues of the earlier stages. Rooted as they well may be in instinctive patterns (preformed potentials activated by specific environments), they are also products of active and delicate syntheses. For generativity and care to occur, archaic modalities of trust and hope, autonomy and will, initiative and purpose, as well as more complex capacities such as industry and competence, identity and fidelity, intimacy and love, must come together in one grand synthesis whereby one finds one's highest fulfillment and most commanding sense of meaning in the establishment and care of succeeding generations.

Before we finish our discussion of love, we must be reminded that love as generativity and care is not offered on these pages as exhaustive of the full meaning of love. Psychoanalytic reflection may have something to learn about the meaning of love from the grand historic visions to be found in the traditions of world culture, both East and West. This is the question with which this study ends: What is the relationship between love and care as exhibited in generative man and the meaning of love in the great religious traditions of mankind, especially in Judaism and in Christianity? If the concept of generativity grants us a glimpse of man's archaeology as well as of his teleology, what must it mean, then, for man's final self-understanding? We assume that man's long journey through the centuries, the accumulated experience and the wealth of symbols which it has bestowed upon him, provides a potential meaning which psychoanalytic reflection does not exhaust. Yet we are also so bold as to suggest that the vision of generative man may indeed come to occupy a privileged position in the pantheon of Western myths. It may reveal the archaeological foundations of these myths; but in addition, its own implicit teleology may come to occupy an interpretative perspective from which older myths will be reinterpreted or assigned new meaning.

Erikson himself believes that there may be meanings in life which transcend the task of the "maintenance of the world" in the cycle of the generations. The last stages of life point to these more transcendent realms of meaning. So Erikson defines the capacity for *integrity* and the virtue of *wisdom* as the strength to accept one's individual life cycle "as something that had to be." [20] There must be, then, in old age a double movement of "acceptance" and "resignation" if the shadows of regret, despair, and disappointment are to be overcome. Resignation cannot come, of course, unless one is able to relativize one's own history as readily as one can accept it as inevitable. The detachment and transcendence of old age must, for generative man, still be focused in an active concern with the maintenance of the world. "Wisdom, then, is detached concern with life itself, in the face of death itself," writes

Erikson. This dialectic of detachment and concern, of transcendent yet active involvement, marks the tension present in generative man in his later years. But it also points to the tension between generativity as a sphere of meaning and the hermeneutics of all possible symbols of transcendence.

Generative Man and the Meaning of Time

Generative man has a discernible experience of time. The center of his time perspective is in the present, but it is a present that grows out of the past and actively leans toward the future. Although he is free from domination by the past, he is renewed by its "creative beginnings" and guided by its traditions. At the same time, his orientation toward the future is a higher statement of that original hope first experienced at the beginning of life; it is a delicate balance of passive openness and active mastery.

Generative man lives under a regime of relaxed and flexible ego mastery; this is the reason why the center of his time perspective is in the present. Whereas the superego is the organ of the blind past and the id is the organ of the utopian future, the ego is the organ of the present.[21]

Generative man, although freed from domination by the past, still uses the past as a resource. He orients himself to the past in two senses. First, he selectively affirms the past as a source to present mastery. "To the ego," Erikson tells us, "the past is not an inexorable process, experienced only as preparation for an impending doom; rather, the past is part of a present mastery which employs a convenient mixture of forgetting, falsifying, and idealizing to fit the past to the present, but usually to an extent which is neither unknowingly delusional nor knowingly dishonest." [22] This orientation to the past we have already discussed in our earlier review of generative man's relation to morality and to the superego.

But there is a second use of the past as a resource. Here the past provides a ground of renewal, an original beginning, which becomes a present source of strength for the ego. This orientation to the past is suggested by Ernst Kris's concept of "regression in service of the ego." It is what Heinz Hartmann meant by "regressive adaptation." For Erikson, this means a controlled regression on the part of the ego to that state of basic trust which characterizes the first stages of life. Such a state is often recaptured, not by literal regression to infancy, but by a return to those basic *modalities* most in balance then. Often certain experiences later in life can activate these modalities. Erikson believes that prayer, the Scriptures, and the concept of justification by faith did just this for Luther. For in all these things, Luther found a higher "matrix"—not a mother substitute, but a motherly mode—which helped him to recapture a "passivity" which was really "only a regained ability to be active with his oldest and most neglected modes." [23] Erikson believes that the German word *passivisch* contains much of what both he and Luther might have in mind. *Passivisch* "is more actively passive, as passific would be." Erikson writes:

> I think that the difference between the old modalities of *passive* and *active* is really that between *erleben* and *handeln,* of being in the state of *experiencing* or of *acting.* Meaningful implications are lost in the flat word *passivity*—among them the total attitude of living receptively and through the senses, of willingly "suffering" the voice of one's intuition and of living a *Passion:* that total passivity in which man regains, through considered self-sacrifice and self-transcendence, his active position in the face of nothingness, and thus is saved. Could this be one of the psychological riddles in the wisdom of the "foolishness of the cross"? [24]

It is often in the face of nothingness, the situation of next to total collapse, that one is forced to rediscover and regain these past modalities of the beginning. Erikson finds such a phenomenon in the drive for the so-called "rock bottom" experience present in so many young people who are suffering from identity confusion.[25] They, too, in a way often quite uncontrolled, plunge toward a regressed state in search of a basic foundation of trust. Sometimes, with the help of an interested and understanding therapist, such a ground of trust is rediscovered and a process of rebuilding begins. Sometimes this search for the rock bottom fails, partially because it was never solidly established in the first place.

This subtle dialect of passive and active as an experience of renewal from the past is the ground for generative man's orientation toward the future. As we have seen, it is the ground of his hope. One's hope for the future evolves out of a past where one has learned that the "things" and "people" of the world will reciprocate "one's physical and emotional needs in expectable ways." [26] This kind of hope, once established, remains "independent of the verifiability of 'hopes'" for specifically wished for things. Because hope in the large sense of the word exists, smaller renunciations become easier to accept. The ego, as the irreducible center of perception and memory, "learns" to "train . . . expectations on what promises to prove possible." Yet this orientation is not merely passive; it does not simply open itself to the blessings and accept the disappointments of the future. It is also active: "it proves itself able to change facts, even as faith is said to move mountains." [27] Hence, Erikson, as always, gives us an ecological definition of time based on the concept of "mutual regulation." Generative man, through his hope, regulates the future as the future regulates him. As Erikson writes, "from an evolutionary point of view, it seems that hope must help man to approximate a measure of that rootedness possessed by the animal world, in which instinctive equipment and environment, beginning with the maternal response, verify each other, unless catastrophe overtakes the individual or the species." [28]

Erikson's ecological view of time presents a different equation between past, present, and future than can be found in the work of any of the other authors we are studying—even Fromm, with whom he has the greatest affinity. Viewed from the category of time, psychological man is all "present" just as we said earlier that he is all "activity." The distance between psychological man and his past, his early superego as well as his infantile spontaneity and trust, amounts to estrangement. The ego as technical reason is so much in control that it has little to learn from either the past or the present. Similarly, psychological man would find it strange indeed, I fear, to speak of hope. Certainly, things will keep "running" and "moving." He may look forward to the small pleasures that tomorrow may bring, just as he enjoys those of the present, but psychological man receives the future no more spontaneously than he does the past. He who expects nothing from the past can certainly expect nothing from the future. Psychological man's spontaneous continuities with the past and the future are broken; all has been filtered through the skepticisms of consciousness and the analytic restraint of technical reason. For generative man, much more is unconscious and far more is spontaneous. Since the ego, for generative man, is a larger, mostly unconscious organ of organization and regulation than is the case with the ego of psychological man, much of the past and the future is unconsciously experienced, tasted, and sorted before the higher processes of consciousness ever come into play. Hence, generative man enjoys a more spontaneous continuity with both the past and the future even though finally he has a sense of active yet flexible mastery over both.

Dionysian man, of course, is really all past, all nostalgia for the union he once knew but has lost. His project is to recapture the past, at least the past as union. At the same time, he seeks to repudiate all false moralities and superego formations of that past ruled by the dominion of the death instinct. Dionysian man has no future. Or, more accurately, we should say that his future is his reclaimed past. That is his hope. When the past and the present come together, there will be no future, only the present, i.e., only eternity. Generative man indeed knows, as does Dionysian man, that the future and the past are intimately related. The hope for the future is grounded, for both Dionysian man and generative man, on the trusts of the past. But because generative man experienced the growth, differentiation, and complexification of experience as real, and not simply as the result of repression, the hope for the future is a *new hope* for a higher union. It is a higher union of differentiated bodies and conscious minds in reciprocal relation to one another. In addition, it is a hope still very much concerned about the mundane affairs of men. One has the impression that even in heaven, generative man will spend his time looking down at his progeny, applauding their victories and mourning their defeats. Although Erikson says nothing about it, one feels that he might appreciate the Christian concept of the "community of the saints." For here the concept of the continuity of the generations is preserved, even if it now takes the form of the continuity between the living and the dead.

As we have seen, productive man rejects the past as superego and morality on both the individual and the collective levels. On the other hand, he affirms the past as a ground and a model for the higher union sought for in the future. But productive man's orientation toward the future is far more active, far more Promethean, than is the case with generative man. Although Fromm celebrates the virtues of the spontaneous life, when it comes to the future he seems to reject the idea that the future in the form of God, nature, or time will bring its gifts independent of man's active efforts to form and shape them. Whereas generative man is a balance between active and passive modalities, productive man is predominantly activeness; the messianic time will come when man brings it, and not before. Skeptical of all eschatologies which overemphasize the passiveness of the role of man, Fromm suddenly becomes Faustian when speaking about man's project for the future. Here, more than anywhere else, the true lack of spontaneity, the latent hyperrationality of productive man, reveals itself. In the end, productive man trusts neither the past nor the future as much as he should. We suspect that he wants to think and plan and work for everything. We fear that productive man, regardless of his rhetoric about play and spontaneity, is, indeed, not entirely unlike his creator —a trifle too serious.

Generative Man and the Social World:
Life as Creative Ritualization

We have called generative man a creative ritualizer. Some people will think that this is a contradiction in terms. To many, ritual is associated with the routine, the boring, and the compulsive. To them ritual is the very opposite of creativity. The fact that the two terms belong together in describing generative man goes to the heart of his uniqueness.

Creative ritualization, I will argue, sums up generative man's attitude toward his social world. Generative man is a special kind of political man, yet he is different from most men of politics as we see them today. Generative man believes in institutions, just as does political man. But political man today is very busy building or changing institutions; he knows very little about living with institutions, caring for them, and maintaining them.

Generative man is political man with an extra measure. He not only creates, he maintains; he not only gives birth, he cares and sustains. He not only knows how to plan, but he has a sense of the unconscious and organic factors pertinent to special traditions, particular moralities, and regional identities which must be included before any plan can become a living reality. Generative man limits his creativity to that which he can comfortably and responsibly live with from day to day.

Generative man is a man very much concerned with institutions, both large and small. Erikson certainly is aware of the importance of large institutions; he has documented the importance of salmon-fishing for the Yurok, of buffalo-hunting for the Sioux, and of industrialization for modern man.

Erikson is also interested in small institutions; more than that, he is interested in the continuity between the large and the small. In our day, small institutions suffer greatly from the dislocations produced by the vicissitudes of the gigantic secondary institutions of modern society. If the modern world is to regain its health, Erikson believes that small institutions must regain their strength, and a new continuity between small institutions and large ones must be discovered or established. And finally, a new ideology, containing both universal and particular elements, must be found to give meaning, solidarity, and controlled change to both.

Erikson sees the modern world simultaneously fragmented by a plethora of contemporary pluralisms and stultified by the silent advance of deadening conformity. How can both of these things be true? Erikson's answer is this: modern life, marked as it is by an irresponsible expansiveness, is devoid of *the fundamental ritualizations that protect individuality and produce real community*. Without a ritual fabric to life, community becomes conformity and individuality becomes normless privatism and destructive egoism.

Erikson gives us an epigenetic theory of ritualization. In contrast to Fromm, who seems primarily interested in the grand ritualizations of public and cultic life, Erikson is interested in both the everyday rituals and the grand official rituals as well as in the continuity between the two. In defining ritual, Erikson turns away from clinical definitions, which often equate it with the repetition compulsion, and from anthropological definitions, which often equate it with "rites" conducted by a community of adults. Instead, he looks to ethology and to new developments in psychoanalysis. The greeting ritual between the newborn gosling and its mother described so eloquently by Konrad Lorenz is an excellent example. At the human level, ritual is an "agreed-upon interplay between at least two persons who repeat it at meaningful intervals and in recurring contexts; and this interplay should have adaptive value for the respective egos of both participants." [29] To understand ritual better, Erikson tries to define it at the level of the earliest and first instance of the joint action of smiles, offered breast, and searching mouth found in the feeding situation between mother and child. Erikson writes:

> If observed for several days (and especially in a milieu not one's own) it becomes clear that this daily event is highly formalized, in that the mother seems to feel obliged (and to be not a little pleased) to repeat a performance arousing in the infant predictable responses, which encourage her, in turn, to proceed. Such formalization, however, is hard to describe. It is at the same time *highly individual* ("typical for the mother") and also tuned to the particular infant; and yet it is also *stereotyped* along traditional lines—as we can see best in cultures, classes, or families other than our own. The whole procedure is, of course, superimposed on the periodicity of vital physical needs; it is an *enhanced routine* which keeps close to the requirements of survival. We have every reason to believe, however, that it is much more than this, and that, as an *emotional* as well as a *practical* necessity for both mother and infant, it can be properly evaluated only as a small but tough link in the whole formidable sequence of generations.[30]

Later, Erikson lists some of the polar elements to be found in all vital ritual. Vital ritual is always based on the "reciprocal needs" of at least two people. It is a "practical" activity, yet it has "symbolic" meaning. It is highly "personal," yet it involves a style characteristic of a "larger" group. It heightens a sense of individual "belongingness," yet it protects a sense of personal "distinctiveness." It is "playful," yet it is "formalized" both in detail and in the entire procedure. It is "familiar" through repetition, yet full of the "surprise of recognition" renewed. It provides an "unambiguous" context in which to pursue and satisfy needs, yet it helps overcome the "ambiguity" which besets those who daily care for and minister to one another.

These are the marks of effective ritual. The epigenetic principle means that these elements can be found in both the ontogenetic early and late, both the phylogenetic simple and complex. But the epigenetic principle, as it applies to ritualization, means more than this. Ritualization also gives expression to the schedule of development as Erikson has described it. Erikson develops a very complex theory of the relationship between the developmental schedule, the phase-specific rituals which men devise to meet specific developmental crises, and the grand adult institutions of *religion, law, theater, technology, ideology,* and *marriage.*

When psychiatrists talk, stouter intellectual types who stalk the corridors of universities tend to close their minds, assuming that, as always, the psychiatrist is up to his old tricks of reducing everything to a childhood complex. This habit of mind of men who generally pride themselves on their broad-mindedness has made it difficult for Erikson's social psychology of institutions to be fully understood. The epigenetic principle means that the rudiments of things late are always to be found in things early, and that the broadened form of things early is always to be found in things late. We need not labor Erikson's correlation of adult institutions with childhood crises. Let it simply be noted that Erikson believes that the early "numinous" experience of an affirming presence and a confirming face receives a higher statement in adult *religion;* that adult institutions related to the *law* are continuous with those first experiences of limitation and those first "judicious" discriminations of right and wrong which generally emerge during the second year of life; and that adult *stories* and *dramas* of guilt and restitution are an advanced form of those first experiences of self-recrimination inevitably connected with the initiatives of the age of play. Erikson never tires of assuring his reader that he is "not suggesting a simple causal relationship between the infantile stage and the adult institution, in the sense that adult rituals 'only' satisfy persisting infantile needs in disguise." [31] Nor is the image of God on the mature level " 'only' a replica of the mother's inclined face or the father's powerful countenance." To the contrary:

> Man's epigenetic development assures that each of his distinct and protracted childhood stages specializes in one of the major elements (i.e., the numinous, the judicial) which hold together human institutions, each binding together a new set of instinctive patterns and of instinctual energies, of mental and of social capacities so as to assure the continuity of that element, throughout the individual's life and through the sequence of generations. In all epigenetic development, however, a ritual element, once evolved, must be progressively reintegrated on each higher level, so that it will become an essential part of all subsequent stages. The numinous element, for example, reappears in judicial ritualizations and in judiciary rituals as the aura which attaches to a personified or abstract image of Justice, or to the concrete persons who as justices are invested with the symbolism and the power of that image. But this also means that neither the numinous nor the judicial elements, although they can dominate a particular stage or a particular institution, can "make up" a ritual all by themselves: always, the whole inventory must be present. [32]

But here Erikson describes an ideal state of things. Modern institutions lack the very unity and integrity about which he speaks. Religious institutions seem devoid of judiciousness, and legal institutions appear to be without the confirming presence that gives judiciousness its sense of humanity.

During the school years and at adolescence, young people search for ways to fit their acquired skills and their broadened historical perspectives into adult rituals both in the realm of technology and in the sphere of political ideology. Generative man is the one who can bring about "coherence and continuity between childhood ritualization and pervasive technological and political trends." But if generative man is to be a ritualizer, he too must have his rituals. This is the true story which modern liberals must learn, for it is they who—reducing all to reason, clarity, debate, and tentativeness—threw away old rituals and replaced them with nothing new. Having no rituals of their own, they had no sanction to become ritualizers of their children or of subsequent generations. There is a place for *official* ritualizations. For these "sanction the adult in his double role as the agent of daily ritualization in the life of the younger generation and as the consumer, as it were, of those formalized rituals which integrate his own childhood ritualizations." Erikson gives credit to Heinz Hartmann when he asserts that the adult ego has its need for a " 'detour through the archaic' in order to gather up the strands of re-progression to a higher level of integration." [33]

Generative man is a religious man. His religion provides him with a commanding world image and a vigorous ritual enactment which sums up, yet somehow renews and enriches, the rituals of everyday life, both those of his children and of himself, and those of his own childhood. His religion sanctions him to indulge in a "generalized generativity of institutions." [34] He too must become, to some extent, a "numinous model" and must learn to act as the "judge and the transmitter of traditional ideals or of innovating ideas."

Yet he accomplishes this task by keeping in close contact with the needs and energies of the young, both in himself and in others. Institutions are kept strong because they are constantly made to contribute to the acquisition of "strength" and "virtue" in the young. When institutions actively contribute to the strength of the young, they in turn will receive energy and devotion from the young.

> I would posit a mutual activation and replenishment between the virtues emerging in each individual life cycle and the strengths of human institutions. In whatever way we may learn to demonstrate this, virtue in the individual and the spirit of institutions have evolved together, are one and the same strength. . . . Without them [the virtues and strengths of youth], institutions wilt; but without the spirit of institutions pervading the patterns of care, love, instruction and training, no virtue could emerge from the sequence of generations.[35]

There is little doubt that generative man will fulfill this mandate by striving to prune the chaotic largeness and expansiveness of modern life in its cities, its industries, its government, and its science. Generative man will not only attempt to make the world more man-sized, he will work to make it more child-sized. No society has ever excluded its children so completely from contact and participation in its adult societies as has modern society. Modern society's pace, its specialization, its psychological and spatial isolation, its rapid innovation, and its total lack of continuity with the schedules and rituals of the young should leave us with little wonder that young people grow up hating the very institutions (almost without exception) which they are supposed someday to join. There is little doubt that generative man will be much like productive man; he too will probably be committed to some kind of communitarian society (if not a communitarian socialism). About such things Erikson says very little. He does believe, however, that tomorrow's world will be built upon the emerging industrial and technological capacities of modern man. But there is little doubt that generative man will exercise a firm if not ruthless grip, an unflinching control over their thoughtless proliferation. Generative man will doubtless be an industrialist and technologist *of a sort*. But more than any of his recent predecessors, he will be interested in the ritual fabric and the ecological integrity of the society that technology serves. The neighborhood, the home, the church, and the school, as well as his public life, factory, store, business, and assembly will be given a "participatory" character. Yes, generative man believes in participatory democracy. Why should he not, since his is a psychology of mutual recognition? He believes in the face-to-face encounter and the heightened sense of activeness and mastery that it provides. But participatory democracy will have for him *its ritual patterns and its regulated actions*. Generative man does not need to call for a vote every time the toilet is cleaned, nor does he feign competence or exercise power in all spheres of life. He is not hyperpolitical, as is productive man; nor is he hyperconscious about all of the world's goings-on.

Because all situations are reciprocal to generative man, he can both exercise authority and delegate it to others. He is willing in certain places and for certain tasks to have followers, just as he is willing, at times, to be a follower of others. By definition, he can be a leader and a teacher of children, and this, we would hope, with consummate skill. In an age when teachers are generally held in disrepute (not because of their incompetence but because society's values are elsewhere), the teacher will once again become the man accorded great respect. Generative man can share his wisdom freely with the young, yet he can also let their growing strengths gain their own autonomy and style. His role as teacher will not prevent him from being renewed, strengthened, instructed, and possibly even corrected by those he teaches.

Generative man will try to slow the world down. He will assume a more leisurely pace, not because he is lazy, but because he wants to spread his energies, in a measured way, over a broader field. Yet he knows that the world will not stop. He is fully aware that social change and cultural readjustment have become an inevitable part of the modern world. He knows, then, that the time span in the cycle of the generations has become shortened. Fathers must remain fathers, both in the symbolic and literal senses. But they may, in the future, be more frequently assisted by older sons and young men and women just entering adulthood. So Erikson writes that the younger generation, "too, will be (or already is) divided more clearly into the older- and the younger-young generation, where the older young will have to take over (and are eager to take over) much of the direction of the conduct of the younger young." [36] Erikson believes that it is the great task of generative man to develop the "ethical potential of our older youth—those who are so close to their own childhood, so close to full adulthood, and so intensively sensitive to the ethical and generational needs of both. Generative man in the generative society will compose himself into a chain of interacting and responsible people, all of whom have their age-specific ethical responsibilities and roles, all of which are aimed at giving generative strength to individuals and generative integrity to society as a whole.

Generative Man and the "Other"

Generative man is both a specialist and a universalist. By a specialist, we mean that generative man is a member of a pseudospecies, and a pseudospecies is by definition a community with a specialized perspective on life. Generative man shares in the particularity of his pseudospecies and in its rationalization and defense of provincial moralities and ideologies. But generative man is also a universalist and strives for a universal generative style relevant to all people and to the children of all people. But his universalism is not a discarnate universalism; he does not speak abstractly about love, goodness, truth, and beauty from some point in the sky midway between heaven and earth. Yet he does indeed believe that such values exist. Universal values, for generative man, grow out of particular histories and they always carry their developmental and epigenetic origins with them even though they may transform them as they evolve.

This is why generative man is something of a synthesis of the dominant polarity marking Western civilization—the polarity between the new *technologist* and the new *universalist*. This polarity, as we have seen, is best expressed in all its brute antagonism by the divisions which beset the youth cultures of Western societies—the divisions between the technologists who "know what they are doing" and the humanist youth who "mean what they are saying."

To say that generative man is a technologist is not to say that he is exclusively or even predominantly a technologist. We are saying simply that he can accept his continuity with immediately preceding character types which have evolved from the specializations of his pseudospecies, i.e., Protestant man, mercantile man, industrial man, and now technological man. Generative man is primarily generative and only secondarily technological. And of course to suggest that he is even secondarily a technologist does not mean that he is necessarily a technologist in the specifically professional sense. Generative man can live in the technological world and sympathize with its strengths even as he guards against its weaknesses. *Most concretely, however, it means that he can work on the ideological border line between the moralities of technology and a universal generative ethic.*

Generative man can live with, sometimes defend, but never absolutize, the specializations of his pseudospecies. Yet, in contrast to some universalists—debased forms of humanist, Christian, existential, mystical, or communist men—he never deludes himself into thinking that man can live without his specializations. This is part of the key to his capacity to relate to the "other." Accepting the necessity of specialization without absolutizing his own, he can permit others to have their specializations without feeling unduly threatened by them. Specializations of a community of people are the particular ways in which they have had to organize their lives: they are doing "their thing," so to speak. These specializations are a result of a combination of regional circumstances, inherited wisdom, accidental discoveries, and applied intelligence, all elaborated and given special meaning by the imagination and playful synthesizing capacities of the better minds of a given culture. These specializations impose order and familiarity on the lives of the people who subscribe to them; everything outside this specialized culture often appears chaotic, formless, and evil. Generative man, however, because of his twofold commitment to the pseudospecies of which he is immediately a part as well as to the larger species of which he is genuinely a part, refuses to regard the specializations of others as mere chaos, evil, or threat. In the same vein, he is able to accept his own inherited specializations without undue remorse or pride.

The universal perspective of generative man impels him to take seriously the provincialities of the stranger; in fact, he tries always to discern the relationship between the universal and the particular in the other. Yet he goes even farther than this. Generative man is likely to look at another specialization as a "strength" which his own pseudospecies has failed (often for both good and bad reasons) to develop. This is where generative man differs so profoundly from the new technological man. The technologist is likely to consider his perspective on life as evolutionarily superior to those of other people. The technological youth feels there are no limits to his specializations. Erikson writes:

> No need is felt to limit expansionist ideals so long as certain old-fashioned rationalizations continue to provide the hope (a hope that has long been

an intrinsic part of an American ideology) that in regard to any possible built-in evil in the very nature of super-organizations, appropriate brakes, corrections, and amendments will be invented in the nick of time and without any undue investment of strenuously new principles.[37]

The technologist believes that unlimited power and invention will balance themselves out in the long run. In view of possible foreign and domestic conflicts which come from the mad rush for power and the shocks of uncontrollable change, technological man believes that his specialization will prove workable and is willing to do a reasonable amount of "killing and of dying" to prove that he is right. It seldom occurs to the technological true believer that his own specialization may have its weaknesses and that the specialization of the other may have its strengths and may contain wisdom which he must not only tolerate but learn to include within his own growing identity.

The assumptions of technological man are often shared by the contemporary social science disciplines in the United States. Erikson has frequently contributed special articles to symposia on certain groups in American life often considered problematic, e.g., blacks and women. These groups can also sometimes appear as the "other"—as people who do not quite fit into the scheme of things in American life. In writing about the American Negro and about American women, Erikson gives us insight into the mentality of generative man as he contemplates the so-called "other." Erikson seems to be perpetually reversing the logic generally found in the social sciences. Other social scientists are forever telling us what is different and problematic about these groups. Erikson is forever discerning their strengths and what it is that technological man has to learn from them.

For instance, it is commonly assumed in social science literature that the American Negro suffers from a negative identity. It is also widely assumed that this negative identity has been imposed upon the black community by the dominant white community, that it is in many of its details the reverse or the opposite of the positive identity of white people, and that the Negro community not only has accepted this stereotype in order to survive but has embellished it and sometimes viciously used it against itself. But Erikson sees in the Negro community something more than "cultural deprivation" and sees in its so-called negative identity something more than simply "defensive adjustments to the dominant white majority." Erikson asks: "Do we (and can we) know enough about the relationship of positive and negative elements *within* the Negro personality and within the Negro community? This alone would reveal how negative is negative and how

positive, positive." [38] Erikson also asks: When psychological tests given
to blacks characterize Negro males, as "feminine" (because some of
them "want to be a singer") or as having "strong feelings," does this
not reveal something about the one-sided image of masculinity which
reigns over the middle-class males of the white majority? Why can
black men (or men from Naples) not sing and feel strongly without
becoming subject to the charge of being effeminate? Furthermore, can
the emerging black identity afford to write off the Negro mother as
"dominating" and "controlling" without determining the deeper meaning of the stability that she granted and the affirmation she freely
bestowed on every child whether legitimate or illegitimate, wanted or
unwanted? Or can the premature sensuality of the crowded and hope-
less ghetto be sociologically rationalized without comprehending the
deeper intrinsic values of affirmation and joy which even these tran-
sient relationships often bestowed upon their partners?

With regard to womanhood, especially in the Western world, Erikson turns the tables in a similar fashion. In so doing, he steers a pre-
carious course between progressivists who assert no difference what-
soever between men and women and those others who continue to
emphasize differences to the distinct disadvantage of the individual
and the social dignity of women. The distorted and unhealthy image
of women prevalent in Western society must be understood in relationship to the one-sidedness of the Western understanding of men and
of the society which men have made and indeed dominate. Men—
following the propensity of their body styles to intrude, to build, to
build high, to go fast, and to dramatize collisions, collapse, or down-
fall—have turned Western society into a parody of a little boy's play-
room. What is an evolutionary and ecologically vital tendency in men
to be concerned with the *exterior* of things—to construct, to aggress,
and sometimes to attack—has now become disconnected from the
larger task of generating and maintaining the species. Erikson asks:
"Do we not see the themes of the toy microcosm dominating an expanding human space: height, penetration, and speed; collision, ex-
plosion—and cosmic superpolice?" [39]

It is in relationship to an imprudent and uncontrolled masculine
expansionism that Erikson assesses the so-called negative identity of
women—their alleged passivity, their weakness, their preoccupation
with the private, the inner, and things pertaining to nurture and care.
Behind this negative identity Erikson believes there lies hidden a more
positive truth; in the context of the divided functions of the species,
women may indeed have more of a propensity toward the intimate

details of care, nurture, continuity, and protection. Certainly these tendencies, to some extent grounded in the very morphology of woman's generative capacities, have often been used to assign to her an inferior place in society. And certainly at times she has accommodated herself to this domination with "masochistic" self-denial and a self-accepted sense of inferiority. Erikson supports the drive for feminine equality. And this means to him full access to the public, political, and professional world with all its rewards, demands, and responsibilities. But to him, equality must never mean equivalence. He hopes that women will enter the public world not simply to imitate men. To emphasize divided function is not to discriminate. Life must have its polarities. Yet these polarities must always be mutual, reciprocal, and overlapping; they must never be discrete, overdifferentiated, or antagonistic. Hence, women must integrate their true feminine potentials into their own consciousness and into the wider society of which they must necessarily become a part. In addition, men must bring their masculine preoccupations into closer proximity with the central tasks of nurture and the maintenance of the cycle of the generations. "Each sex," we are told, "can transcend itself to feel and to represent the concerns of the other. For even as real women harbor a legitimate as well as a compensatory masculinity, so real men can partake of motherliness— if permitted to do so by powerful mores." [40] But if woman gains emancipation and liberation, she must do it on her own terms and not on the basis of those laid down by men. "A truly emancipated woman . . . ," Erikson believes, "would refuse to accept comparisons with more 'active' male proclivities as a measure of her equivalence, even when, or precisely when, it has become quite clear that she can match man's performance and competence in most spheres of achievement. True equality can only mean the right to be uniquely creative." [41]

At all points, then, generative man finds in the "other" a particularity that contains a truth which is often complementary to his own partial truth. The evolution of this great congress of conflicting identities into a larger, "more inclusive identity" is the grand task of generative man at the cultural level. The coming universal technology will pose the demand (but not the specific details) for wider and more inclusive identities. If wider identities are to come about, the past of old identities must be incorporated (although inevitably reworked) into the more universal elements of a new future. It is, as we have said before, the work of ideology to bridge the gap between old moralities and universal ethics. It is Erikson's firm belief that man must learn to handle the threats to identity caused by rapid social change, pluralism, and cultural dislocation which in turn are produced by the emerging technology. To do this, man must develop a program whereby provincial identities are made ever more inclusive. Unless this is done, the people will gradually tear the world apart in an effort to defend and rebuild those struggling pseudospecies, both old and new, which seem ever more intensely bent upon exterminating one another.

We should not be surprised, then, to learn that Erikson, a Western psychoanalyst and a disciple of Freud, turns to the East and to Gandhi for the ultimate solution to the treatment of the "other." (Actually, Gandhi is a strange combination of East and West.) For Gandhi's philosophy of Satyagraha is indeed a marvelous synthesis; it is the first great application of the Christian doctrine of love to the field of political life. Yet it is more than this. It is something very instinctual, yet controlled and guided by the highest reaches of intelligence and insight. As a method to advance the evolution of man toward more inclusive identities in the present conflict of classes and nations, it integrates what is most fundamental in animals to the highest level of human reflection and self-discipline. It is the supreme method for generative man in his effort to be true to both the pseudospecies and the universal species in the grand project of generating and caring for the cycle of the generations.

Erikson sees important parallels between Gandhi's method of Satyagraha, the basic meaning of the Golden Rule, the ritual conflicts between animals, and the true essence of the psychoanalytic relationship. Erikson sees an important relationship between the meaning of the Golden Rule, as he interprets it, and the true meaning of Satyagraha. In a 1963 essay entitled "The Golden Rule in the Light of New Insight," Erikson defines this ancient truth found in various forms in so many cultures and religions in the following way:

> *Truly worthwhile acts enhance a mutuality between the doer and the other—a mutuality which strengthens the doer even as it strengthens the other.* Thus, the "doer" and "the other" are partners in one deed. Seen in the light of human development, this means that the doer is activated in whatever strength is *appropriate to his age, stage, and condition,* even as he activates in the other the strength appropriate to *his* age, stage, and condition. Understood this way, the Rule would say that it is best to do to another what will strengthen you even as it will strengthen him—that is, what will develop his best potentials even as it develops your own.[42]

In his book on Gandhi, Erikson states his amended Golden Rule somewhat differently: "I suggested that (ethically speaking) a man should act in such a way that he actualizes both in himself and in the other such forces as are ready for a heightened mutuality." [43] Gandhi himself had his own version of the Golden Rule which he enunciated one day under the babul tree in Ahmedabad in his first full employment of the principles of Satyagraha against the millowners of this city. Here he said: *"That line of action is alone justice which does not harm either party to a dispute.'"* [44] This, for Gandhi, was the principle of ahimsa. Erikson is certain that the "harm" to which Gandhi refers means more than simple bodily harm; it includes an "inseparable combination of economic disadvantage, social indignity, loss of self-esteem, and latent vengeance." In other words, ahimsa implies a pledge not "to violate another person's essence."

Hence, the principle of Satyagraha was a method of finding "truth in action." It was a method of finding the "true" and the "good" for both parties locked in the potential antagonism of divided functions. The truth that Gandhi sought was always a "relative" truth; it was a truth relative to the demands for justice in a limited situation and it was a truth relative to readiness (both developmental and historical) of the parties involved in the conflict. "The truth in any given encounter," Erikson tells us, "is linked with the developmental stage of the individual and the historical situation of his group: together, they help to determine the *actuality*, i.e., the potential for unifying action at a given moment." [45] In the context of the specific conflict in Ahmedabad, this meant securing "the good of the workers while safeguarding the good of the employers." [46]

But Satyagraha also meant being willing to die for the "truth" even though the truth to be sought and found was a relative one. But the willingness to die was always the last step. To apply Satyagraha, one must follow a set of clearly defined steps which are, in fact, a *ritual pattern* for conflict with the other in the name of truth. For instance, the injustice to be redressed is always carefully *studied* and clearly *defined* and circumscribed. Then an offer for arbitration is proposed. If this is refused or if arbitration breaks down, then further *preparation* of both parties through *publicity* and *announcement* of intentions must occur. Forms of *noncooperation* are decided upon by an action committee, *ultimatums* are announced, but resistance and nonviolent force are used with a measure never exceeding that which is necessary to reach a *defined goal*. Issues which are selected are always of immediate *practical* significance for the disadvantaged party, although generally they are of wider *symbolic* significance for the total community. At all times the resister is *willing to persuade* and *to be persuaded* as he attempts to find the truth which will actualize both parties to the dispute. [47]

Erikson believes that this kind of ritual conflict is grounded in the primitive animal instinctual tendency only recently clarified by the findings of ethology. The violence and brutality that man often ascribes to the beasts of the jungle is only a projection of a behavior which seems to be indeed limited only to the human species. For years, Erikson has been in dialogue with ethology, especially with the work of Konrad Lorenz on the *instinctive pacific behavior* of certain social animals.[48] Rather than positing an instinct to aggress or an instinct toward pacific behavior (as Lorenz himself appears to do), Erikson believes that there are in social animals (and possibly also in man) instinctive tendencies and potentialities which can, in certain circumstances, call upon quantities of drive energy for actualization. It is important to note that animals do not attack senselessly or randomly. They kill only for hunger and protection and then often without visible signs of anger. Moreover, conflict between members of a single species seems well regulated by dependable rituals which appear to be designed to determine the victor without bringing death or total humiliation to the loser. The example of ritual conflict among the Damstags seems to have impressed Erikson most. Here two stags trot parallel to each other and then turn to confront each other, never turning too quickly or taking unfair advantage through a surprise attack. When they are both ready, there is a powerful but harmless confrontation. The victor of this harmless wrestling is the stag which holds out the longer. The loser concedes defeat by means of a "ritualized disengagement" which normally stops the tournament. Erikson reaffirms Lorenz' observations when he writes: "Lorenz suggests that there are untold numbers of analogous rituals of pacification among the higher animals; but he also points out (most importantly for us) that de-ritualization at any point results in violence to the death." [49]

Erikson is certainly not saying that the kind of moral action which one finds in Satyagraha is simply a product of instinct. Yet he is saying that in "such ritualization" one may see "an evolutionary antecedent of man's inborn propensity for a moral inhibition that prevents undue violence." [50] What one sees in Satyagraha is, Erikson insists, "an instance of man's capacity to let inspiration, insight, and conviction 'cure' his instinctual complexity and to reinstate on a human level what in the animal is so innocently and yet so fatefully given." [51]

Erikson himself may be indulging in a bit of historical remythologizing when he points to the similarities between Satyagraha and the method of psychoanalytic treatment discovered and employed by Freud. And yet, what Erikson tells us here may indeed tell us much about what the moral meaning of psychoanalysis has *become,* not only because of the influence of Freud, but also because of the influence of a great army of followers, not the least of which is Erikson himself. Hence, in both encounters—the psychoanalytic and the one guided by Satyagraha—it has been revealed that

> only the militant probing of a vital issue by a nonviolent confrontation can bring to light what insight is ready on both sides. Such probing must be decided on only after careful study, but then the developing encounter must be permitted to show, step by step, what the power of truth may reveal and enact. At the end only a development which transforms both partners in such an encounter is truth in action; and such transformation is possible only where man learns to be nonviolent toward himself as well as toward others. Finally, the truth of Satyagraha and the "reality" of psychoanalysis come somewhat nearer to each other if it is assumed that man's "reality testing" includes an attempt not only to think clearly but also to enter into an optimum of mutual activation with others. But this calls for a combination of clear insight into our central motivations and pervasive faith in the brotherhood of man.[52]

Hence, Erikson gives us a combination of both history and synthesis. More than that, he has given us a new ideology for generative man. Generative man will have the simultaneous commitment of reducing the size, speed, and gigantism of modernity while slowly developing a more inclusive identity. He cherishes the past (his own as well as the past of the other) as well as seeking a more universal future. But he works actively to keep the future within manageable proportions; only then can the step from the past to a universal future be successfully taken.

Generative man works on the border line between ideology and universality just as he works with historical actualities. Therefore he treats the other in vastly different ways than does psychological man or Dionysian man or productive man. Psychological man sees the whole world forgetting its past and becoming like the West—simultaneously technological, affluent, and interior. Dionysian man can affirm only a universalism of regression. He fails to take particularity seriously even if that particularity is erroneously to be considered as only symptom and disease. Productive man can affirm only a universalism of progressive truth; he neither knows nor respects the relativities and historical actualities in which the universal is always to be found. Only generative man, of all the psychoanalytic types, seeks a universal generative ethic while respecting and profiting from each man's particular self-understanding and current historical actuality.

I must confess with apology that there is no tangible sociological evidence that generative man is indeed emerging as a dominant character type in the Western world. I cannot predict the future; rather, I raise only a possibility. I do not even say with certainty that generative man is a complete picture of the good man in the context of modernity. Generative man, as portrayed in these pages, has yet to confront in mature dialogue the great historical prototypes, in both the East and the West. Most specifically, I have not answered the question, posed at the beginning of this study, as to the final relationship between generative man and the great Christian image of man which has fed, in one way or another, most of the historical prototypes of the Western world. I have only answered what I believe to be the central testimony of the growing, most clinically responsible part of the psychoanalytic tradition.

That I admire generative man somewhat can hardly be denied. As a listener to the Christian tradition and as someone with some experience in the therapeutic arts, I find generative man a challenge to my imagination. I have little doubt that he is indeed a good man—in fact, a better man than any other we presently have. We could do far worse, and we may not be able to do better. I am convinced that the psychoanalytic tradition and its allied disciplines will continue in our midst for a long time, and it is my simple hope that their moral implications will be properly understood.

Yet I see no irreversible course to history which guarantees that generative man is an inevitability. Young people appear to be searching for someone like generative man, but I have yet to hear a young person mention his name or give tribute to another resembling him. Psychological man and Dionysian man seem to be vastly more popular for some. Technological man, the other-directed man, or the marketing man seem to be more tangible possibilities for others. The David Riesmans, the Philip Rieffs, the Marshall McLuhans, the Herman Kahns, with their respective predictions about the future of man, all may be on better sociological grounds. Productive man, the closest visible relative to generative man, seems to have been clearly repudiated by nearly everyone. Generative man may indeed suffer the same fate.

Yet there are stirrings which indicate that generative man could have a welcome reception. In the recent concern with ecology and with birth control, and in the concern to guarantee each child throughout the world a wanted and cared-for existence, we see some of the impulses that make up the moral sensibility of generative man. In the present-day experimentation with a more communitarian social existence, with smaller and more manageable units of social life, and with new forms of official and unofficial ritualization, we see evidence of some of the social concerns that have motivated Erikson for years, long before they became popular at the mass level. In the new realism about the limits of technology, in the new fears about uncontrolled urban expansionism and overcrowding, in the recent speculations about the effects of unbelievably rapid social change and "future shock," we find an emerging sensibility which may see generative man as a source of hope.

It seems strange that all the psychoanalytic ethicists reviewed here have shared a common faith in culture. Although social and biological forces are always given sufficient respect, each of these men believes that important and creative ideas engendered by fertile minds are ultimately the real inspiration for the dynamics of history. I can agree. What happens in the future will indeed be a "work of culture." If generative man is to have a place among the prototypes of the future, it will be because Erikson and men like him have successfully worked on the border line between the images of the past and the emerging cultural disciplines of the present to help form a grand new world image which will bridge our march from the present toward a more inclusive and universal future.

EPILOGUE

Generativity and Advance:
Postscript on Generative Man and Religion

A few months after Norman Brown finished the main body of *Life Against Death,* he added a final chapter entitled "The Resurrection of the Body." In it he argues that psychoanalysis is not the only resource present today which aspires to liberate the body from repression and sublimation. Most specifically, he cites the philosophy of organism espoused by Alfred North Whitehead and amplified by Joseph Needham in *Science and Civilization in China.* Brown tells us that "the resurrection of the body has been placed on the agenda not only by psychoanalysis, mysticism, and poetry, but also by the philosophical criticism of modern science." [1] He continues in this vein when he writes:

> Whitehead's criticism of scientific abstraction is, in psychoanalytical terms, a criticism of sublimations. His protest against "The Fallacy of Misplaced Concreteness" is a protest on behalf of the living body as a whole. [2]

Nothing could demonstrate more clearly Brown's undisciplined use of the history of ideas than this strange attempt to find an affinity between himself and Whitehead. It is true that Whitehead opposed the abstractionistic tendencies of modern science and that he celebrated the fullness of the human body. But it is also true that he believed that the evolutionary struggle for the survival of the human species is an authentic part of the human project and not a wicked consequence of sublimation, repression, and a perverse fear of death. In addition, evolution for Whitehead entails a real element of creative advance. Ferenczi's theory, set forth in *Thalassa* (and readily accepted by Brown), that biological evolution was triggered by a protoplasmic irritation from which biological life has ever since been attempting to free itself would have seemed absurd to Whitehead.[3] Furthermore, although the heart of Whitehead's philosophy of organism was indeed a critique of the overdependence of modern science on that abstracting and distancing mode of perception which he called "presentational immediacy," it would scarcely have occurred to him to attribute this excess to the dynamics of repression or sublimation. Presentational immediacy, to Whitehead, was a fundamental mode of human perception, just as human—although somewhat less primordial—as that more fully organismic mode of perception he sometimes referred to as "causal efficacy." [4]

The difference between Brown and Whitehead can be seen clearly when one reflects on Whitehead's characterization of the goals of the life process. All of life exhibits a threefold urge: "(1) to live, (2) to live well, (3) to live better." [5] These three urges constitute the "art of life" and it is the "function of reason" to promote them.

> In fact the art of life is *first* to be alive, *secondly* to be alive in a satisfactory way, and *thirdly* to acquire an increase in satisfaction. It is at this point of our argument that we have to recur to the function of Reason, namely the promotion of the art of life.[6]

Since in one way or another Brown has associated each of these urges with sublimation and repression, his efforts to enlist the support of the philosophy organism for his cause can hardly be taken seriously. And since, as I have demonstrated, Rieff makes most of the same metapsychological mistakes as does Brown, if any of our quartet has the right to claim affinity with the school of emergent evolution as exemplified by the philosophy of Whitehead, certainly Fromm and Erikson —and especially Erikson—would have the greater right to do so.

The disciplines of man are various foci or perspectives on a common subject matter. Sometimes the interpretations of the various disciplines contradict one another; at other times certain perspectives very much correspond to and support other points of view outside their own focus. I have already suggested that Erikson has far more correspondence with contemporary ethological and ecological perspectives on man than does orthodox psychoanalytic theory. It is also true that he has far more coherence than the rest of psychoanalysis with contemporary evolutionary theory in general and with the emergent evolutionary philosophy of Whitehead in particular.

It is in the spirit of Erikson's own work that I dare to suggest this general compatibility between his psychology and various efforts to develop a philosophy of evolution such as Whitehead attempted. Erikson has shown how ideology is important for identity. Ideology seeks to synthesize historical experience, inherited religious and cultural symbols, and current states of knowledge. The most commanding single factor touching in some way all the contemporary disciplines of man is evolutionary theory. The most exciting current developments in psychoanalytic theory are those which are striving to align psychoanalysis more systematically with current developments in evolutionary theory. Toward this end, Erikson's work has indeed been pioneering.[7] It is my conviction that it is of central importance for modern man's ideological integrity that the disciplines of man enter into a grand dialogue in an effort to develop a sense of coherence between the disciplines, man's religious and cultural heritage, and the growing body of evolutionary theory and knowledge. Only when this happens will the modern world have a resource for the development and guidance of a positive culture.

In their important book entitled *Ego in Evolution*, Esther and William Menaker make a distinction between "the ego" and "ego." "The ego" is the central organizing agency of the human organism coordinating ontogenetic development. "Ego" is a phylogenetic concept and refers to the central organizing capacities of the human organism which have guided and coordinated the adaptive processes of man down through the ages.[8] "The ego" in the ontogenetic sense (a particular person's ego) is grounded in "ego" in the phylogenetic sense. It follows, then, that the ego in both the phylogenetic sense and the ontogenetic sense functions according to many of the same principles of operation. The Menakers observe that although the physical universe as a whole is losing energy according to the second law of thermodynamics, biological evolution has taken another direction and seems to be elaborating, organizing, and complexifying its forms of energy.[9] It is clear that Erikson's ontogenetic concept of ego epigenesis assumes a more fundamental phylogenetic conception of the ego as the central organizing agent in the evolutionary course of the cycle of the generations. Much of what Erikson writes about deals indirectly with the ego's phylogenetically grounded tendency to elaborate, organize, and complexify experience in the context of its struggle to establish and maintain the cycle of the generations.

In their outstanding book entitled *Ego and Instinct: The Psychoanalytic View of Human Nature*, Daniel Yankelovich and William Barrett make an important observation about Erikson. After suggesting certain similarities between Erikson and the German phenomenologists Husserl and Heidegger, Yankelovich and Barrett write that Erikson's thought also has "similarities to Whitehead's concept of organism as an emergent structure." [10] Taking Yankelovich and Barrett as my point of departure, I will suggest certain ways of conceiving of these similarities.

Psychoanalytic literature lists a variety of functions of the ego. Perception, thinking, memory, defense, adaptation, synthesis, continuity, effectance, play, and exploration are all sometimes mentioned as functions and needs of the ego. For the purpose of our argument, let us summarize these various functions under two headings—survival and play. In order for man to survive, the central organizing functions of the ego must adapt to the environment (both alloplastically and autoplastically), maintain some sense of continuity (both within the self and between young and old in the cycle of the generations), and defend the organism from dangerous stimuli (from the external environment as well as from the inner world of impulse). To perform these functions of survival, the mechanisms of perception, thinking, and memory (all of which have their own phylogenetic grounding) perform vital services. Under the category of play, we must list the need for effectance, exploration, function pleasure, and new experience, which were discovered by a number of present-day researchers and summarized by Robert White in *Ego and Reality in Psychoanalytic Theory*. What is important in White's discussion of ego psychology is his insistence upon the close relationship between adaptation and play. When man is simply playing in a relaxed manner—experiencing and exploring his world with no visible purpose, and manipulating the objects of his environment without attempting to satisfy his needs for hunger, thirst, or sex—he is indeed undergoing valuable learnings. He is experiencing, differentiating, and integrating a stable sense of his world which has important implications for adaptation in the larger sense of that word. In his view of things, adaptation, or the struggle for survival, is not all work; it includes within it those relaxed modalities of play and wonder which have so often been thought to be the very opposite of adaptive processes.

A similar point of view is found, I believe, in the dialectical processes of assimilation and accommodation in Piaget's description of the total process of adaptation. In order for man to survive in this world, he must know how to play in it. And in the process of playing in his world, man makes important syntheses, develops new responses, and makes new discoveries which enhance his efforts to survive, adapt, defend himself, and maintain a viable sense of continuity not only within himself but also between those members of the species who compose the cycle of the generations.

These two functions of ego—survival (adaptation) and play—are summarized by Erikson's concept of mastery. The ego's efforts to gain mastery and wholeness include for Erikson, in intimate dialectical association, the relaxed functions of playful synthesis as well as the more mobilized functions of adaptation. When man's attempts to order and adapt his world are at their best, they include significant elements of play and wonder. At the same time, man's acts of play and wonder have important, although often indirect, consequences for his evolutionary struggle to order and master his world and maintain his species.

One can see at a glance the close similarity between Erikson's characterization of the functions of the ego and Whitehead's definition of the processes of life—i.e., to live, to live well, and to live better. Every organism, from the lowest animal all the way up to man, exhibits these tendencies. The two goals of living *well* and living *better* are found, by Whitehead, in the tendency, pervasive among all living beings, to aim at an "intensity of feeling, (a) in the immediate subject, and (b) in the relevant future." [11] Intensity of feeling is accomplished when inherited and experienced feelings and qualities are synthesized into vivid patterns of harmony and contrast. Man, for Whitehead, seeks to survive; but in addition, he seeks to experience his world playfully and to integrate his experiences into an increasingly more coherent yet diversified sense of inner richness. It is not stretching the point, I believe, to say that in both psychoanalytic ego psychology and in process philosophy a vision is emerging which sees man's primary aims as including the elements of both survival *and* advance.

Evolutionary theory has always been important for both psychology and philosophy in the nineteenth and twentieth centuries. But early interpretations of Darwin's theory of natural selection were subject to a variety of misuses by philosophy and the social sciences. It led to an overemphasis upon the practical and utilitarian dimensions of adaptation. It has led to an interpretation of adaptation that reduced it to a struggle for the immediate satisfaction of basic physiological needs such as food, water, and sex. It gave exaggerated emphasis to the "survival of the fittest" and the factors of competition, conflict, and power as central elements in the adaptive process. This ethos led to behaviorism and functionalism in the social sciences, to social Darwinism in political theory, and to pragmatism in philosophy. These cultural disciplines helped rationalize and support the emergence of a power-oriented culture in the Western world committed to competitive capitalism, industrial expansion, and efficiency. In psychoanalytic ego psychology and in the philosophy of organism, the struggle for life—survival and adaptation—has been expanded to include the dimensions of play and of creative advance. Wonder and play serve the aims of life just as much as do struggle, conflict, and competition.

This overemphasis upon evolution as a practical and utilitarian struggle has led to a variety of reactions. Many of these reactions have argued that play itself is crucial to the evolution of human life. Some scholars have argued that play is central to processes of cultural creativity; others have argued that the play impulse is the basis of all religious symbolism and ritual activity. The importance of play as a factor in cultural creativity has been convincingly argued by Johan Huizinga. He writes:

> The view we take . . . is that culture arises in the form of play, that it is played from the very beginning. . . . It is through this playing that society expresses its interpretation of life and the world. By this we do not mean that play turns into culture, rather that in its earliest phases culture has the play-character that it proceeds to shape and the mood of play.[12]

Huizinga also extended his understanding of the role of play in cultural creativity to the phenomena of myth and cult. Adolf Jensen, following Huizinga, investigated further the relationship of play to myth and cult. He writes:

> There is no question that Huizinga succeeded in arriving at insights basic to the cultural sciences by his characterization of play. It is important for our context that he finds all the essential criteria of play repeated in cult. . . . Though there were predecessors, it was Huizinga who expanded the connections between play and cult into a system.[13]

Although Huizinga and Jensen differ on certain details, both argue that play is an important element in cultural creativity, myth, and ritual. In addition, they believe that the functions of play transcend the utilitarian struggle for purely material and physical survival. However, as we have already observed in an earlier chapter, their tendency to emphasize the nonpractical and nonutilitarian aspects of play overlooks the contribution made by play to higher and more general adaptational activity. As Erikson—and Piaget—point out, play is a more relaxed modality of the self designed to bring a more human order, mastery, and wholeness into actuality. Play is primarily an effort to bring synthesis to the dichotomies, polarities, and contrasts of human existence. In myth and cult, play gives narrative expression and dramatic demonstration to this constructed wholeness. In myth and cult, play serves adaptive processes by founding and enacting an inclusive wholeness which gives order to the widest dimensions of man's experience of the world. As I have indicated, the need to survive and the need to play are functions of the human ego. Culture, myth, and cult are efforts on the part of the human ego to order the world so that man can *live, live well, and live better.*

In many ways, however, it has been the nature of modern Western societies to emphasize the evolutionary goals of creativity, advance, and growth at the expense of the more conservative impulses connected with survival, i.e., continuity, maintenance, and defense. As we have seen—especially with the help of Erikson, but also with the aid of Sidney Mead, R. W. B. Lewis, and Alvin Toffler—a commitment to experimentation, creativity, rapid change, mobility, and unlimited economic and scientific experimentation has characterized American life for a good part of its history. And, increasingly, what has been typical for American life has become typical for other Western nations as well.

The thrust of our argument (taking our cues from Erikson and from psychoanalytic ego psychology) is to take seriously both the more conservative *and* the more progressive forces—both the drives for individual and generational survival *and* the needs for play—and to see them as fundamental givens of man's central organizing capacities which we call the ego. In this way, we differ from Brown and Rieff who see these progressive forces as simple products of sublimation, repression, and desexualization. On the other hand, following Erikson, we have argued that although these more progressive forces of man are valid and necessary aspects of his human equipment, it is now time to give new emphasis to those more conservative impulses which strive toward preservation, continuity, and maintenance. If these elements are not emphasized, the processes of change and experimentation will fragment the human community beyond recognition. There must be some grounds upon which to resist the rampant growth and expansionism of contemporary society without launching a misconceived attack on man's innate tendencies to expand (differentiate) and synthesize (integrate) experience playfully.

It is important to understand that religion is a product of both of the functions of the ego which we have been discussing. Religion promotes survival *and* play; it seeks to promote the generation *and* the regeneration of life (survival, continuity, maintenance), and it seeks to thrust life toward higher and more inclusive levels of experience (play, growth, creative advance, and synthesis).

Or to state it more accurately, religion seeks to generate and regenerate life and it seeks to elaborate this generative thrust to successively more inclusive levels of experience. Religion always contains the themes of generation and regeneration. These themes apply to the cycle of the generations—to the entire community of young and old. The themes of the generation and renewal of life apply also to primitive and archaic religions which see these themes played out in cyclical myths of eternal return. They also apply to the great religions such as Judaism, Christianity, and Islam in which these themes are manifested in historical events against the background of linear, or noncyclical, concepts of time. They also apply equally to worldly or otherworldly religions—religions with naturalistic or supernaturalistic sensibilities. Birth and rebirth, generation and regeneration, life and the renewal of life—these are the universal themes to be found in the religions of man.

Species everywhere seek to preserve themselves. In some circumstances, individuals within the species will undergo extreme hardship and possibly death in order that the species may continue its cycle of generation and regeneration. The fortunes of environmental change and the capricious processes of biological mutation have brought many species to their end. For this reason, evolutionary theory since Darwin has been reluctant to speak of final causality and purpose in the drama of evolution. But it is clear that the processes of natural selection everywhere seek to preserve and maintain life and will succeed if the variables of mutation and environment cooperate. In man, this impulse to preserve and maintain the species is unstable and easily misguided. Yet there is every reason to believe it is still a part of his nature. Erikson's vision of generative man assumes that the generational urge is still present in man and constitutes the ground of his impulses to establish and care for succeeding generations. Because of man's capacity for imagination and historical vision, he can sometimes express this impulse at the level of a generalized concern for mankind as a whole.

Theodosius Dobzhansky has recently pointed to the importance of generative themes for the history of religions; furthermore, he has explicitly related these themes to fundamental evolutionary processes. He writes:

In a larger sense, it may be said that modern variants of cults of fertility supply the meaning of existence to many millions of persons now living.

Man (or woman) strives for sexual gratification, then for family attachments, and finally for the security and welfare of the progeny. These strivings form designs for living which are so firmly anchored in the genetically
established instinctoid drives that their meaningfulness is taken for
granted by almost everyone and is questioned by few. Although un-
deniably biological in their roots, these strivings on the human level easily
take on the cultural elaborations and embellishments of symbolism, myth,
mysticism, poetry, and art. Motherhood is esteemed as meritorious or even
sacred by most peoples. The Madonna and Child became hallowed
symbols of Christianity. We need not go so far as to see here the ancient
Mother Goddess who has reclaimed her ancient dignity; the deep emotional appeal of the mother image is, however, evident.[14]

In this passage, it is clear that Dobzhansky shares many of the themes
which run through the thought of Erikson. A fundamental ground of
human meaning is found in generativity itself. Generativity and parental care, although rooted in instinctual tendencies, can express themselves in higher cultural activities; and, finally, they can constitute a
fundamental theme in man's religious self-understanding.

However, Dobzhansky questions whether generativity itself as a
process of endless repetition in the never-ending chain of human existence can alone provide man with all the meaning that man, the
self-conscious animal, needs. He asks:

May one, then, be satisfied to live to be alive, to be alive to leave more
life, life which will continue the chain of living, one hopes forever? To
many people, this is the only plausible answer to the problem of the
meaning of life, and the endless chain of living the only believable kind
of immortality. If it were possible for an animal to ask what is the
meaning of its life, the only answer would be that the meaning of life is
life itself. But is this answer good enough for man? An animal capable
of asking such questions would have to be human! [15]

It is clear that Dobzhansky believes that life which "continues the
chain of living"—what Erikson would call the "cycle of the generations"—constitutes a basic substratum to the religious meaning of life.
But he also thinks that to many "common" as well as "uncommon"
people this "amounts only to a senseless repetition. We wish to see,"
he says, "or at least to hope for, something not only novel but also
better." [16]

Dobzhansky believes that the two themes which we have been discussing (variously referred to as survival, or generativity, *and* play, or
advance) as dimensions of the evolutionary process are synthesized in
the mystical philosophy of Pierre Teilhard de Chardin. I have said that

hints of such a synthesis are found in Whitehead's philosophy of organism. And, of course, it has been the persistent argument of this book that the psychoanalytic theory of Erik Erikson constitutes just such a synthesis at the level of psychology. A few additional words, however, about Dobzhansky and Teilhard may prove helpful.

Dobzhansky is critical of the particular way in which Teilhard attempted to formulate the dimension of final causality, which Teilhard believed to be present in the process of evolution. The *direction,* or *orientation,* of evolution was thought, by Teilhard, to be determined by what he called "orthogenesis." Orthogenesis assumes that the rudiments needed to produce all evolutionary developments are present in the most elementary particles of primordial life. Orthogenesis implies that evolution occurs as the unfolding of "preexisting rudiments, like the development of a flower from a bud."

Dobzhansky believes that this view represents evolution as far too settled, inflexible, and predetermined. It overlooks the significant elements of chance and purely random mutation, which Mendelian recombination and environmental change "introduce into the evolutionary picture." However, Dobzhansky, writing decades after Teilhard and with the benefit of momentous developments in biological theory not available to Teilhard, does agree that evolution has an overall orientation. Evolution, throughout its history, has moved toward greater diversity and higher complexity of forms. In man, with his increased capacities for thought and communication, a new stage of evolution has been entered. This new phase Teilhard calls "planetisation" or "mega-synthesis." These neologisms refer to an extension at the level of human psychology of simple processes quite familiar to any student of evolution. These processes tend toward ever greater complexity and ever greater unification. To illustrate this, Teilhard makes reference to processes very similar to those which are brought to mind by the idea of "generativity."

> First the molecules of carbon compounds with their thousands of atoms symmetrically grouped; next the cell which, at the very smallest, contains thousands of molecules linked in a complicated system; then the metazoa in which the cell is no more than an almost infinitesimal element; and later the manifold attempts made by the metazoa to enter into symbiosis and raise themselves to a higher biological condition.
>
> And now, as a germination of planetary dimensions, comes the thinking layer which to its full extent develops and intertwines its fibres, not to confuse and neutralise them but to reinforce them in the living unity of a single tissue.

Really I can see no coherent, and therefore scientific, way of grouping this immense succession of facts but as a gigantic psychobiological operation, a sort of *mega-synthesis*, the "super-arrangement" to which all the thinking elements of the earth find themselves today individually and collectively subject.[17]

A similar vision of the trend of evolution can be found in Whitehead's understanding of an actual entity's subjective aim as tending toward intensification of feeling through the harmonizing of diversity and contrasts of experience. And, of course, both views of evolution suggest much the same vision of man as that entertained by Erikson when he speaks of a variety of pseudospecies synthesizing their own peculiar moralities and ideologies into a new concept of humanity which would contain both universal and particular dimensions.

Of course the weighty terminology of "planetisation" and "mega-synthesis" is foreign to the modest style of a thinker such as Erikson. And although there are similarities of vision between his understanding of the progressive forces in man and evolution and those of Teilhard, Dobzhansky, and Whitehead, we must not forget the essential psychoanalytic sensibility which Erikson brings to the discussion. Generativity is the core of meaning bringing significance to human life and man may indeed tend to elaborate his sense of generativity *progressively* (and *playfully*) to successively higher and more universal levels of experience; but man, Erikson tells us, must constantly remember his origins if his progressively oriented generative odyssey is to make sense and endure. As man moves into the future, he must remember his archaic foundations. He must remember the child and the primitive within himself. Evolution must have its continuities as well as its discontinuities, its reverence for the past as well as its creativity in the present and in the future. Psychoanalysis is the custodian of that special corner of man's archaeology which relates the child and the adult within each man. His sensitivity and appreciation for the special contributions of each of these aspects within himself marks the peculiar genius of generative man.

NOTES

INTRODUCTION

1. Charles Reich, *The Greening of America* (Random House, Inc., 1970); Theodore Roszak, *The Making of a Counter Culture* (Doubleday & Company, Inc., 1969).

CHAPTER 1
Psychoanalysis and Modernity

1. Philip Rieff, *The Triumph of the Therapeutic: Uses of Faith After Freud* (Harper & Row, Publishers, Inc., 1966), pp. 1–47. (Hereafter cited as *TTT*.)
2. Under the category of serious studies, in addition to the writings by the four authors reviewed here, I would list Heinz Hartmann's *Psychoanalysis and Moral Values* (International Universities Press, Inc., 1960); John C. Flügel's *Man, Morals and Society: A Psychoanalytical Study* (The Viking Press, Inc., 1961); Paul Ricoeur's *Freud and Philosophy*, tr. by Denis Savage (Yale University Press, 1970); Thomas Szasz's *The Ethics of Psychoanalysis: The Theory and Method of Autonomous Psychotherapy* (Basic Books, Inc., Publishers, 1965); Joseph Margolis' *Psychotherapy and Morality: A Study of Two Concepts* (Random House, Inc., 1966). Among the very bad studies I would list Richard La Piere's *The Freudian Ethic* (Duell, Sloan & Pearce, Inc., 1959); and O. Hobart Mowrer's *The Crisis in Psychiatry and Religion* (Insight Book, D. Van Nostrand Company, Inc., 1961).
3. Rieff, *TTT*, pp. 1–47.
4. Peter Berger, *The Sacred Canopy: Elements of a Sociological Theory of Religion* (Doubleday & Company, Inc., 1967), p. 146; Thomas Luckmann, *The Invisible Religion: The Problem of Religion in Modern Society* (The Macmillan Company, 1967), p. 99; Talcott Parsons and Robert Bales, *Family, Socialization and Interaction Process* (Free Press, 1955); Robert

Bellah, *Beyond Belief: Essays on Religion in a Post-Traditional World*
(Harper & Row, Publishers, Inc., 1970).

5. Flügel, *Man, Morals and Society.*
6. La Piere, *The Freudian Ethic.*
7. *Ibid.;* Mowrer, *The Crisis in Psychiatry and Religion.*
8. Ricoeur, *Freud and Philosophy.*
9. Margolis, *Psychotherapy and Morality;* Flügel, *Man, Morals and Society.*
10. For a detailed history of the cultural influence of psychoanalysis on the American scene, see Hendrik M. Ruitenbeek, *Freud and America* (The Macmillan Company, 1966). Also see David Shakow and David Rapaport, *The Influence of Freud on American Psychology* (International Universities Press, Inc., 1964); Celia Burns Stendler, "New Ideas for Old: How Freudianism Was Received in the United States," *Journal of Educational Psychology,* Vol. 37 (1947), pp. 193–206.
11. Wilhelm Dilthey, *Pattern and Meaning in History: Thoughts on History and Society,* ed. and with an introduction by H. P. Rickman (Harper Torchbook, Harper & Row, Publishers, Inc., 1962); Paul Ricoeur, *Le Conflit des interprétations* (Paris: Éditions du Seuil, 1969), p. 8.
12. See David Riesman, *The Lonely Crowd* (Yale University Press, 1961), p. 19; for Erich Fromm's concept of the "marketing character" (to be discussed in detail later), see Erich Fromm, *Man for Himself: An Inquiry Into the Psychology of Ethics* (Rinehart & Company, Inc., 1947), p. 67. (Hereafter cited as *MFH.*)
13. Ivan Illich, *Celebration of Awareness* (Doubleday & Company, Inc., 1969); Paulo Freire, *Pedagogy of the Oppressed* (Herder & Herder, Inc., 1970). Also, Fromm's interest in the South American scene and in the practical implications of his thought for the problems of developing nations is now visible in the impressive volume coauthored with Michael Maccoby entitled *Social Character in a Mexican Village* (Prentice-Hall, Inc., 1970). This ambitious application of Fromm's theory of social character to the study of social anthropology may spark a new wave of interest in Fromm's thinking among members of the academic community.
14. The typology of accommodational (Rieff), regressive (Brown), progressive (Fromm), and dialectically progressive (Erikson) responses to modernity makes sense in the light of more scientifically oriented psychological and sociological studies of modernity. Progressive responses to modernity can be seen in the work of Alex Inkeles and the Harvard Center for International Affairs. Although his work has a somewhat different meaning than that of Fromm, Inkeles' tendency to see modern man in rather radical discontinuity with traditional man justifies us in characterizing him as a progressive and a modernist. Inkeles assigns ten characteristics to modern man. Modern man (1) has a readiness for change and innovation, (2) is interested in issues beyond his own immediate affairs, (3) is democratic, (4) is oriented toward the present and future rather than toward the past, (5) is oriented toward planning and organization, (6) has a sense of

efficacy and believes he can control his environment, (7) sees the world as calculable, (8) believes in the dignity of man, (9) has faith in science and technology, and (10) believes in distributive justice according to merit. For Inkeles, the forces which produce these characteristics are (1) education; (2) urbanization; (3) mass communication; (4) the national state with its apparatus of government, bureaucracy, and political parties; and (5) modern factory and other productive and administrative enterprises. See Alex Inkeles, "The Modernization of Man," in *Modernization: The Dynamics of Growth*, ed. by Myron Weiner (Basic Books, Inc., Publishers, 1966), pp. 151–163. This characterization of modern man seems to correspond with the assumptive world of Cyril E. Black in *The Dynamics of Modernization: A Study in Comparative History* (Harper & Row, Publishers, Inc., 1966) and Shmuel N. Eisenstadt in *Modernization: Protest and Change* (Prentice-Hall, Inc., 1966). A more complicated view of the effects of modernization on personality is suggested by Vytautas Kavolis. This writer suggests that the forces of modernization tend to produce two kinds of responses—the response of acceptance and the response of rejection, or refusal. Kavolis isolates a variety of modernizing trends and then specifies the response of acceptance (the modernist variant) and the response of refusal (the underground variant). For example, in response to the trend of bureaucratization, he discusses the response of "rational organization and formalism" (the modernist variant) and the "response of expressionism" and "informality" (the underground variant). Centralization of social control produces the response of "focusing of personality" (modernistic) or "rejection of constraints" and "defocusing of personality" (underground). The trend toward acceleration of change produces the response of "constant experimentation" (modernistic) or a "sense of getting nowhere" and a "recovery of the primeval" (underground). See Vytautas Kavolis, "Post-Modern Man: Psychocultural Responses to Social Trends," *Social Problems*, Vol. 17 (Spring, 1970), pp. 435–448. In the light of Kavolis' observations, it is possible to see Rieff and Fromm as variants of the modernist response, although this is much less true of Fromm. Of course, neither Fromm nor Rieff fits neatly into Kavolis' specific understanding of the modernist response. Norman Brown's concept of Dionysian man (along with Charles Reich and Herbert Marcuse) fits the more rejecting and regressive response of Kavolis' underground variant. Erikson, we believe, has the virtue of combining some of the dimensions of both the modernist variant and the underground variant. This is why I characterize his understanding of generative man as dialectically progressive.

15. For Paul Ricoeur's understanding of how the sciences of man can constitute a diagnosis suggestive of man's reflection about himself, see *Freedom and Nature: The Voluntary and the Involuntary*, tr. by Erazim V. Kohák (Northwestern University Press, 1966), pp. xv, 8–13, 371; also see *Freud and Philosophy*, p. 436.

16. Charles Frankel, *The Case for Modern Man* (Beacon Press, Inc., 1959), p. 29.

17. Endless and ever accelerating social and technological change seems

to be central to Erikson's intuitions about the nature of modernity. The cultural vision that produces uncontrolled economic and technological expansionism is at the heart of his concerns. In this respect, Erikson's analysis is closer to Alvin Toffler's diagnosis in *Future Shock* (Random House, Inc., 1970). The speed of social change (and its accompanying identity confusion) takes precedence for Erikson over the corporate state described by Reich in *The Greening of America* or the "myth of objective consciousness" discussed by Roszak in *The Making of a Counter Culture* as the central factor in the experience of modernity, although Erikson is very much aware of these dimensions as well.

18. I list here representative writings dealing with the issue of character and modernity. Talcott Parsons and Winston White, "The Link Between Character and Society," in Seymour Martin Lipset and Leo Lowenthal (eds.), *Culture and Social Character: The Work of David Riesman Reviewed.* (The Free Press of Glencoe, Inc., 1961), pp. 89–135; Riesman, *The Lonely Crowd;* Winston White, *Beyond Conformity* (The Free Press of Glencoe, Inc., 1961); C. Wright Mills, *White Collar: The American Middle Classes* (Oxford University Press, 1956); William Whyte, *The Organization Man* (Simon & Schuster, Inc., 1956); Edward Shils, "The Theory of Mass Society," *Diogenes,* Vol. 39 (Fall, 1962), pp. 45–66; Eisenstadt, *Modernization: Protest and Change;* Daniel Lerner, *The Passing of Traditional Society: Modernizing the Middle East* (The Free Press of Glencoe, Inc., 1958); and Black, *The Dynamics of Modernization.*

19. For a discussion of the need for stable organizing categories to guide comparative work in personality and culture, see Alex Inkeles and Daniel Levinson, "National Character: The Study of Modal Personality and Sociocultural Systems," in Gardner Lindzey and Elliot Aronson (eds.), *The Handbook of Social Psychology,* 2d ed., Vol. IV, *Group Psychology and Phenomena of Interaction* (Addison-Wesley Publishing Company, Inc., 1969), pp. 447–452. It should be noted that the categories I use are different from those suggested by Inkeles and Levinson. I make no claim that mine are exhaustive, but they should prove helpful.

CHAPTER 2
Philip Rieff: Psychological Man and
the Penultimate Ethic of the Abundant Life

1. Philip Rieff, *Freud: The Mind of the Moralist* (Anchor Book, Doubleday & Company, Inc., 1961), p. 391. (Hereafter cited as *FMM.*)

2. *Ibid.*

3. *Ibid.*

4. *Ibid.*, *FMM*, p. 392.

5. Rieff, *TTT*, p. 6.

6. Philip Rieff, "The American Transference: From Calvin to Freud," *Atlantic*, Vol. 208 (July, 1961), pp. 105–107.

7. Rieff, *TTT*, p. 6. (Italics mine.)

8. Philip Rieff, "History, Psychoanalysis, and the Social Sciences," *Ethics*, Vol. 63 (Jan., 1953), p. 116. For further elaboration of Rieff's view of the way in which elites influence history, see "Disraeli: The Chosen of History; Uniting the Old Jerusalem and the New," *Commentary*, Vol. 13 (Jan., 1952), pp. 22–33.

9. Rieff, *TTT*, p. 12.

10. *Ibid.*, p. 14.

11. *Ibid.*, p. 17.

12. *Ibid.*, p. 15.

13. *Ibid.*, p. 22.

14. Cf. Eisenstadt, *Modernization: Protest and Change*, and Black, *The Dynamics of Modernization*.

15. For examples of how the principle of structural differentiation is employed in sociological literature to explain the new psychological styles of modern man, see the following: Peter Berger and Thomas Luckmann, *The Social Construction of Reality: A Treatise in the Sociology of Knowledge* (Doubleday & Company, Inc., 1966), pp. 125, 163–173; Luckmann, *The Invisible Religion*, pp. 69–106.

16. Berger, *The Sacred Canopy*, p. 167.

17. Although Berger seems to give "culture" a place in his understanding of the social world, it is clear that he gives greater weight to social processes and social structures. One can consistently see this in his tendency to write off "psychology" as a mere epiphenomenon of the forces of division of labor, structural differentiation, and pluralism, and their tendency to produce individualism, privatism, and subjectivism in the population of advanced countries. See *The Sacred Canopy*, pp. 165–171.

18. Rieff, *TTT*, p. 31.

19. Rieff, *FMM*, p. xi.

20. *Ibid.*, p. xvii.

21. Rieff, *TTT*, pp. 31–32.

22. Rieff, *FMM*, p. 284.

23. *Ibid.*, p. 6.

24. *Ibid.*, p. 11.

25. *Ibid.*

26. *Ibid.*, p. 12.

27. *Ibid.*, p. 20.

28. *Ibid.*, p. 21.

29. *Ibid.*, p. 63; see also "Freudian Ethics and the Idea of Reason," *Ethics*, Vol. 67 (April, 1957), pp. 172–174, and "Origin of Freud's Political Philosophy," *Journal of History of Ideas*, Vol. 17 (April, 1956), p. 240.

30. Rieff, *FMM*, p. 165.

31. *Ibid.*, p. 22.

32. *Ibid.*, p. 354.

33. *Ibid.*, p. 352.

34. *Ibid.*, pp. 353–354.

35. Rieff, *TTT*, pp. 85–86.

36. Rieff, *FMM*, p. 105.

37. *Ibid.*, p. 66.

38. *Ibid.*, p. 158. (Italics mine.)

39. Ricoeur, *Freud and Philosophy*, pp. 115–116, 134–150, 455–457; Jacques Lacan, *Écrits* (Paris: Éditions du Seuil, 1966), pp. 237–322.

40. Rieff, *FMM*, p. 29.

41. *Ibid.*, p. 35.

42. *Ibid.*

43. Heinz Hartmann, *Ego Psychology and the Problem of Adaptation*, tr. by David Rapaport (International Universities Press, Inc., 1958), p. 36 (hereafter cited as *EPAPA*); Robert White, *Ego and Reality in Psychoanalytic Theory: A Proposal Regarding Independent Ego Energies* (International Universities Press, Inc., 1963), p. 161 (hereafter cited as *ERPT*).

44. Rieff, *FMM*, p. 387.

45. *Ibid.*, p. 386.

46. For the influence of Piaget's work on psychoanalytic ego psychology, see the following works: Peter Wolff, *The Developmental Psychologies of Jean Piaget and Psychoanalysis* (International Universities Press, Inc., 1960); Robert R. Holt (ed.), *Motives and Thought: Psychoanalytic Essays in Honor of David Rapaport* (International Universities Press, Inc., 1967); and White, *Ego and Reality in Psychoanalytic Theory*. As we shall see later, Piaget makes important contributions to the thought of both Fromm and Erikson. For an excellent article on the similarities between Erikson and Piaget, see Peter Wolff's "Cognitive Considerations for a Psychoanalytic Theory of Language Acquisition," in Holt (ed.), *Motives and Thought: Psychoanalytic Essays in Honor of David Rapaport*.

47. Jean Piaget, *Play, Dreams, and Imitation in Childhood* (W. W. Norton & Company, Inc., 1962), p. 163.

48. For a discussion of the deeper regulatory capacities of the total organism, see the writings of the following organismic theorists: Carl Rogers, *Client-Centered Therapy* (Houghton Mifflin Company, 1951); Heinz Werner, *Comparative Psychology of Mental Development*, rev. ed. (International Universities Press, Inc., 1957); Kurt Goldstein, *Human Nature in the Light of Psychopathology* (Harvard University Press, 1940).

49. For a continuation of this line of thought in Rieff, see his recent article entitled "The Impossible Culture," in *Encounter*, Vol. 35 (Sept., 1970), p. 39. Here he represents Freud as standing solidly against the modern cultural attitude, so eloquently expressed by Oscar Wilde toward weakening civility and restraint and giving "expression to everything." In

opposition to this trend, Freud upholds the "no" of culture. Of course, for Freud, this meant the "no" of prudent psychoanalytic instinct.

50. Rieff, *FMM*, p. 174.

51 Rieff, *TTT*, p. 57.

52. Philip Rieff, "The Bullitt-Freud 'Wilson,'" *Encounter*, Vol. 28 (April, 1967), p. 84.

53. Philip Rieff, "The Mirage of College Politics," *Harper's Magazine*, Vol. 223 (Oct., 1961), pp. 156–163.

54. Philip Rieff, "The Theology of Politics: Reflections on Totalitarianism as the Burden of Our Time," *The Journal of Religion*, Vol. 32 (Spring, 1952), p. 126.

55. Rieff, *TTT*, pp. 252–254.

56. *Ibid.*, p. 34.

57. Rieff, "The Authority of the Past: Sickness and Society in Freud's Thought," *Social Research*, Vol. 21 (1954), pp. 428–450; see also his "The Meaning of History and Religion in Freud's Thought," *The Journal of Religion*, Vol. 31 (April, 1951), pp. 114–131.

CHAPTER 3

Norman Brown: Dionysian Man and the Resurrection of the True Christian Body

1. Thomas B. Morgan, "How Hieronymus Bosch and Norman O. Brown Would Change the World," *Esquire*, Vol. 59 (March, 1963), p. 135.

2. Susan Sontag, *Against Interpretation and Other Essays* (Delta Book, Dell Publishing Company, Inc., 1967), p. 260.

3. Paul Robinson, *The Freudian Left: Wilhelm Reich, Géza Róheim, Herbert Marcuse* (Harper & Row, Publishers, Inc., 1969), pp. 216–244; Roszak, *The Making of a Counter Culture*, pp. 84–123.

4. Roszak, *The Making of a Counter Culture*, p. 88.

5. Norman O. Brown, *Hermes the Thief: The Evolution of a Myth* (University of Wisconsin Press, 1947); also see *Hesiod's Theogony*, tr. by Norman O. Brown (The Liberal Arts Press, 1953).

6. Norman O. Brown, *Love's Body* (Random House, Inc., 1966), p. 187. (Hereafter cited as *LB*.)

7. Norman O. Brown, "Apocalypse: The Place of Mystery in the Life of the Mind," *Harper's Magazine*, Vol. 222 (May, 1961), p. 47.

8. Sontag, *Against Interpretation*, p. 258; Lionel Abel, "Important Nonsense: Norman Brown," *Dissent*, Vol. XV (March, 1968), p. 153.

9. Daniel Bell, *The Reforming of General Education* (Columbia University Press, 1966), pp. 308–310.

10. Rieff, *TTT*, p. 199.

11. Sigmund Freud, "Beyond the Pleasure Principle," *Standard Edition of the Complete Psychological Works of Sigmund Freud*, Vol. 18 (London: The Hogarth Press, 1955), p. 52; Sigmund Freud, "The Ego and the Id," *Standard Edition*, Vol. 19 (1961), pp. 40–47 (hereafter cited as *EAI*); Sigmund Freud, "New Introductory Lectures on Psychoanalysis," *Standard Edition*, Vol. 22 (1964), pp. 112–157.

12. Norman O. Brown, *Life Against Death: The Psychoanalytical Meaning of History* (Wesleyan University Press, 1959), p. 40. (Hereafter cited as *LAD*.)

13. *Ibid.*, p. 41.

14. *Ibid.*, p. 43.

15. *Ibid.*

16. *Ibid.*, p. 45.

17. Brown, *LB*, p. 36.

18. *Ibid.*, p. 50.

19. The writings of Paul Tillich can be cited to support this interpretation of the nature of the fall. See his *Systematic Theology*, 3 vols. (The University of Chicago Press, 1951, 1957, 1963).

20. Brown, *LAD*, p. 113.

21. *Ibid.*, p. 90.

22. *Ibid.*

23. *Ibid.*

24. *Ibid.*, p. 118.

25. Brown, *LB*, p. 52.

26. Frederick Crews, "Love in the Western World," *Partisan Review*, Vol. 34 (Spring, 1967), p. 286.

27. Morgan, "How Hieronymous Bosch and Norman O. Brown Would Change the World," p. 104.

28. Brown, *LAD*, p. 322. (Italics mine.)

29. Brown, *LB*, pp. 52–53.

30. *Ibid.*, p. 53.

31. *Ibid.*, p. 54.

32. Brown, *LAD*, p. 107.

33. *Ibid.*, p. 105.

34. *Ibid.*, p. 169.

35. *Ibid.*, p. 174.

36. *Ibid.*, p. 159.

37. *Ibid.*, p. 163.

38. *Ibid.*, p. 239.

39. *Ibid.*, p. 288.

40. *Ibid.*, p. 222.

41. *Ibid.*, p. 223.

42. Brown, *LB*, pp. 3–31.

43. Norman O. Brown, "A Reply to Herbert Marcuse," *Commentary*, Vol. 43 (March, 1967), p. 83.

44. Brown, *LB*, pp. 176–177.

45. Brown, *LAD*, p. 292.

46. *Ibid.*, p. 303.

47. Brown, *LB*, p. 217.

48. *Ibid.*, p. 207.

49. Norman O. Brown, "From Politics to Metapolitics," *Caterpillar I* (Oct., 1967), p. 69.

50. Norman O. Brown, "Daphne, or Metamorphosis," in *Myths, Dreams, and Religion,* ed. by Joseph Campbell (E. P. Dutton & Co., Inc., 1970), p. 93.

51. See Robert Bellah's "Brown in Perspective: A Commentary on Love's Body," *Soundings,* Vol. 54 (Winter, 1971), pp. 450–459. Bellah's article tries to save Brown from nihilistic readings typical of the many reviews of Brown's writings. Bellah does this by arguing that Brown is speaking in poetry. It is through poetry that Brown wants to integrate the conscious and the unconscious and in this way to overcome the literalness of twentieth-century rationalism. However, the article makes several mistakes. (1) Bellah overlooks or minimizes the fact that the content of the unconscious for Brown is playful release aiming toward death. (2) Bellah fails to realize that this gives Brown's so-called poetry a univocal and literal meaning. Integrating the unconscious into consciousness does not abrogate the fact that all symbols for Brown have only one meaning—the literal drive toward death as union with the mother. (3) Bellah misperceives the function of "regression in service of the ego." This concept, as handled especially by Erikson and Hartmann, does not mean simply (as he presumes) that the unconscious is "expressed" in such a way as not to interfere with "rational processes." Rather, for these ego psychologists, regression in service of the ego means real participation of the "intact" ego in the lower-order wisdom of the unconscious.

52. Ludwig Binswanger, *Being-in-the-World: Selected Papers of Ludwig Binswanger,* tr., and with an introduction to Binswanger's existential psychoanalysis by Jacob Needleman (Basic Books, Inc., Publishers, 1963), p. 78.

53. Ernest Jones as quoted by Needleman in Binswanger, *ibid.*, p. 61.

54. *Ibid.*, p. 72.

55. Ricoeur, *Freud and Philosophy*, pp. 1–47; also see Ricoeur, "Le Problème du double sens comme problème herméneutique et comme problème sémantique," *Le Conflit des interprétations* (Paris: Éditions du Seuil, 1969), pp. 64–78.

56. Brown, *LB*, p. 264.

57. Brown, *LAD*, p. 284.

58. *Ibid.*, p. 93.

59. Brown, *LB*, p. 207.

60. Nothing to contradict this interpretation of Brown's attitude toward politics and government can be found in his more recent statement on the subject in "From Politics to Metapolitics," pp. 62–94.

61. In "Daphne, or Metamorphosis," Brown writes: "Literature is as collective as the unconscious; private authorship or ownership is not to be respected. It is all one book, which includes the gospel according to Ovid, Saint Ovid the Martyr (Ovid moralise): and Petrarch, and Marvell, and Keats, and Rilke, and Yeats, and André Gide, and Pound. And also the ravings of every poor Crazy Jane. Every poor schizophrenic girl is a Delphic priestess." This is further evidence that for Brown, there is only one logos, one Word, one meaning, and one religion. Particularity is something Brown equates with repression—further evidence of his literal-mindedness. See *Myths, Dreams, and Religion,* ed. by Campbell, p. 109.

CHAPTER 4
The Ego, Play, and Individuation

1. Sigmund Freud, "Project for a Scientific Psychology," in *The Origins of Psychoanalysis: Letters to Wilhelm Fliess, Drafts and Notes: 1887–1902* (Basic Books, Inc., Publishers, 1954).

2. Sigmund Freud, "Two Principles in Mental Functioning," *Standard Edition,* Vol. 12 (1958), p. 219.

3. *Ibid.*

4. Freud, *EAI,* p. 25.

5. Sigmund Freud, "Mourning and Melancholia," *Standard Edition,* Vol. 14 (1957), pp. 243–258.

6. Sigmund Freud, "On Narcissism," *Standard Edition,* Vol. 14 (1957), pp. 73–102.

7. Freud, *EAI,* p. 46.

8. *Ibid.*

9. *Ibid.,* p. 44.

10. *Ibid.,* p. 17.

11. *Ibid.,* p. 26.

12. Sigmund Freud, "Inhibitions, Symptoms, and Anxiety," *Standard Edition,* Vol. 20 (1959), p. 174.

13. *Ibid.,* pp. 132–143.

14. It can hardly be denied that Freud never overcame his theory of reductive energetics even though, in many ways, it became less and less important for his thought in later years. Efforts to show that there are two kinds of language in Freud—the language of energy and the language of meaning—as Paul Ricoeur attempts to do, are entirely justified. It is also justified, as Peter Homans has cogently suggested, to give Freud an iconic reading. See Peter Homans, *Theology After Freud: An Interpretive Inquiry* (The Bobbs-Merrill Company, Inc., 1970). Culture, religion, and the transference situation in therapy provided important resources for Freud's

thought. The point is that the two kinds of language contaminate each other and become mutually distorted. We cannot see culture, religion, symbolism, or energetics quite correctly because of the distorting consequences of Freud's fundamental energetic, which he never completely outgrew, even though his later thought strongly hints of its inadequacy.

15. Hartmann, *EPAPA*, p. 105.

16. Sigmund Freud, "Three Essays on the Theory of Sexuality," *Standard Edition*, Vol. 7 (1953), pp. 177–178.

17. Sigmund Freud, "Analysis Terminable and Interminable," *Standard Edition*, Vol. 23 (1964), pp. 240–241.

18. Otto Fenichel, "Early Stages of Ego Development," in Otto Fenichel, *Collected Papers: First and Second Series*, ed. by Hanna Fenichel and David Rapaport, Vol. 2 (W. W. Norton & Company, Inc., 1954), p. 29.

19. Anna Freud, *The Ego and the Mechanisms of Defense*, tr. by Cecil Baines (International Universities Press, Inc., 1946).

20. Hartmann, *EPAPA*, pp. 8–9.

21. *Ibid.*

22. Heinz Hartmann, "Notes on the Reality Principle," in Heinz Hartmann, *Essays on Ego Psychology: Selected Problems in Psychoanalytic Theory* (International Universities Press, Inc., 1964), pp. 245–246. (Italics mine.)

23. Hartmann, *EPAPA*, p. 102.

24. *Ibid.*

25. *Ibid.*, p. 51.

26. *Ibid.*, p. 27.

27. *Ibid.*, p. 24.

28. *Ibid.*, p. 54.

29. Heinz Hartmann, Ernst Kris, and Rudolph M. Loewenstein, "Comments on the Formation of Psychic Structure," in *The Psychoanalytic Study of the Child, 1945–1946: An Annual*, Vol. II (International Universities Press, Inc., 1946), pp. 11–38.

30. Hartmann, *Essays on Ego Psychology*, p. xii.

31. Hartmann, *EPAPA*, p. 47.

32. *Ibid.*, p. 48.

33. *Ibid.*, p. 49.

34. *Ibid.*

35. *Ibid.*, p. 36.

36. *Ibid.*

37. Ernst Kris, *Psychoanalytic Explorations in Art* (International Universities Press, Inc., 1952).

38. For an interesting attempt to relate the work of Heinz Hartmann to certain classical views of the nature and function of reason, see Homer Bain, "Rational and Irrational Action: A Comparison of the Thought of Thomas Aquinas and Heinz Hartmann." (Unpublished Ph.D. dissertation for the Divinity School of the University of Chicago, 1971.)

39. Alfred North Whitehead, *The Function of Reason* (Beacon Press, Inc., 1958), p. 4.

40. White, *ERPT*, p. 24. Also see Robert White, "Motivation Reconsidered: The Concept of Competence," *The Psychological Review*, Vol. 66 (Sept., 1959), pp. 297–333.

41. White, *ERPT*, p. 35.

42. *Ibid.*

43. K. C. Montgomery, "The Role of the Exploratory Drive in Learning," *Journal of Comparative and Physiological Psychology*, Vol. 47 (1954), pp. 6–64.

44. R. A. Butler and H. F. Harlow, "Discrimination Learning and Learning Sets to Visual Exploration Incentives," *Journal of General Psychology*, Vol. 57 (1957), pp. 257–264.

45. White, *ERPT*, p. 28.

46. Desmond Morris, *The Naked Ape* (Dell Publishing Company, Inc., 1969), p. 107.

47. White, *ERPT*, p. 30.

48. *Ibid.*, p. 32.

49. *Ibid.*, p. 35.

50. *Ibid.*, p. 39.

51. *Ibid.*, p. 85.

52. *Ibid.*, p. 91.

53. *Ibid.*, p. 77.

54. *Ibid.*, p. 79.

55. *Ibid.*, p. 138.

56. *Ibid.*, p. 195. (Italics mine.)

57. *Ibid.*

58. Ricoeur, *Freud and Philosophy*, pp. 453–470.

CHAPTER 5

Erich Fromm: The Productive Personality
and the Coming of the Messianic Time

1. See John H. Schaar, *Escape from Authority: The Perspectives of Erich Fromm* (Basic Books, Inc., Publishers, 1961); J. Stanley Glen, *Erich Fromm: A Protestant Critique* (The Westminster Press, 1966).

2. For evidence of Fromm's importance for many practicing psychologists and psychoanalysts as well as the general esteem granted to him in the scholarly community, see the recent symposium *In the Name of Life: Essays in Honor of Erich Fromm*, ed. by Bernard Landis and Edward S. Tauber (Holt, Rinehart & Winston, Inc., 1971).

3. See Will Herberg, "Freud, Religion, and Social Reality," *Commentary*, Vol. 23 (Fall, 1957), pp. 277–284.

4. White, *Beyond Conformity*, pp. 37–49.

5. "The Rotten Middle Class," *Time*, Jan. 25, 1963. Here the reviewer seems upset most of all that Fromm would suggest, "Marx is a figure of world historical significance with whom Freud cannot even be compared."

6. A. I. Titarenko, "Erich Fromm in the Chains of Illusion," *Science and Society*, Vol. 29 (Summer, 1965), pp. 319–329.

7. For a review of the contradictory uses the student generation sometimes makes of Fromm's thought, see David Riesman, "Notes on Education Reform," in *In the Name of Life: Essays in Honor of Erich Fromm*, ed. by Landis and Tauber, pp. 193–217.

8. Herbert Marcuse, *Eros and Civilization: A Philosophical Inquiry Into Freud* (Beacon Press, Inc., 1955), pp. 216–251.

9. David Riesman, *The Lonely Crowd*, abridged ed. (Yale University Press, 1961), pp. 4, 5, 19n., 22n.

10. Lipset and Lowenthal (eds.), *Culture and Social Character*.

11. Erich Fromm, *Escape from Freedom* (Farrar & Rinehart, Inc., 1941), p. 26. (Hereafter cited as *EFF*.)

12. Fromm, *MFH*, p. 219.

13. There is evidence that although Fromm remained aloof from the development of psychoanalytic ego psychology, his thought may have had some influence upon the development of this strand of psychoanalytic theory. See David Rapaport's discussion of Fromm's contributions in "The Points of View of Metapsychology," given at the William Alanson White Institute of Psychiatry and Psychoanalysis, May 22–23, 1959. Also see *The Collected Papers of David Rapaport*, ed. by Merton M. Gill (Basic Books, Inc., Publishers, 1967), p. 921. I am indebted for these references to David Schecter's "Of Human Bonds and Bondage," in *In the Name of Life: Essays in Honor of Erich Fromm*, ed. by Landis and Tauber, pp. 84–99. Schecter's article is also helpful in demonstrating the usefulness of some of Fromm's concepts for the study of early ego development.

14. Ernest G. Schachtel, *Metamorphosis: On the Development of Affect, Perception, Attention and Memory* (Basic Books, Inc., Publishers, 1959), p. 43.

15. Fromm, *MFH*, p. 83.

16. For a definitive statement of the ethical neutrality of classical psychoanalytic theory, see Hartmann's *Psychoanalysis and Moral Values*. It is, in part, the purpose of this present book to demonstrate that psychoanalysis does indeed have an implied ethical vision, but that it has difficulty rendering its basic concepts consistent with the positive ethical view it often holds.

17. Ricoeur, *Freedom and Nature: The Voluntary and the Involuntary*, p. 13.

18. For this exchange, see the following articles: Herbert Marcuse, "Social Implications of Freudian Revisionism," *Dissent*, Vol. 2 (Summer,

1955), pp. 221–240; Erich Fromm, "The Human Implications of Instinctual 'Radicalism,'" *Dissent*, Vol. 2 (Fall, 1955), pp. 342–349; Marcuse, "A Reply to Erich Fromm," *Dissent*, Vol. 3 (Winter, 1956), pp. 79–81; Erich Fromm, "A Counter-Rebuttal," *Dissent*, Vol. 3 (Winter, 1956), pp. 81–83.

19. Marcuse, *Eros and Civilization*, pp. 203–251.

20. *Ibid.*, p. 5.

21. Roszak, *The Making of a Counter Culture*, pp. 84–123.

22. See the following exchange between Marcuse and Brown on the issue of political versus cultural (read mystical) revolution. Herbert Marcuse, "Love Mystified: A Critique of Norman O. Brown," *Commentary*, Vol. 43 (Feb., 1967), pp. 71–75; Norman O. Brown, "A Reply to Herbert Marcuse," pp. 83–84.

23. Marcuse, *Eros and Civilization*, p. 193.

24. Freud, "Beyond the Pleasure Principle," p. 62.

25. Herbert Marcuse, *One Dimensional Man: Studies in the Ideology of Advanced Industrial Society* (Beacon Press, Inc., 1964); *Soviet Marxism: A Critical Analysis* (London: Routledge & Kegan Paul, Ltd., 1958).

26. Fromm, *EFF*, pp. 24–39; also D. T. Suzuki and others, *Zen Buddhism and Psychoanalysis*, ed. by Erich Fromm (Grove Press, Inc., 1963), p. 92.

27. Fromm, *MFH*, p. 40; also Erich Fromm, *Psychoanalysis and Religion* (Yale University Press, 1950), p. 22 (hereafter cited as *PAR*); and Erich Fromm, *The Sane Society* (Rinehart & Company, Inc., 1955), pp. 23–24 (hereafter cited as *TSS*).

28. Fromm, *MFH*, p. 42.

29. *Ibid.*, p. 43.

30. Reinhold Niebuhr, *The Nature and Destiny of Man: A Christian Interpretation* (Charles Scribner's Sons, 1941), pp. 186–207. Note, however, that Niebuhr tends to derive the fleshly or sensual orientations from the orientations of pride. "The Biblical and Christian thought has maintained with a fair degree of consistency that pride is more basic than sensuality and that the latter is, in some way, derived from the former" (p. 186).

31. Søren Kierkegaard, *Fear and Trembling*, tr. by Walter Lowrie (Doubleday & Company, Inc., 1954), p. 80.

32. Fromm, *MFH*, p. 60.

33. Fromm, *EFF*, p. 298.

34. Fromm, *MFH*, p. 57.

35. *Ibid.*, p. 36.

36. Fromm, *EFF*, pp. 295–296.

37. Fromm, *MFH*, p. 58.

38. *Ibid.*, p. 88.

39. *Ibid.*, p. 111. For a more detailed discussion of the orientations of socialization, see Fromm, *EFF*, pp. 136–206. Here he calls them mechanisms of escape. It should be noted that Fromm's theory of character orientation has been changed and adapted somewhat to fit the circumstances of recent research he has done on social character in a Mexican village. Specifically, he

has added a new set of categories dealing with sociopolitical orientations. See his *Social Character in a Mexican Village*, pp. 80–82.

40. Fromm, *MFH*, pp. 62–82.

41. *Ibid.*, pp. 54–61.

42. *Ibid.*, p. 80.

43. *Ibid.*, pp. 65–67.

44. Fromm, *TSS*, p. 166. See also Richard Evans, *Dialogue with Erik Erikson* (Harper & Row, Publishers, Inc., 1967), p. 28 (hereafter cited as *DEE*); Erich Fromm, *The Revolution of Hope* (Bantam Books, Inc., 1968), p. 40 (hereafter cited as *ROH*). Fromm's recent publication of his research on social character in a Mexican village demonstrates how decisively the Mexican peasant is affected by the consumer-oriented attitudes found in more sophisticated urban populations. Old traditions are swept away and nothing replaces them except the vague dreams of a remote consumer paradise. Fromm and Maccoby also discovered that efforts to develop the village economically tended to support the social advancement of individuals formerly considered deviant by the more traditional culture. These individuals who became the new entrepreneurs were productive-exploitative type characters who, under new economic circumstances, tended to gain wealth and ended up being the leaders of the village.

45. Erich Fromm, *The Heart of Man: Its Genius for Good and Evil* (Harper & Row, Publishers, Inc., 1964), pp. 37–61.

46. Erich Fromm, *Sigmund Freud's Mission: An Analysis of His Personality and Influence* (Harper & Brothers, 1959), p. 112.

47. Fromm, *MFH*, p. 18.

48. *Ibid.*, p. 30.

49. Fromm, *PAR*, pp. 4–6.

50. *Ibid.*, p. 61.

51. Fromm, *EFF*, p. 261.

52. *Ibid.*, p. 259.

53. Fromm, *MFH*, p. 84.

54. *Ibid.*

55. *Ibid.*

56. *Ibid.*, pp. 102–106.

57. Erich Fromm, *The Art of Loving* (Harper & Brothers, 1956), p. 23. (Hereafter cited as *AOL*.)

58. *Ibid.*, p. 23.

59. *Ibid.*, p. 33.

60. *Ibid.*, p. 24.

61. *Ibid.*, p. 25.

62. *Ibid.*, p. 26.

63. *Ibid.*, p. 28.

64. *Ibid.*

65. Erich Fromm (ed.), *Marx's Concept of Man* (Frederick Ungar Publishing Company, 1961), p. 28. (Hereafter cited as *MCOM*.)

66. *Ibid.*, p. 35.

67. Erich Fromm and Ramón Xirau (eds.), *The Nature of Man: A Reader* (The Macmillan Company, 1968), p. 219; also see *MCOM*, pp. 34, 101.

68. Fromm, *MCOM*, p. 33. Also see Erich Fromm, *Beyond the Chains of Illusion: My Encounter with Marx and Freud* (Simon & Schuster, Inc., 1962), pp. 27–32, for further discussion of Marx's early concept of man.

69. Fromm, *MFH*, p. 113.

70. *Ibid.*, pp. 113–114.

71. Fromm, *ROH*, p. 11.

72. *Ibid.*, p. 12.

73. *Ibid.*, p. 15.

74. Fromm, *PAR*, p. 21.

75. Fromm, *ROH*, p. 73.

76. Fromm, *PAR*, pp. 37–51.

77. *Ibid.*, p. 49. Here he writes, "God is not a symbol of power over man, but of man's own powers."

78. Noam Chomsky, *Syntactic Structures* (The Hague: Mouton & Co., N.V., 1957).

79. Lawrence Kohlberg, "Development of Moral Character and Moral Ideology," *Review of Child Development Research*, Vol. 1, ed. by Martin L. Hoffman and Lois W. Hoffman (Russell Sage Foundation, 1964), pp. 383–431.

80. Fromm, *PAR*, p. 29.

81. Fromm, *EFF*, p. 37.

82. Erich Fromm, *You Shall Be as Gods: A Radical Interpretation of the Old Testament and Its Tradition* (Holt, Rinehart & Winston, Inc., 1966), pp. 123–124.

83. *Ibid.*, p. 72.

84. *Ibid.*, p. 138.

85. *Ibid.*, p. 125.

86. *Ibid.*, p. 128.

87. *Ibid.*, p. 133, and Leo Baeck, *Judaism and Christianity: Essays*, tr. by Walter Kaufmann (The Jewish Publication Society of America, 1958), p. 31.

88. Fromm, *MFH*, p. 167.

89. *Ibid.*, p. 139.

90. Fromm, *TSS*, p. 276.

91. Fromm, *PAR*, p. 21.

92. Fromm, *TSS*, p. 347.

93. Fromm, *PAR*, p. 63.

CHAPTER 6
Erik Erikson: Generative Man and the Household of God

1. Erik H. Erikson, *Gandhi's Truth: On the Origins of Militant Non-violence* (W. W. Norton & Company, Inc., 1969), p. 399. (Hereafter cited as *GT*.)

2. Erik H. Erikson, *Identity and the Life Cycle: Selected Papers*, Psychological Issues Monograph, Vol. I, No. 1 (International Universities Press, Inc., 1959), p. 97. (Hereafter cited as *IALC*.) Also see Erik H. Erikson, *Childhood and Society*, 2d ed., rev. and enlarged (W. W. Norton & Company, Inc., 1963), p. 267. (Hereafter cited as *CS*.) Also see Erik H. Erikson, *Identity: Youth and Crisis* (W. W. Norton & Company, Inc., 1968), p. 138. (Hereafter cited as *IYC*.)

3. Erik H. Erikson, *Insight and Responsibility: Lectures on the Ethical Implications of Psychoanalytic Insight* (W. W. Norton & Company, Inc., 1964), p. 132. (Hereafter cited as *IAR*.)

4. Erikson, *IALC*, p. 97.

5. Erikson, *IAR*, p. 131.

6. Erikson, *GT*, p. 132.

7. See David Elkind, "Erik Erikson's Eight Ages of Man," *The New York Times Magazine*, April 5, 1970, pp. 25–27, 84–92, 110–119; Robert Coles, "Profiles: The Measure of Man, I," *The New Yorker*, Vol. 46, No. 38 (Nov. 7, 1970), pp. 55–131; "Profiles: The Measure of Man, II," *The New Yorker*, Vol. 46, No. 39 (Nov. 14, 1970), pp. 59–138. This was a condensation of a book by Robert Coles entitled *Erik H. Erikson: The Growth of His Work* (Atlantic Monthly Press, Little, Brown & Company, 1970).

8. Erik H. Erikson, "Autobiographic Notes on the Identity Crisis," *Daedalus*, Vol. 99, No. 4 (Fall, 1970), p. 742.

9. *Ibid.*, p. 748.

10. *Ibid.*

11. *Ibid.*, p. 744.

12. *Ibid.*, p. 748.

13. Erikson, *IYC*, p. 36; also see Evans, *DEE*, p. 36.

14. Erikson, *CS*, p. 418.

15. *Ibid.; IYC*, p. 75.

16. Erikson, *IAR*, p. 29.

17. *Ibid.*

18. *Ibid.*, p. 44.

19. *Ibid.*, p. 237.

20. Erikson, *CS*, p. 424.

21. Erikson, *IAR*, p. 237.

22. Jean-Paul Sartre, *Being and Nothingness: An Essay in Phenomenological Ontology*, tr. by Hazel Barnes (Citadel Press, 1964).

23. Martin Buber, *I and Thou*, 2d ed., tr. by Ronald Gregor Smith (Charles Scribner's Sons, 1958).

24. For an example of current research on the nature of the human smiling response, see the following: D. G. Friedman, "Smiling in Blind Infants and the Issue of Innate vs. Acquired," *Journal of Child Psychology and Psychiatry*, Vol. 5 (Dec., 1964), pp. 171–184; Rene A. Spitz, *The Smiling Response: A Contribution to the Ontogenesis of Social Relations*, Genetic Psychological Monograph, Vol. 34 (Journal Press, 1946), pp. 57–125; J. A. Ambrose, "The Development of the Smiling Response in Early Infancy," *Determinants of Infant Behaviour*, ed. by Brian M. Foss (London: Methuen & Company, Ltd., 1961), pp. 179–196.

25. Erikson, *IAR*, p. 231.

26. Konrad Lorenz, *On Aggression*, tr. by Marjorie K. Wilson (Bantam Books, Inc., 1970), p. 83.

27. Erikson, *IYC*, p. 222; also see Hartmann, *Ego Psychology and the Problem of Adaptation*.

28. Erikson, *IAR*, p. 151.

29. *Ibid.*, p. 176.

30. *Ibid.*, p. 149.

31. *Ibid.*, pp. 145, 149, 228.

32. Erikson, *IYC*, p. 218.

33. Evans, *DEE*, p. 27; Erikson, *IAR*, p. 122.

34. Erikson, *IYC*, p. 81.

35. Erik H. Erikson, *Young Man Luther: A Study in Psychoanalysis and History* (W. W. Norton & Company, Inc., 1958), p. 208. (Hereafter cited as *YML*.)

36. Erikson, *IAR*, p. 165.

37. David Rapaport, "A Historical Survey of Psychoanalytic Ego Psychology," Introduction to Erikson, *IALC*, p. 14.

38. Erikson, *IALC*, p. 52; *CS*.

39. Erikson, *CS*, pp. 48–97.

40. Evans, *DEE*, pp. 86–87.

41. Peter Wolff, "Cognitive Considerations for a Psychoanalytic Theory of Language Acquisition," in *Motives and Thought: Psychoanalytic Essays in Honor of David Rapaport*, ed. by Holt, pp. 330–335. See also Robert White's discussion of Erikson's modes and modalities in *ERPT*, pp. 19–20.

42. I am happy to see that this way of interpreting Erikson is shared by William Barrett and Daniel Yankelovich in *Ego and Instinct: Psychoanalysis and the Science of Man* (Random House, Inc., 1969), pp. 314–317.

43. Erikson, *IAR*, p. 165.

44. *Ibid.*, p. 113.

45. *Ibid.*, p. 115.

46. For a perceptive discussion of Erikson from the perspective of a

theory of culture, see Benjamin Nelson, "Actors, Directors, Roles, Cues, Meanings, Identities," *The Psychoanalytic Review,* Vol. 51 (Spring, 1964), pp. 135–160. In terms of Nelson's categories, Erikson should be seen as emphasizing a "dramatic" and "directive" theory of culture in addition to the standard psychoanalytic emphasis upon the defensive functions of culture. Nelson also performs the helpful function of calling attention to the relationship between the psychological concept of "identity" and the sociological concept of anomie and the need to bring some unification to the two concepts.

47. Erikson, *IALC,* p. 97. (Italics mine.)

48. Erikson, *CS,* p. 267; *IYC,* p. 138.

49. Erikson, *CS,* p. 267; *IALC,* p. 97; *IYC,* p. 138.

50. Erikson, *IYC,* p. 138. (Italics mine.)

51. Erikson, *CS,* p. 267; *IYC,* p. 138.

52. Erikson, *IALC,* p. 97; *CS,* p. 267; *IYC,* p. 138.

53. Erikson, *IAR,* p. 130.

54. *Ibid.,* p. 131.

55. Erikson, *IALC,* p. 89; *CS,* p. 261. (Italics mine.)

56. Erikson, *IALC,* p. 22. (Italics mine.) See also *CS,* p. 412, footnote.

57. Erikson, *YML,* p. 41.

58. Erikson, *IAR,* p. 171. Erikson believes that this "historical perspective" is related to the adolescent's emerging capacity for "hypothetical" and "deductive" thinking, which was investigated and verified by Jean Piaget and Bärbel Inhelder in *The Growth of Logical Thinking from Childhood to Adolescence: An Essay on the Construction of Formal Operational Structures,* tr. by Anne Parsons and Stanley Milgram (Basic Books, Inc., Publishers, 1958).

59. Erikson, *IYC,* p. 41.

60. *Ibid.,* p. 132.

61. Erikson, *IALC,* p. 37.

62. Erikson, *IAR,* p. 95.

63. *Ibid.,* p. 96.

64. Erikson, *YML,* p. 208.

65. *Ibid.,* pp. 238–239.

66. Erikson, *CS,* p. 286.

67. Seymour Martin Lipset, *The First New Nation: The U.S. in History and Comparative Perspective* (Doubleday & Company, Inc., 1967), pp. 115–158.

68. It is also clear that Charles Reich in *The Greening of America* falls into much the same kind of thinking. His distinction between Consciousness I (the Protestant ethic), Consciousness II (meritocracy), and Consciousness III (self-acceptance, lack of competitiveness, personal responsibility) seems to emphasize discontinuity much in the style of Riesman and Fromm.

69. Erikson, *CS,* p. 286. (Italics mine.)

70. *Ibid.,* pp. 114–165.

71. *Ibid.,* pp. 166–186. Erikson also presents in *Childhood and Society*

interesting and perceptive studies of the importance of space-time factors in the formation of the national identity of the Russian and the German people.

72. Sidney E. Mead, *The Lively Experiment: The Shaping of Christianity in America* (Harper & Row, Publishers, Inc., 1963), p. 5.

73. *Ibid.*, p. 6.

74. R. W. B. Lewis, *The American Adam: Innocence, Tragedy, and Tradition in the Nineteenth Century* (The University of Chicago Press, 1955), p. 40.

75. *Ibid.*, p. 91.

76. Kenneth Keniston, *Young Radicals: Notes on Committed Youth* (Harcourt, Brace and World, Inc., 1968), pp. 257–290; also his "Youth, Change, and Violence," *American Scholar*, Vol. XXXVII (1968), pp. 227–245.

CHAPTER 7

The Empirics of Generative Man

1. Representative works reflecting the positions of these men and some of the issues within their debate are as follows: Jean-Paul Sartre, *Being and Nothingness;* Claude Lévi-Strauss, *Tristes Tropiques,* tr. by John Russell (Atheneum Publishers, 1964) and *The Savage Mind* (The University of Chicago Press, 1966); Paul Ricoeur, *Freedom and Nature;* Maurice Merleau-Ponty, *Phenomenology of Perception,* tr. by Colin Smith (London: Routledge & Kegan Paul, Ltd., 1962).

2. Erikson, *YML*, p. 208.

3. For extended discussion of *basic trust* and *hope,* see the following sections of Erikson's writings: Erikson, *IALC*, pp. 55–65; *CS*, pp. 247–251; *IYC*, pp. 96–107; *IAR*, pp. 115–118.

4. For extended discussion of *autonomy* and *will,* see the following sections of Erikson's writings: Erikson, *IALC*, pp. 65–74; *CS*, pp. 251–254; *IYC*, pp. 107–115; *IAR*, pp. 118–120.

5. Erikson, *IALC*, pp. 73, 166.

6. For extended discussions of *initiative* and *purpose,* see Erikson, *IALC*, pp. 74–82; *CS*, pp. 255–258; *IYC*, pp. 115–122; *IAR*, pp. 120–122.

7. Erikson, *CS*, p. 222.

8. *Ibid.*, p. 212.

9. *Ibid.*, p. 220.

10. Piaget, *Play, Dreams, and Imitation in Childhood,* pp. 169–212.

11. Johan Huizinga, *Homo Ludens: A Study of the Play-Element in Culture* (Beacon Press, Inc., 1955); Adolf Jensen, *Myth and Cult Among Primitive Peoples,* tr. by Marianna Tax Choldin and Wolfgang Weissleder (The University of Chicago Press, 1963).

12. Erikson, *IALC*, pp. 88–94, 101–164; *CS*, pp. 261–263; *IAR*, pp. 124–127; *IYC*, pp. 128–135, 142–179.

13. Erikson, *IAR*, p. 125.

14. *Ibid.*, p. 126.

15. Erikson, *IALC*, p. 116.

16. Erikson, *IALC*, pp. 95–97; *CS*, pp. 263–266; *IAR*, pp. 127–130; *IYC*, pp. 135–138.

17. Erikson *IAR*, pp. 127–128.

18. *Ibid.* The general point of view which Erikson sets forth resonates well with Desmond Morris' belief that sexuality, over and above its specific role in procreation, has the additional function of interpreting and rewarding the pair bond. And, of course, the function of the pair bond is to provide a consistent and effective environment for the purpose of raising mankind's highly dependent infants. See Desmond Morris, *The Naked Ape*, p. 55.

19. Erikson, *IAR*, p. 129.

20. Erikson, *IALC*, p. 98; *CS*, pp. 268–269; *IYC*, pp. 139–141; *IAR*, pp. 132–134.

21. Erikson, *YML*, p. 218.

22. *Ibid.*, p. 217.

23. *Ibid.*, p. 208.

24. *Ibid.*, pp. 208–209.

25. Erikson, *IALC*, pp. 133–136.

26. Erikson, *IAR*, p. 117.

27. *Ibid.*

28. *Ibid.*

29. Erikson, "Ontogeny of Ritualization," in *Psychoanalysis—A General Psychology: Essays in Honor of Heinz Hartmann*, ed. by Rudolph M. Loewenstein and others (International Universities Press, Inc., 1966), pp. 602–603.

30. *Ibid.*, p. 603.

31. *Ibid.*, p. 613.

32. *Ibid.*

33. *Ibid.*, p. 619.

34. *Ibid.*

35. Erikson, *IAR*, pp. 155–156.

36. Erikson, "Memorandum on Youth," *Daedalus*, Vol. 96, No. 3 (Summer, 1967), p. 868.

37. *Ibid.*, p. 865.

38. Erikson, *IYC*, p. 306.

39. Erikson, *IYC*, p. 274. It appears even in the early months after the storm created by the publication of Kate Millett's *Sexual Politics* (Doubleday & Company, Inc., 1970) that her heated attack on Erikson's view of women is already being exposed as having been built on a noncontextual reading of the basic intent of Erikson. With characteristic sensitivity, Erikson has helped to reveal both the function and the limitations of her style

of politics. In a recent statement in *Newsweek*, he writes: "Maybe, in a revolution, one should not complain too much if one gets shoved; and we do need angry Milletts who insist on demonstrating that in our civilization the social order has recklessly enslaved the personal and the somatic order (in both sexes) in the service of the oldest establishment: male dominance." But then he presses his own position by adding: "And no sneer from either sex will prevent me from hoping that when women succeed in claiming full participation, they will add maternal concern to the cares of the world governing" (*Newsweek*, Dec. 21, 1970).

40. Erikson, *IYC*, pp. 285–286.
41. *Ibid.*, pp. 290–291.
42. Erikson, *IAR*, p. 233.
43. Erikson, *GT*, p. 413.
44. Erikson, *IAR*, p. 239.
45. Erikson, *GT*, p. 413.
46. Erikson, *IAR*, p. 239.
47. Erikson, *GT*, pp. 415–416.
48. Konrad Lorenz, *On Aggression*, pp. 104–132.
49. Erikson, *GT*, p. 426.
50. *Ibid.*, p. 428.
51. *Ibid.*, p. 418.
52. *Ibid.*, p. 439.

EPILOGUE

Generativity and Advance:
Postscript on Generative Man and Religion

1. Brown, *LAD*, p. 314.
2. *Ibid.*
3. Sándor Ferenczi, *Thalassa: A Theory of Genitality*, tr. by Henry Alden Bunker (Psychoanalytic Quarterly, Inc., 1938).
4. Alfred North Whitehead, *Process and Reality: An Essay in Cosmology* (The Macmillan Company, 1960), pp. 255–279.
5. Whitehead, *The Function of Reason*, p. 8.
6. *Ibid.*
7. Three recent works that have made important contributions toward this goal are Esther Menaker and William Menaker, *Ego in Evolution* (Grove Press, Inc., 1965); Barrett and Yankelovich, *Ego and Instinct;* Emanuel Peterfreund, *Information, Systems, and Psychoanalysis: An Evolutionary Biological Approach to Psychoanalytic Theory* (International Universities Press, Inc., 1971).
8. Menaker and Menaker, *Ego in Evolution*, pp. 1–10.

9. *Ibid.,* p. 12.

10. Barrett and Yankelovich, *Ego and Instinct,* p. 150.

11. Whitehead, *Process and Reality,* p. 41.

12. Huizinga, *Homo Ludens,* p. 46.

13. Jensen, *Myth and Cult Among Primitive Peoples,* p. 48.

14. Theodosius Dobzhansky, *The Biology of Ultimate Concern* (The New American Library, Inc., 1967), pp. 87–88.

15. *Ibid.,* pp. 88–89.

16. *Ibid.,* p. 107.

17. Pierre Teilhard de Chardin, *The Phenomenon of Man,* tr. by Bernard Wall (Harper & Row, Publishers, Inc., 1959), pp. 243–244.

BIBLIOGRAPHY

Abel, Lionel, "Important Nonsense: Norman Brown," *Dissent*, Vol. XV (March, 1968), pp. 147–157.

Ambrose, J. A., "The Development of the Smiling Response in Early Infancy," in *Determinants of Infant Behaviour*, ed. by Brian M. Foss. London: Methuen & Company, Ltd., 1961. Pp. 179–196.

Baeck, Leo, *Judaism and Christianity: Essays*, tr. by Walter Kaufmann. The Jewish Publication Society of America, 1958.

Bain, Homer, "Rational and Irrational Action: A Comparison of the Thought of Thomas Aquinas and Heinz Hartmann." Unpublished Ph.D. dissertation, the Divinity School of the University of Chicago, 1971.

Barrett, William, and Yankelovich, Daniel, *Ego and Instinct: Psychoanalysis and the Science of Man*. Random House, Inc., 1969.

Bell, Daniel, *The Reforming of General Education*. Columbia University Press, 1966.

Bellah, Robert, *Beyond Belief: Essays on Religion in a Post-Traditional World*. Harper & Row, Publishers, Inc., 1970.

Berger, Peter, *The Sacred Canopy: Elements of a Sociological Theory of Religion*. Doubleday & Company, Inc., 1967.

Berger, Peter, and Luckmann, Thomas, *The Social Construction of Reality: A Treatise in the Sociology of Knowledge*. Doubleday & Company, Inc., 1966.

Binswanger, Ludwig, *Being-in-the-World: Selected Papers of Ludwig Binswanger*, tr., and with an introduction to Binswanger's existential psychoanalysis by Jacob Needleman. Basic Books, Inc., Publishers, 1963.

Black, Cyril E., *The Dynamics of Modernization: A Study in Comparative History*. Harper & Row, Publishers, Inc., 1966.

Brown, Norman O., "Apocalypse: The Place of Mystery in the Life of the Mind," *Harper's Magazine*, Vol. 222 (May, 1961), pp. 46–49.

——— "Daphne, or Metamorphosis," in *Myths, Dreams, and Religion*, ed. by Joseph Campbell. E. P. Dutton & Co., Inc., 1970.

——— "From Politics to Metapolitics," *Caterpillar I* (Oct., 1967), pp. 62–94.

——— *Hermes the Thief: The Evolution of a Myth*. University of Wisconsin Press, 1947.

———— (tr.), *Hesiod's Theogony*. The Liberal Arts Press, 1953.

———— *Life Against Death: The Psychoanalytical Meaning of History*. Wesleyan University Press, 1959.

———— *Love's Body*. Random House, Inc., 1966.

———— "A Reply to Herbert Marcuse," *Commentary*, Vol. 43 (March, 1967), pp. 83–84.

Buber, Martin, *I and Thou*, 2d ed., tr. by Ronald Gregor Smith. Charles Scribner's Sons, 1958.

Butler, R. A., and Harlow, H. F., "Discrimination Learning and Learning Sets to Visual Exploration Incentives," *Journal of General Psychology*, Vol. 57 (1957), pp. 257–264.

Chomsky, Noam, *Syntactic Structures*. The Hague: Mouton & Co., N. V., 1957.

Coles, Robert, *Erik H. Erikson: The Growth of His Work*. Atlantic Monthly Press, Little, Brown & Company, 1970.

———— "Profiles: The Measure of Man, I," *The New Yorker*, Vol. 46, No. 38 (Nov. 7, 1970), pp. 51–131; "Profiles: The Measure of Man, II," *The New Yorker*, Vol. 46, No. 39 (Nov. 14, 1970), pp. 59–138.

Crews, Frederick, "Love in the Western World," *Partisan Review*, Vol. 34 (Spring, 1967), pp. 272–287.

Dilthey, Wilhelm, *Pattern and Meaning in History: Thoughts on History and Society*, ed. and with an introduction by H. P. Rickman. Harper Torchbook, Harper & Row, Publishers, Inc., 1962.

Dobzhansky, Theodosius, *The Biology of Ultimate Concern*. The New American Library, Inc., 1967.

Eisenstadt, Shmuel N., *Modernization: Protest and Change*. Prentice-Hall, Inc., 1966.

Elkind, David, "Erik Erikson's Eight Ages of Man," *The New York Times Magazine*, April 5, 1970, pp. 25–27, 84–92, 110–119.

Erikson, Erik H., "Autobiographic Notes on the Identity Crisis," *Daedalus*, Vol. 99, No. 4 (Fall, 1970), pp. 730–759.

———— *Childhood and Society*, 2d ed., rev. and enlarged. W. W. Norton & Company, Inc., 1963.

———— "Erikson Speaks Out: Interview," *Newsweek*, Vol. 76 (Dec. 21, 1970), pp. 85–89.

———— *Gandhi's Truth: On the Origins of Militant Nonviolence*. W. W. Norton & Company, Inc., 1969.

———— *Identity and the Life Cycle: Selected Papers*, Psychological Issues Monograph, Vol. I, No. 1. International Universities Press, Inc., 1959.

———— *Identity: Youth and Crisis*. W. W. Norton & Company, Inc., 1968.

———— *Insight and Responsibility: Lectures on the Ethical Implications of Psychoanalytic Insight*. W. W. Norton & Company, Inc., 1964.

———— "Memorandum on Youth," *Daedalus*, Vol. 96, No. 3 (Summer, 1967), pp. 860–870.

———— "Ontogeny of Ritualization," in *Psychoanalysis—A General Psychol-*

ogy: Essays in Honor of Heinz Hartmann, ed. by Rudolph M. Loewenstein and others. International Universities Press, Inc., 1966. Pp. 601–621.

———— *Young Man Luther: A Study in Psychoanalysis and History.* W. W. Norton & Company, Inc., 1958.

Evans, Richard, *Dialogue with Erik Erikson.* Harper & Row, Publishers, Inc., 1967.

Fenichel, Otto, "Early Stages of Ego Development," in Otto Fenichel, *Collected Papers: First and Second Series,* ed. by Hanna Fenichel and David Rapaport, Vol. 2. W. W. Norton & Company, Inc., 1954. Pp. 25–48.

Ferenczi, Sándor, *Thalassa: A Theory of Genitality,* tr. by Henry Alden Bunker. Psychoanalytic Quarterly, Inc., 1938.

Flügel, John C., *Man, Morals and Society: A Psychoanalytical Study.* The Viking Press, Inc., 1961.

Frankel, Charles, *The Case for Modern Man.* Beacon Press, Inc., 1959.

Freire, Paulo, *Pedagogy of the Oppressed.* Herder & Herder, Inc., 1970.

Freud, Anna, *The Ego and the Mechanisms of Defense,* tr. by Cecil Baines. International Universities Press, Inc., 1946.

Freud, Sigmund, "Project for a Scientific Psychology," in *The Origins of Psychoanalysis: Letters to Wilhelm Fliess, Drafts and Notes: 1887–1902.* Basic Books, Inc., Publishers, 1954. Pp. 347–445.

———— *Standard Edition of the Complete Psychological Works of Sigmund Freud.* London: The Hogarth Press, 1964.

"Analysis Terminable and Interminable," Vol. 23 (1964), pp. 216–253.

"Beyond the Pleasure Principle," Vol. 18 (1955), pp. 7–64.

"The Ego and the Id," Vol. 19 (1961), pp. 12–66.

"Inhibitions, Symptoms, and Anxiety," Vol. 20 (1959), pp. 77–174.

"The Interpretation of Dreams," Vols. 4 and 5 (1953).

"Mourning and Melancholia," Vol. 14 (1957), pp. 243–258.

"New Introductory Lectures on Psychoanalysis," Vol. 22 (1964), pp. 3–182.

"On Narcissism," Vol. 14 (1957), pp. 73–102.

"Three Essays on the Theory of Sexuality," Vol. 7 (1953), pp. 130–243.

"Two Principles in Mental Functioning," Vol. 12 (1958), pp. 213–226.

Friedman, D. G., "Smiling in Blind Infants and the Issue of Innate vs. Acquired," *Journal of Child Psychology and Psychiatry,* Vol. 5 (Dec., 1964), pp. 171–184.

Fromm, Erich, *The Art of Loving.* Harper & Brothers, 1956.

———— *Beyond the Chains of Illusion: My Encounter with Marx and Freud.* Simon & Schuster, Inc., 1962.

———— "A Counter-Rebuttal," *Dissent,* Vol. 3 (Winter, 1956), pp. 81–83.

———— *The Dogma of Christ: And Other Essays on Religion, Psychology and Culture.* Doubleday & Company, Inc., 1966.

———— *Escape from Freedom.* Farrar & Rinehart, Inc., 1941.

———— *The Heart of Man: Its Genius for Good and Evil.* Harper & Row, Publishers, Inc., 1964.

—— "The Human Implications of Instinctual 'Radicalism,'" *Dissent,* Vol. 2 (Fall, 1955), pp. 342–349.

—— *Man for Himself.* Rinehart & Company, Inc., 1947.

—— (ed.), *Marx's Concept of Man.* Frederick Ungar Publishing Company, 1961.

—— *May Man Prevail? An Inquiry Into the Facts and Fictions of Foreign Policy.* Doubleday & Company, Inc., 1961.

—— *Psychoanalysis and Religion.* Yale University Press, 1950.

—— *The Revolution of Hope.* Bantam Books, Inc., 1968.

—— *The Sane Society.* Rinehart & Company, 1955.

—— *Sigmund Freud's Mission: An Analysis of His Personality and Influence.* Harper & Brothers, 1959.

—— (ed.), *Socialist Humanism: An International Symposium.* Doubleday & Company, Inc., 1965.

—— *You Shall Be as Gods: A Radical Interpretation of the Old Testament and Its Tradition.* Holt, Rinehart & Winston, Inc., 1966.

—— (ed.), *Zen Buddhism and Psychoanalysis,* by D. T. Suzuki and others. Grove Press, Inc., 1963.

Fromm, Erich, and Maccoby, Michael, *Social Character in a Mexican Village.* Prentice-Hall, Inc., 1970.

Fromm, Erich, and Xirau, Ramón (eds.), *The Nature of Man: A Reader.* The Macmillan Company, 1968.

Glen, J. Stanley, *Erich Fromm: A Protestant Critique.* The Westminster Press, 1966.

Goldstein, Kurt, *Human Nature in the Light of Psychopathology.* Harvard University Press, 1940.

Hartmann, Heinz, *Ego Psychology and the Problem of Adaptation,* tr. by David Rapaport. International Universities Press, Inc., 1958.

—— "Notes on the Reality Principle," in Heinz Hartmann, *Essays on Ego Psychology: Selected Problems in Psychoanalytic Theory.* International Universities Press, Inc., 1964. Pp. 241–267.

—— *Psychoanalysis and Moral Values.* International Universities Press, Inc., 1960.

Hartmann, Heinz; Kris, Ernst; and Loewenstein, Rudolph M., "Comments on the Formation of Psychic Structure," in *The Psychoanalytic Study of the Child, 1945–1946: An Annual,* Vol. II. International Universities Press, Inc., 1946. Pp. 11–38.

Herberg, Will, "Freud, Religion, and Social Reality," *Commentary,* Vol. 23 (Fall, 1957), pp. 277–284.

Holt, Robert R. (ed.), *Motives and Thought: Psychoanalytic Essays in Honor of David Rapaport.* International Universities Press, Inc., 1967.

Homans, Peter, *Theology After Freud: An Interpretive Inquiry.* The Bobbs-Merrill Company, Inc., 1970.

Huizinga, Johan, *Homo Ludens: A Study of the Play-Element in Culture.* Beacon Press, Inc., 1955.

Illich, Ivan, *Celebration of Awareness*. Doubleday & Company, Inc., 1969.

Inkeles, Alex, "The Modernization of Man," in *Modernization: The Dynamics of Growth*, ed. by Myron Weiner. Basic Books, Inc., Publishers, 1966. Pp. 151–163.

Inkeles, Alex, and Levinson, Daniel, "National Character: The Study of Modal Personality and Sociocultural Systems," in Gardner Lindzey and Elliot Aronson (eds.), *The Handbook of Social Psychology*, 2d ed., Vol. IV, *Group Psychology and Phenomena of Interaction*. Addison-Wesley Publishing Company, Inc., 1969. Pp. 418–506.

Jensen, Adolf, *Myth and Cult Among Primitive Peoples*, tr. by Marianna Tax Choldin and Wolfgang Weissleder. The University of Chicago Press, 1963.

Kavolis, Vytautas, "Post-Modern Man: Psychocultural Responses to Social Trends," *Social Problems*, Vol. 17 (Spring, 1970), pp. 435–448.

Keniston, Kenneth, *Young Radicals: Notes on Committed Youth*. Harcourt, Brace and World, Inc., 1968.

———— "Youth, Change, and Violence," *American Scholar*, Vol. XXXVII (1968), pp. 227–245.

Kierkegaard, Søren, *Fear and Trembling*, tr. by Walter Lowrie. Doubleday & Company, Inc., 1954.

Kohlberg, Lawrence, "Development of Moral Character and Moral Ideology," in *Review of Child Development Research*, ed. by Martin L. Hoffman and Lois W. Hoffman, Vol. 1. Russell Sage Foundation, 1964. Pp. 383–431.

Kris, Ernst, *Psychoanalytic Explorations in Art*. International Universities Press, Inc., 1952.

Lacan, Jacques, *Écrits*. Paris: Éditions du Seuil, 1966.

Landis, Bernard, and Tauber, Edward S. (eds.), *In the Name of Life: Essays in Honor of Erich Fromm*. Holt, Rinehart & Winston, Inc., 1971.

La Piere, Richard, *The Freudian Ethic*. Duell, Sloan & Pearce, Inc., 1959.

Lerner, Daniel, *The Passing of Traditional Society: Modernizing the Middle East*. The Free Press of Glencoe, Inc., 1958.

Lévi-Strauss, Claude, *The Savage Mind*. The University of Chicago Press, 1966.

———— *Tristes Tropiques*, tr. by John Russell. Atheneum Publishers, 1964.

Lewis, R. W. B., *The American Adam: Innocence, Tragedy, and Tradition in the Nineteenth Century*. The University of Chicago Press, 1955.

Lipset, Seymour Martin, *The First New Nation: The U. S. in History and Comparative Perspective*. Doubleday & Company, Inc., 1967.

Lipset, Seymour Martin, and Lowenthal, Leo (eds.), *Culture and Social Character: The Work of David Riesman Reviewed*. The Free Press of Glencoe, Inc., 1961.

Lorenz, Konrad, *On Aggression*, tr. by Marjorie K. Wilson. Bantam Books, Inc., 1970.

Luckmann, Thomas, *The Invisible Religion: The Problem of Religion in Modern Society*. The Macmillan Company, 1967.

Marcuse, Herbert, *Eros and Civilization: A Philosophical Inquiry Into Freud.*
Beacon Press, Inc., 1955.
——— "Love Mystified: A Critique of Norman O. Brown," *Commentary,*
Vol. 43 (Feb., 1967), pp. 71–75.
——— *One Dimensional Man: Studies in the Ideology of Advanced In-
dustrial Society.* Beacon Press, Inc., 1964.
——— "A Reply to Erich Fromm," *Dissent,* Vol. 3 (Winter, 1956), pp.
79–81.
——— "Social Implications of Freudian-Revisionism," *Dissent,* Vol. 2
(Summer, 1955), pp. 221–240.
——— *Soviet Marxism: A Critical Analysis.* London: Routledge & Kegan
Paul, Ltd., 1958.
Margolis, Joseph, *Psychotherapy and Morality: A Study of Two Concepts.*
Random House, Inc., 1966.
Mead, Sidney E., *The Lively Experiment: The Shaping of Christianity in
America.* Harper & Row, Publishers, Inc., 1963.
Menaker, Esther, and Menaker, William, *Ego in Evolution.* Grove Press, Inc.,
1965.
Merleau-Ponty, Maurice, *Phenomenology of Perception,* tr. by Colin Smith.
London: Routledge & Kegan Paul, Ltd., 1962.
Millett, Kate, *Sexual Politics.* Doubleday & Company, Inc., 1970.
Mills, C. Wright, *White Collar: The American Middle Classes.* Oxford Uni-
versity Press, 1956.
Montgomery, K. C., "The Role of the Exploratory Drive in Learning,"
Journal of Comparative and Physiological Psychology, Vol. 47 (1954),
pp. 6–64.
Morgan, Thomas B., "How Hieronymus Bosch and Norman O. Brown Would
Change the World," *Esquire,* Vol. 59 (March, 1963), pp. 100–105, 135.
Morris, Desmond, *The Naked Ape.* Dell Publishing Company, Inc., 1969.
Mowrer, O. Hobart, *The Crisis in Psychiatry and Religion.* Insight Book, D.
Van Nostrand Company, Inc., 1961.
Nelson, Benjamin, "Actors, Directors, Roles, Cues, Meanings, Identities,"
The Psychoanalytic Review, Vol. 51 (Spring, 1964), pp. 135–160.
Niebuhr, Reinhold, *The Nature and Destiny of Man: A Christian Interpre-
tation.* Charles Scribner's Sons, 1941.
Parsons, Talcott, and Bales, Robert, *Family, Socialization and Interaction
Process.* Free Press, 1955.
Parsons, Talcott, and White, Winston, "The Link Between Character and
Society," in *Culture and Social Character: The Work of David Riesman
Reviewed,* ed. by Seymour Martin Lipset and Leo Lowenthal. The
Free Press of Glencoe, Inc., 1961. Pp. 89–135.
Peterfreund, Emanuel, *Information, Systems, and Psychoanalysis: An Evolu-
tionary Biological Approach to Psychoanalytic Theory.* International Uni-
versities Press, Inc., 1971.

Piaget, Jean, *Play, Dreams, and Imitation in Childhood*. W. W. Norton & Company, Inc., 1962.

Piaget, Jean, and Inhelder, Bärbel, *The Growth of Logical Thinking from Childhood to Adolescence: An Essay on the Construction of Formal Operational Structures*, tr. by Anne Parsons and Stanley Milgram. Basic Books, Inc., Publishers, 1958.

Rapaport, David, *The Collected Papers of David Rapaport*, ed. by Merton M. Gill. Basic Books, Inc., Publishers, 1967.

—————— "A Historical Survey of Psychoanalytic Ego Psychology," Introduction to *Identity and the Life Cycle: Selected Papers*, Psychological Issues Monograph, Vol. I, No. 1. International Universities Press, Inc., 1959. Pp. 5–17.

—————— "The Points of View of Metapsychology." A paper delivered at the William Alanson White Institute of Psychiatry and Psychoanalysis, May 22–23, 1959.

Reich, Charles, *The Greening of America*. Random House, Inc., 1970.

Ricoeur, Paul, *Le Conflit des interprétations*. Paris: Éditions du Seuil, 1969.

—————— *Freedom and Nature: The Voluntary and the Involuntary*, tr. by Erazim V. Kohák. Northwestern University Press, 1966.

—————— *Freud and Philosophy*, tr. by Denis Savage. Yale University Press, 1970.

Rieff, Philip, "The American Transference: From Calvin to Freud," *Atlantic*, Vol. 208 (July, 1961), pp. 105–107.

—————— "The Authority of the Past: Sickness and Society in Freud's Thought," *Social Research*, Vol. 21 (1954), pp. 428–450.

—————— "The Bullitt-Freud 'Wilson,' " *Encounter*, Vol. 28 (April, 1967), pp. 84–89.

—————— "Disraeli: The Chosen of History; Uniting the Old Jerusalem and the New," *Commentary*, Vol. 13 (Jan., 1952), pp. 22–33.

—————— *Freud: The Mind of the Moralist*. Anchor Book, Doubleday & Company, Inc., 1961.

—————— "Freudian Ethics and the Idea of Reason," *Ethics*, Vol. 67 (April, 1957), pp. 169–183.

—————— "History, Psychoanalysis, and the Social Sciences," *Ethics*, Vol. 63 (Jan., 1953), pp. 107–120.

—————— "The Impossible Culture," *Encounter*, Vol. 35 (Sept., 1970), pp. 33–44.

—————— "The Meaning of History and Religion in Freud's Thought," *The Journal of Religion*, Vol. 31 (April, 1951), pp. 114–131.

—————— "The Mirage of College Politics," *Harper's Magazine*, Vol. 223 (Oct., 1961), pp. 156–163.

—————— "Origin of Freud's Political Philosophy," *Journal of History of Ideas*, Vol. 17 (April, 1956), pp. 235–249.

—————— "The Theology of Politics: Reflections on Totalitarianism as the

Burden of Our Time," *The Journal of Religion*, Vol. 32 (Spring, 1952), pp. 119–126.

———— *The Triumph of the Therapeutic: Uses of Faith After Freud*. Harper & Row, Publishers, Inc., 1966.

Riesman, David, *The Lonely Crowd*, abridged ed. Yale University Press, 1961.

———— "Notes on Education Reform," in *In the Name of Life: Essays in Honor of Erich Fromm*, ed. by Bernard Landis and Edward S. Tauber. Holt, Rinehart & Winston, Inc., 1971. Pp. 193–217.

Robinson, Paul, *The Freudian Left: Wilhelm Reich, Géza Róheim, Herbert Marcuse*. Harper & Row, Publishers, Inc., 1969.

Rogers, Carl, *Client-Centered Therapy*. Houghton Mifflin Company, 1951.

Roszak, Theodore, *The Making of a Counter Culture*. Doubleday & Company, Inc., 1969.

Ruitenbeek, Hendrik M., *Freud and America*. The Macmillan Company, 1966.

Sartre, Jean-Paul, *Being and Nothingness: An Essay in Phenomenological Ontology*, tr. by Hazel Barnes. Citadel Press, 1964.

Schaar, John H., *Escape from Authority: The Perspectives of Erich Fromm*. Basic Books, Inc., Publishers, 1961.

Schachtel, Ernest G., *Metamorphosis: On the Development of Affect, Perception, Attention and Memory*. Basic Books, Inc., Publishers, 1959.

Schecter, David, "Of Human Bonds and Bondage," in *In the Name of Life: Essays in Honor of Erich Fromm*, ed. by Bernard Landis and Edward S. Tauber. Holt, Rinehart & Winston, Inc., 1971. Pp. 84–99.

Shakow, David, and Rapaport, David, *The Influence of Freud on American Psychology*. International Universities Press, Inc., 1964.

Shils, Edward, "The Theory of Mass Society," *Diogenes*, Vol. 39 (Fall, 1962), pp. 45–66.

Sontag, Susan, *Against Interpretation and Other Essays*. Delta Book, Dell Publishing Company, Inc., 1967.

Spitz, Rene A., *The Smiling Response: A Contribution to the Ontogenesis of Social Relations*, Genetic Psychological Monograph, Vol. 34. Journal Press, 1946. Pp. 57–125.

Stendler, Celia Burns, "New Ideas for Old: How Freudianism Was Received in the United States," *Journal of Educational Psychology*, Vol. 37 (1947), pp. 193–206.

Szasz, Thomas, *The Ethics of Psychoanalysis: The Theory and Method of Autonomous Psychotherapy*. Basic Books, Inc., Publishers, 1965.

Teilhard de Chardin, Pierre, *The Phenomenon of Man*, tr. by Bernard Wall. Harper & Row, Publishers, Inc., 1959.

Tillich, Paul, *Systematic Theology*, 3 vols. The University of Chicago Press, 1951, 1957, 1963.

Time magazine, "The Rotten Middle Class," Vol. 81 (Jan. 25, 1963), p. 88.

Titarenko, A. I., "Erich Fromm in the Chains of Illusion," *Science and Society*, Vol. 29 (Summer, 1965), pp. 319–329.

Toffler, Alvin, *Future Shock*. Random House, Inc., 1970.

Werner, Heinz, *Comparative Psychology of Mental Development*, rev. ed. International Universities Press, Inc., 1957.

White, Robert, *Ego and Reality in Psychoanalytic Theory: A Proposal Regarding Independent Ego Energies*. International Universities Press, Inc., 1963.

———— "Motivation Reconsidered: The Concept of Competence," *The Psychological Review*, Vol. 66 (Sept., 1959), pp. 297–333.

White, Winston, *Beyond Conformity*. The Free Press of Glencoe, Inc., 1961.

Whitehead, Alfred North, *The Function of Reason*. Beacon Press, Inc., 1958.

———— *Process and Reality: An Essay in Cosmology*. The Macmillan Company, 1960.

Whyte, William, *The Organization Man*. Simon & Schuster, Inc., 1956.

Wolff, Peter, "Cognitive Considerations for a Psychoanalytic Theory of Language Acquisition," in *Motives and Thought: Psychoanalytic Essays in Honor of David Rapaport*, ed. by Robert R. Holt. International Universities Press, Inc., 1967. Pp. 299–343.

———— *The Developmental Psychologies of Jean Piaget and Psychoanalysis*. International Universities Press, Inc., 1960.

INDEX

Abel, Lionel, 63
Adaptation, 95, 190, 221, 222
Apollo, 74, 75
Apollonian character, 26, 60, 61, 75, 79, 185
Arendt, Hannah, 57, 105

Bachelard, Gaston, 64
Barrett, William, 220–221
Bell, Daniel, 63
Bellah, Robert, 13
Berger, Peter L., 13, 39, 40
Binswanger, Ludwig, 80, 159
Black, Cyril E., 29, 39
Brown, Norman O., 8, 12, 15, 16, 18, 19, 29, 31, 36, 60–82, 83–86, 100, 111, 112, 117, 123, 154–155, 164, 165, 172, 184, 187, 218, 224
Buber, Martin, 120, 152, 153
Bultmann, Rudolf, 132, 168

Calvin, John, 13, 35, 36, 74, 172
Care, 128, 163, 164
Chomsky, Noam, 132
Competence, 100–104, 190
Controlling symbolic, 13
Counter culture, 8
Crews, Frederick, 71
Culture, 37, 167, 217
    symbolic for, 8
    theory of, 35–38

Dewey, John, 48
Diagnostics, 24, 25, 110
Dilthey, Wilhelm, 17

Dionysian man, 12, 19, 21, 22, 30, 60–82, 123, 199, 215
    Dionysian Christian, 74, 78–82
Disraeli, Benjamin, 74
Dobzhansky, Theodosius, 225–228
Dulles, John Foster, 56
Durand, Gilbert, 64
Durkheim, Émile, 36, 77

Ecology, 7, 151–156
Effectance, 97–104, 221
Ego, 83–104
    in Brown, 75, 79, 84
    independent, 27, 83–104, 224
    in Erikson, 154–162, 170, 197, 199, 220, 221, 222
    in Freud, 46, 86–90
    in Fromm, 138
    in Hartmann, 90–96
    in Menaker, 220
    in Rieff, 46, 55, 84
    in White, 96–104, 221
Eisenstadt, Shmuel N., 29, 39
Eliade, Mircea, 29, 36, 64, 77, 133
Epigenesis, 156, 157, 181
Epigenetic principle, 22, 136, 137
Erikson, Erik H., 8, 9, 12, 16, 21–24, 29, 31, 83, 145–228
    biographical information, 148–149
    developmental   interrelationships in, 182
    ego, 154–162, 170, 197, 199, 220, 221, 222
    evolution, 219–223, 227
    identity, 166–178
    ideology, 167–168
    life cycle, 181–197

Erikson, Erik H. (*continued*)
  other (the stranger), 207–217
  play, 188–190
  self, 179–197
  social world, 201–207
  time, 197–200
Ethics, 124, 125, 152, 167, 169
Evolution, 161, 162, 219–228

Ferenczi, Sándor, 72, 219
Flügel, John C., 14, 16
Frankel, Charles, 25
Freire, Paulo, 20
Freud, Anna, 46, 90, 146
Freud, Sigmund, 12, 13, 18, 25, 32,
  33, 36, 37, 40, 41, 45–54, 66,
  68, 69, 86–90, 102, 167, 189,
  190, 215
Frobenius, Leo, 63
Fromm, Erich, 8, 12, 16, 18, 19, 20–
  21, 25, 29, 31, 105–144, 168,
  185, 187, 200, 202
  biographical information, 106

Galbraith, John Kenneth, 105
Gandhi, 15, 24, 149, 167, 189, 212,
  213
Generative man, 9, 12, 22, 23, 30,
  120, 143, 145–178, 179–217
Genital personality, 125
God, 132, 204
Golden Rule, 212
Goldstein, Kurt, 101–102, 108, 109,
  111
Good man, four theories of the, 30
Guilt, 185, 203

Hartmann, Heinz, 14, 15, 16, 46, 48,
  83, 86, 89, 90–96, 97, 102, 104,
  109, 146, 152, 154, 159, 167,
  180, 197, 204–205
Hegel, G. W. F., 77, 112, 129
Heidegger, Martin, 29, 112, 159, 221
Homo consumens, 122, 124
Homo economicus, 74–77, 79
Homo religiosus, 149
Horney, Karen, 48, 53, 112
Huizinga, Johan, 189, 223
Husserl, Edmund, 110, 159, 221

Id, 14, 48, 94–96, 197
Identity, 148, 166–178, 211, 215,
  220
Ideology, 150, 167, 168, 211, 215,
  220
Illich, Ivan, 20
Individuation, 73, 83–104
Instinct, 47

Jensen, Adolf E., 133, 189, 223
Jung, Carl, 36, 38, 58, 61, 63

Keniston, Kenneth, 177
Kierkegaard, Søren, 116, 117, 168
Klages, Ludwig, 63
Kohlberg, Lawrence, 132
Kris, Ernst, 15, 83, 94, 109, 146, 197

Lacan, Jacques, 47
La Piere, Richard, 14, 16
Lawrence, D. H., 38, 61, 63
Lerner, Daniel, 29
Lessing, Theodore, 63
Lévi-Strauss, Claude, 29, 64, 77,
  133, 180
Lewis, R. W. B., 174, 175, 224
Lipset, Seymour, 174
Loewenstein, Rudolph M., 94, 109
Lorenz, Konrad, 63, 98, 154, 202,
  214
Luckmann, Thomas, 13, 39, 40
Luther, Martin, 15, 24, 77–78, 149,
  154, 167, 172, 189, 198

McCarthy, Eugene, 57
McLuhan, Marshall, 170
Manichaeism, 72, 187
Marcuse, Herbert, 19, 20, 62, 67, 68,
  78, 105, 106, 108, 111, 112,
  113, 114
Margolis, Joseph, 16
Marx, Karl, 36, 77, 105, 112, 129,
  130
Marxism, 17, 20, 105–107, 112
Maslow, Abraham, 17, 130
Mastery, concept of, 164, 222
Mead, Sidney, 174–175, 224
Menaker, Esther and William, 220
Merleau-Ponty, Maurice, 159, 180

Mills, C. Wright, 29, 105
Modernity, 11, 27, 118–124, 166–178
Moral science, 42–45
Morality, 137, 138, 167, 186, 208
Morgan, Thomas B., 60
Morris, Desmond, 64, 99
Mother, 67, 68, 100, 154, 175, 226
Mowrer, O. Hobart, 16
Myth, 223

Needham, Joseph, 218
Needleman, John, 80–81
Niebuhr, Reinhold, 116, 117, 168
Nietzsche, Friedrich Wilhelm, 36, 73

Oedipal project, 70–71
Orthogenesis, 227
Other (the stranger)
    in Brown, 82
    in Erikson, 207–217
    in Fromm, 142
    in Rieff, 58, 59

Parsons, Talcott, 13, 29, 39
Piaget, Jean, 49–50, 99, 108, 109, 111, 127, 184, 189, 221, 223
Play, 49, 65, 83–104, 117, 188–190, 221–223
Productive man, 12, 20, 30, 106–144, 185, 215
Promethean character, 26
Protestant ethic, 27, 165
Protestantism, 172
Psychoanalysis, 12–17, 40–44, 214, 221, 228
Psychological man, 12, 18, 30, 32–35, 38–59, 123, 215

Rapaport, David, 15, 46, 83, 109, 146, 157
Reason, 45, 85, 96, 126, 127, 190, 219
Reich, Charles, 8
Reich, Wilhelm, 20, 38, 58, 61, 63
Religion, 57, 58, 131, 142, 203, 205, 224, 225
Repression, 68–70

Ricoeur, Paul, 16, 17, 24–25, 29, 47, 64, 81, 103, 110, 116, 132, 168, 180
Rieff, Philip, 8, 12, 13, 16, 17, 29, 31, 32–59, 61, 83, 84, 107, 123, 162, 169, 172, 184, 187, 219, 224
Riesman, David, 18, 29, 34, 79, 108, 173, 174
Ritual, 143, 147, 170, 201–204, 214
Robinson, Paul, 62
Roszak, Theodore, 8, 62, 112

Sartre, Jean-Paul, 71, 152, 153, 159, 180, 185
Satyagraha, 212, 213, 214
Schachtel, Ernest G., 109–110, 111, 127, 130
Secularization, 28
Self
    in Brown, 79
    in Erikson, 179–197
    in Fromm, 135
    in Rieff, 51
Shils, Edward, 29
Skinner, B. F., 17
Social world
    in Brown, 82
    in Erikson, 201–207
    in Fromm, 139, 140
    in Rieff, 51–57
Sontag, Susan, 61–62, 63
Spinoza, 71, 110
Sullivan, Harry Stack, 48, 112
Superego, 55, 137, 155, 156, 170, 185, 186, 187, 197
Symbolism, 80, 81, 111

Teilhard de Chardin, Pierre, 226–228
Thass-Thienemann, Theodore, 64
Tillich, Paul, 15, 29, 48, 116, 168
Time
    in Brown, 81
    in Erikson, 197–200
    in Fromm, 139
    in Rieff, 58
Toffler, Alvin, 224

Weber, Max, 36, 74, 77, 78, 120, 172
White, Robert W., 15, 48, 83, 86, 94,
    96–104, 109, 110, 113, 127,
    130, 146, 156, 158, 184, 191,
    221
White, Winston, 29

Whitehead, Alfred North, 96, 218,
    219, 222, 227, 228
Whyte, William, 29, 105
Wolff, Peter, 109, 159

Yankelovich, Daniel, 220, 221